Thinking Children's Rights in Africa

Edited by Isaac Mutelo OP, Joyline Gwara and Monica Nyachowe OP

The Southern African Dominican Series is a joint project led by Southern African Dominican women and men and offers contributions on topics of African Dominican interest and various aspects of Church, theology, culture and religion.

Series editors: Monica Nyachowe OP and Isaac Mutelo OP

Editorial assistant: Donald Kateguru OP

1. *The First Dominican Friars in Boksburg, Brakpan and Springs, South Africa (1917–1927),* Joseph Falkiner, OP, 2024.

Thinking Children's Rights in Africa

Emerging Issues

Edited by Isaac Mutelo OP, Joyline Gwara and Monica Nyachowe OP

Adelaide
2025

© Copyright 2025 with the individual authors for their contributions and with ATF Press for the collection.

All rights reserved no part of the publication may be reproduced, stored in a retrieval system, or transmitted in any form or by any means electronic, mechanical, photocopying, recording or otherwise, without the prior permission of the publisher.

ISBN
978-1-923580-10-7   Softcover
978-1-923580-11-4   Hardcover
978-1-923580-12-1   Epub
978-1-923580-13-8   PDF

Published by:

Making a lasting impact
ATF Africa is an imprint of imprint of the ATF Press Publishing Group
owned by ATF (Australia) Ltd.
PO Box 234
Brompton, SA 5007
Australia
ABN 90 116 359 963
www.atfpress.com

Table of Contents

Preface vii
Acknowledgements ix
Notes on Contributors xi
Introduction to 'Thinking Children's Rights in Africa' xvii

Part 1: Foundations And Frameworks Of Children's Rights In Africa 1

    The African Child as a Person: Child Rights in Traditional African Societies 3

    Reimagining Children's Rights in Africa: An African Philosophical Approach 17

    Normative Content of Selected Rights in the African Children's Charter: The Right to Health 31

    Rethinking the Source of Rights for Learners with Special Educational Needs in Africa 47

Part II: Legal and Policy Dimensions of Child Protection 67

    Understanding the Challenges Faced by Zimbabwean Child Labour Law Enforcement Agencies 69

    Child Rights and Child Protection in Zimbabwe: Counting the Gains, Exploring the Gaps and Drivers 89

    The Roles of Social Workers in Promoting Child Rights in Africa 109

    Online Child Sexual Exploitation and Abuse in South Africa: A Review 135

Part III: Lived Realities and Emerging Child Rights Challenges 153

Child Marriage as a Major Challenge in Rural Communities: A Case Study of Binga District, Zimbabwe 155

Child Marriages in Zimbabwe: Interrogating Culture, girls' rights, and HIV and AIDS in Hurungwe District, Mashonaland West Province 171

Access to Services for Children in Zimbabwean Streets: A Case of Harare Central Business District 181

Child Sexual Abuse in Zimbabwe: A Case of Street Children of the Harare Central Business District 207

Unintended Pregnancies and Substance Abuse among Street Girls of the Harare Central Business District, Zimbabwe 221

Religion and Scourge of Domestic Servant Syndrome in Some Christian Homes in Southwestern, Nigeria 235

Preface

Children remain among the most vulnerable members of society, and the responsibility of protecting their rights requires ongoing intellectual, legal, religious, cultural and social engagement. Since the adoption of the African Charter on the Rights and Welfare of the Child (ACRWC) in 1990, African states have made significant progress in developing legal frameworks and mechanisms protecting children. However, emerging challenges and deep-rooted structural issues continue to hinder the full realisation of children's rights across Africa. *Thinking Children's Rights in Africa: Emerging Issues* is a response to this reality. It is a multidisciplinary volume that brings together a wide range of voices—academics, practitioners, philosophers, theologians, social workers, and child rights advocates—to reflect on the progress, contradictions, and persistent gaps in Africa's child protection landscape.

The volume consists of fourteen chapters and includes the work of more than nineteen contributors, many of whom have conducted empirical research, engaged with policy and existing literature, and/or drawn from years of practical experience. The book begins by exploring traditional and theoretical foundations of children's rights in Africa, emphasising the relevance and tensions between customary norms and contemporary child protection discourses. It then considers the legal and policy dimensions as well as lived realities and emerging challenges, including child marriage, trafficking, sexual abuse, and the situation of children in street contexts. The role of religion, law, and policymakers in shaping the future of child rights on the continent is emphasised.

This book is not just an academic exercise but a call for deeper reflection, bolder advocacy, and more inclusive action in the field of child protection in Africa and beyond. The contributors have not only analysed major challenges; they have also highlighted opportunities for reform, dialogue, and solidarity. We believe this work will be useful to students, scholars, policymakers, faith-based institutions, civil society actors, governments and all those committed to safeguarding the dignity of every child.

Dr Isaac Mutelo, Dr Joyline Gwara and Dr Monica Nyachowe

Acknowledgements

This work represents the collective efforts of many individuals, institutions, and communities whose contributions have made it possible. First, we extend our heartfelt gratitude to the nineteen contributors whose scholarship and dedication shaped this book. Each of them brought a unique perspective and expertise that enriched its thematic depth and diversity. We are equally indebted to our language editors and reviewers, who ensured clarity, consistency, and academic rigour throughout the manuscript. Special appreciation goes to all respondents and communities who participated during data collection for their insights and experiences.

Institutional support from various universities was vital. We particularly acknowledge the Arrupe Jesuit University and the University of Zimbabwe, whose support cannot be underestimated. We are also grateful to scholars and colleagues from other institutions in Zimbabwe, Nigeria, South Africa, and beyond who engaged with this work in various capacities. We also acknowledge the unwavering support of the Mutelo, Gwara, and Nyachowe families. Their love, patience, and encouragement made this endeavour possible. Finally, we are deeply thankful to all those who contributed directly or indirectly, through mentorship, critical feedback, prayers, or logistical help.

We dedicate this work to the children of Africa, whose voices must be heard, whose rights must be protected, and whose future must be safeguarded.

Dr Isaac Mutelo, Dr Joyline Gwara and Dr Monica Nyachowe

Notes on Contributors

Ayegboyin Abimbola Christiana is a lecturer at Bowen University, Nigeria, with over seven years of teaching experience. She is a respected scholar with publications in reputable journals and edited volumes. Her research interests include comparative religion, sociology of religion, and women's studies. She holds a PhD in Religious Studies from Obafemi Awolowo University, Ile-Ife, and is affiliated with the Circle of Concerned African Women Theologians and the Institute of All African Conference of Churches (Young Theologians).

Agber Thaddeus Igbalumun holds a Diploma in Medical Laboratory Sciences from the School of Medical Laboratory Sciences, Mkar Gboko, Nigeria, and a Bachelor of Arts in Philosophy and Humanities from Arrupe Jesuit University, Zimbabwe. He has published journal articles and book chapters and presented at various conferences. His interests include visual art, social justice, and African identity.

Chika Ikeorji holds a Bachelor's degree in Social Work from the University of Calabar, a Master's in Gerontology from the University of Southampton (UK) under the Commonwealth Scholarship, and a Master's in Medical Social Work from the University of Nigeria, Nsukka. She is currently pursuing a PhD in Social Work at the University of Calgary, Canada. Chika is a lecturer at the University of Calabar, and her teaching and research interests include social work, gerontology, community development, and youth work. She is active in qualitative research, data analysis, and academic writing, with publications in both local and international journals.

Esther Musengi holds a Doctor of Education from the University of South Africa, a Master of Education from Great Zimbabwe University, and degrees in Science and Education from the Zimbabwe Open University and the University of Zimbabwe, respectively. She is the Matabeleland South Regional Program Coordinator for Disability and Special Needs Education at the Zimbabwe Open University. Her research interests lie in disability studies, disability justice, deaf education, and sign language rights.

Francis Maushe is a Senior Lecturer in Social Work at Midlands State University. He is a registered social work practitioner and educator with extensive experience in university teaching, service, extension work, and in programming, monitoring, and evaluation. He holds a Master of Social Work, a Bachelor of Social Work Honours, and a Diploma in Social Work from the University of Zimbabwe, as well as a Postgraduate Diploma in Tertiary Education from Bindura University of Science Education. He is currently pursuing a PhD in Social Work at the University of Limpopo, South Africa. His research interests include social exclusion, public policy analysis, and political sociology. He has published widely in the *African Journal of Social Work* and other academic journals.

Isaac Mutelo OP is a Catholic priest belonging to the Dominican Order and currently serves as Lecturer and Director of Quality Assurance, Research and Innovation at Arrupe Jesuit University in Harare, Zimbabwe. He holds a total of eight degrees across Theology (BTh), Philosophy (BA, BA Hons, MA, PhD), Education (PGDE), and Law (PGDHREEL, LLM). Dr Mutelo has authored numerous articles and book chapters on topics including human rights law, environmental issues, politics and religion, artificial intelligence and robotics, interreligious dialogue, and philosophy. He is the author of *Muslim Organisations in South Africa: Political Role Post-1948* (2023) and editor of *Human Rights in Southern Africa: Theory and Practice* (2024). He has presented at several conferences locally and internationally.

Joyline Gwara is a Senior Lecturer in the Department of Philosophy, Religion, and Ethics at the University of Zimbabwe and a Research Fellow with the Decoloniality Research Group at the University of Pretoria. She holds a PhD in Philosophy from the University of KwaZulu-Natal, South Africa, and is the first woman in Zimbabwe to earn a doctorate in Philosophy. Her teaching and research interests centre on African philosophy and related disciplines.

Michelle Brotherton is a postdoctoral research fellow in law at Rhodes University. She previously held a research fellowship at the Centre for Leadership and Ethics in Africa at the University of Fort Hare. Her areas of expertise include health care rights, global justice, human rights, and socio-economic rights, with a particular focus on HIV treatment and resource distribution. She has published widely on these topics and challenges surrounding the notion of resource scarcity.

Monica Nyachowe OP is a Lecturer in the School of Education and Leadership at Arrupe Jesuit University. She holds a PhD in Leadership and Management in Education from the University of KwaZulu-Natal. She currently serves as the Coordinator of the BA Honours in Transformational Leadership programme and is a Certified Coach, trained by the Benedictine Sisters of Pittsburgh, USA. Her research interests focus on leadership and management, anti-human trafficking, and coaching.

Nokukhanya G Ndhlovu holds a PhD in Social Work/Social Development from the University of Fort Hare, as well as a Master's and Honours degree in Social Development from the University of Cape Town. With a strong background in social development, she is deeply passionate about social justice, which informs her research interests in integrated, people-centred development, structural violence, children's rights, gender, and marginalised African masculinities. Committed to engaging both academic and public audiences, her work spans scholarly journals and thought-provoking op-eds. She has published ten journal articles in accredited journals and contributed 3 chapters to edited volumes.

Natalie Simbini is a development practitioner with expertise in resource mobilisation, programme management, and monitoring and evaluation. She holds a Master of Arts in Development Studies and a Bachelor of Humanities and Social Sciences with Honours. Currently working in Business Development, her cross-sectoral research interests include protection, education, health, livelihoods, resilience building, and climate change adaptation.

Olatayo George Olayeye holds a PhD from Obafemi Awolowo University, Ile-Ife, Nigeria, and is a lecturer in the Department of Religious Studies and Philosophy at Redeemer's University, Osun State. His research focuses on comparative religion, African

Indigenous Religion, peace and development, and African theology. He has presented at international conferences and published widely. Dr Olatayo is a recipient of the Chief Barrister Jimoh Ibrahim Prize for Best Doctoral Thesis (2021).

Raymond Taruvinga is a social work academic with over five years of experience in teaching and research across local and regional universities. His work spans child rights, human rights, and social development. He is involved in community development initiatives, including access to justice and faith-based youth guidance, and has collaborated with international agencies on peacebuilding and post-conflict recovery. His academic interests focus on social development, social investment, and human rights.

Takudzwa Chikombe is an academic and social worker. He holds a Master of Social Work and a Bachelor of Social Work from the University of Zimbabwe. An early-career researcher and junior lecturer at the same institution, his interests lie in intervention-based research, child welfare, livelihoods, occupational safety, health, and environmental studies.

Taruvinga Muzingili holds a Bachelor of Social Science Honours and a Master of Social Work from the University of Zimbabwe, as well as a Special Honours and a Master of Science in Monitoring and Evaluation from Lupane State University. He also holds diplomas in Project Management and Mental Health. He has previously lectured at the University of Zimbabwe's School of Social Work, Women's University in Africa, Bindura University of Science Education, and Midlands State University. His research interests include child well-being, family violence, generic social work, and social development.

Tapiwa Musasa holds Doctor of Philosophy (PhD) in Development Studies from the Catholic University of Zimbabwe, MSc in Development Studies from Women University in Africa, BSc in Social Sciences from Great Zimbabwe University, Diploma in Education from Gweru Teachers College, Diploma in Personnel Management from the Institute of Personnel Management Zimbabwe (IPMZ), Executive certificate in Project Management, Monitoring and Evaluation from the University of Zimbabwe, and a certificate in Zimbabwean Sign Language from the Catholic University of Zimbabwe. She is a senior Lecturer at the Catholic University of Zimbabwe. Tapiwa

Musasa's areas of research interest include Child Rights, Gender and Development, Indigenous Knowledge Systems, Human Rights, Food Security, Climate Change, and Disaster Management, among others. Her research publications include 17 journal articles published in accredited journals, as well as 4 book chapters, and one book.

Ruth Oluwakemi Oke holds a Doctorate in Biblical Studies and Gender Issues from the University of Ibadan, Nigeria. She is a Chief Lecturer (equivalent to Professor) at the Federal College of Education, Abeokuta, Ogun State. A member of several academic associations, including the Circle of Concerned African Women Theologians, SBL, NABIS, and NACS, she has presented widely and published in peer-reviewed journals. She was a recipient of the SBL Travel Grant in 2015.

Witness Chikoko is an academic and social worker. He is a Senior Lecturer and Chairperson in the Department of Social Work at the University of Zimbabwe and a Research Fellow in the Department of Social Work at the University of Johannesburg, South Africa. He also serves as an External Examiner at Great Zimbabwe University. He has published extensively on childhood studies, social protection, and disaster management.

Willard Muntanga holds an MSc in Disaster Risk and Livelihood Studies from the Women's University in Africa, a BA in History with Peace and Conflict Studies from Solusi University, and several other qualifications, including a Diploma in Agriculture, Food Security and Livelihoods, and a Special Honours degree in Monitoring and Evaluation from Lupane State University. He is an independent researcher focusing on history, disaster, peace, and conflict in the Zambezi Valley. His research interests include child protection, indigenous child parenting, BaTonga livelihoods, and the intersections of culture, politics, and development.

Introduction to 'Thinking Children's Rights in Africa'

Isaac Mutelo, Joyline Gwara and Monica Nyachowe

Introduction

Children's rights remain a crucial and evolving concept in Africa, shaped by traditional values, cultural law, and socio-economic realities. On 1 July 1990, the African Union (formerly the Organisation of African Unity) adopted the African Charter on the Rights and Welfare of the Child, also known as the African Children's Charter. The Charter remains one of the major legal instruments in promoting and protecting children's rights in Africa. Over the past two decades, many African countries have put in place comprehensive policies and regulations on the protection and promotion of the rights of children. While children under the age of eighteen make up nearly half of Africa's population, their rights to protection, health, education, and dignity remain negatively affected by poverty, harmful cultural practices, lack of enforcement for legal frameworks, and under-resourced social systems. Nevertheless, African countries have adopted several local, regional and international legal instruments to safeguard and guarantee the rights of children within African cultural contexts. Despite progress, implementation remains problematic, and many children remain vulnerable to abuse, exploitation, and neglect through chronic violation of child rights. Having explored the historical evolution of child rights, this introductory chapter outlines the objectives and scope of this work. Organised into three thematic sections, the work explores the indigenous and normative frameworks for child rights, legal and policy dimensions, and grounded case studies of children's lived experiences.

Historical Evolution of Child Rights

The notion of child rights refers to the political, economic, social, cultural, civil, and civil rights universally entitled to children. Child rights guarantee the well-being of children, ensuring that they are protected from all forms of abuse, harm, and exploitation. They also reaffirm the dignity and intrinsic worth of children while promoting their holistic development, access to healthcare, safety, and education, as well as protection from exploitation and violence. The full realisation of child rights ensures that children 'grow up in a safe, nurturing, and supportive environment' (Save the Children Australia, 2023).

The historical development of child rights and the perception of childhood have been gradual. In ancient times, children were perceived as incomplete adults who needed to be integrated into adult life and tasks as they gradually matured. By the 1600s, thinkers such as John Locke began shaping the notion of childhood as a period of innocence and holistic development. Based on tabula rasa theory, John Locke emphasised the importance of upbringing and experience in shaping the mind of the child. Between the eighteenth and nineteenth centuries, the innocence and wondering aspects of childhood were romanticised in literature and art, though many children experienced abuses (HeinOnline, 2020). During this time, child protection and care were regarded as the responsibility of families.

The centrality of child wellbeing and protection became evident during the Industrial Revolution due to increased cases of child labour, which was characterised by harsh and dangerous working conditions. Child labour exploitation and poverty led many families to force children to work for long hours in mines and factories. The concern contributed to the need for child protection and welfare regarding child labour and other challenges. By the early nineteenth century, several countries began developing laws that were meant to protect children. Between 1802 and 1833, the United Kingdom promulgated a series of guidelines that regulated child labour in factories and restricted the employment of children in certain industries. In 1841, France passed policies that were meant to protect children from abusive forms of labour. Similarly, between 1830 and 1852, Massachusetts in the United States passed several child labour guidelines protecting the rights of children.

In 1842, the number of working hours for children was limited, and it became compulsory for adopting parents to be suitable (Pecora et al, 1992:231). Child welfare services were also to remove neglected children from their parents. In 1853, the Children's Aid Society was founded to respond to the challenge of abandoned, neglected, and orphaned children. These regulations were meant to promote the rights of children, especially the right to education, and more and more children were now being enrolled in schools. In 1874, the Case of Mary Ellen Wilson in the United States, which involved the criminal prosecution of a child abuse case, highlighted the centrality of legal protection for children (Tower-Cynthia, 1999). The landmark case contributed to organised efforts against child abuse and maltreatment. Between 1874 and 1877, Switzerland passed regulations that made schooling compulsory for children and raised the minimum working age.

Increasing awareness and campaigns against the harsh and unsafe conditions children were exposed to in industrialised countries fuelled efforts to improve the welfare and holistic well-being of children globally. When the League of Nations was established, improving the living conditions of children and expanding their rights became one of its goals. Through the efforts of the League, in 1919, the international community formed the Child Welfare Committee to focus on the welfare of children by examining the challenges and conditions of children in member states and recommending best practices and guidelines. The same year, 'the Englishwoman Eglantyne Jebb and her sister Dorothy founded Save the Children, which evolved very quickly and, in 1920, gave way to the establishment of the International Save the Children Union, headquartered in Geneva' (Jimeno, 2021:143).

Based on the need for universal rights of children, Eglantyne Jebb drafted the Declaration of the Rights of the Child, which was approved by the League of Nations in 1924. The Geneva Declaration of the Rights of the Child became the first internationally recognised document acknowledging the existence of the rights of children. The Declaration emphasised the need for protection, relief, development and assistance, and assistance.

> Article 1: *The child must be given the means requisite for its normal development, both materially and spiritually.*

> Article 2: The hungry child must be fed; the child that is sick must be nursed; the backwards child must be helped; the delinquent child must be reclaimed; and the orphan and the waif must be sheltered and succoured.
> Article 3: The child must be the first to receive relief in times of distress.
> Article 4: The child must be put in a position to earn a livelihood, and must be protected against every form of exploitation.
> Article 5: The child must be brought up in the consciousness that its talents must be devoted to the service of fellow men (Humanium).

While not legally binding, the Declaration was a landmark document on the rights of children. In 1946, the United Nations took over the Declaration and in 1948 promulgated the Universal Declaration of Human Rights. The Universal Declaration of Human Rights emphasised the rights of all human beings, including children. The freedoms and liberties include the right to life, protection from discrimination, education, and health. This laid a foundation for more specific and comprehensive child rights instruments, such as the Convention on the Rights of the Child, which was adopted in 1989 and came into force in 1990. The Convention on the Rights of the Child was adopted by the United Nations General Assembly as the first legally binding international treaty that recognised children and their economic, social, cultural, and civic rights.

The four general principles of the Convention are non-discrimination, the best interests of the child, the right to life, survival and development, and respect for the views of the child (Office of the United Nations High Commissioner for Human Rights). Following the adoption of the Convention on the Rights of the Child (CRC), several other international protocols and laws have been promulgated to further strengthen the welfare and rights of children. These include the Optional Protocol on the Involvement of Children in Armed Conflict and the Optional Protocol on the Sale of Children, Child Prostitution and Child Pornography (OPSC), which were adopted in 2000 and entered into force in 2002. The International Labour Organisation (ILO) has also promulgated conventions such as the Worst Forms of Child Labour Convention (Convention No. 182) and the Minimum Age Convention (Convention No. 138).

Child Rights in Africa

In Africa, the history of child rights is marked by the influence of traditional and cultural values, colonialism, and the adoption of regional and international legal frameworks. In pre-colonial Africa, children were gradually integrated into the social and economic life of the community as important members. Childbearing was perceived as a communal responsibility, with communities and extended families playing a role in the upbringing of the child (Sindayigaya, 2024:512). Children were progressively introduced to tasks and responsibilities based on their age, and cultural practices were important. During the colonial period in most African territories, Western values and education disrupted the traditional system of child-rearing and welfare. Missionaries introduced schools and orphanages for children, thereby granting them access to care and education with an emphasis on Western religious and cultural values.

The post-colonial era has been marked by significant progress on the rights of children and an emphasis on child welfare, protection, and holistic development. The evaluation of child rights in Africa has also been influenced by international norms, including the Convention on the Rights of the Child (1989). The African Union (formerly the Organisation of African Unity) adopted the African Charter on the Rights and Welfare of the Child (ACRWC) in 1990, which came into force in 1999. This regional instrument addresses the fundamental rights and other issues affecting children in Africa. It addresses specific political, social, cultural, and economic issues affecting children in Africa, including child marriages, child labour, harmful practices, children in armed conflict regions, and children affected by diseases such as HIV/AIDS (Sindayigaya, 2024:510).

There are also several other organisations and actors meant to promote the rights and welfare of children in Africa. These include the African Committee of Experts on the Rights and Welfare of the Child (ACERWC), African Network for the Prevention and Protection Against Child Abuse and Neglect (ANPPCAN), and the Eastern Africa Child Rights Network (EACRN). International organisations such as the United Nations Children's Fund (originally known as the United Nations International Children's Emergency Fund) work with partners to improve the lives and well-being of children in Africa. Despite progress, challenges such as inequality, poverty, sexual and physical violence, exploitation, harmful practices, and conflict continue to affect the promotion and protection of child rights in Africa.

The understanding of the rights of children in Southern Africa is guided by international and continental frameworks, regional initiatives through the Southern African Development Community (SADC), and national efforts in different countries. Countries in Southern Africa have ratified international and regional legal instruments such as the African Charter on the Rights and Welfare of the Child (ACRWC), the United Nations Convention on the Rights of the Child (CRC) and the African Charter on the Rights and Welfare of the Child (ACRWC). In 2016, the SADC Parliamentary Forum adopted a Model Law on Eradicating Child Marriage to help member states develop national laws on child marriages. In 2022, it adopted the revised SADC Code of Conduct on Child Labour to eradicate child labour in the region.

Despite these commitments, several challenges impede the full realisation of children's rights in the region. They include high poverty levels, different forms of child abuse, harmful traditional practices, and diseases such as HIV/AIDS (Chibwana, 2020:106). There are also implementation gaps, as most countries in the region have not adequately domesticated and implemented international and regional conventions, standards, and best practices (Moreira, 2025). The lack of financial resources, awareness about the rights of children, and inadequate participation of children themselves impede the protection and promotion of child rights.

Objectives and Thematic Focus

The main objective of this volume is to comprehensively analyse the progress, persistent gaps, and emerging challenges surrounding the rights of children in Africa. The work identifies and investigates major obstacles hindering the realisation of children's rights, such as child labour, child marriage, and harmful traditional practices, while proposing actionable solutions. The work also analyses the effectiveness of enforcement strategies and mechanisms of child rights in Africa. Ultimately, the volume offers a historical and contemporary roadmap and critical assessment of the frameworks designed to protect children, thereby informing policy, practice, and advocacy efforts for the improvement of child welfare in Africa and beyond. The volume is divided into three parts.

The first part explores the philosophical and cultural foundations for the rights of children in Africa. The authors consider how African traditional societies recognise and protect children and the compatibility of cultural norms with regional and international legal frameworks. The second part of this volume is an appraisal of the legal and institutional mechanisms for the protection and promotion of the rights of children in Africa. The authors examine the effectiveness of protection policies, child labour laws, and the role of social workers in protecting children. The final part presents practical and real-life cases on the violations of children's rights in Africa. Issues such as sexual abuse, child marriages, street life, and substance abuse are discussed. In general, the work systematically and comprehensively covers reflections on traditional values, legal and policy frameworks, and practical challenges affecting children while offering possible solutions.

This work is based on two primary research methodologies. Eight chapters – specifically Chapters One, Two, Three, Four, Seven, Eight, and Fourteen – are based on qualitative methods. In these chapters, the authors critically analyse key issues using existing literature, offering insightful reflections, policy recommendations, and practical directions. The remaining chapters—Chapters Five, Six, Nine, Ten, Eleven, Twelve, and Thirteen—adopt a mixed-methods approach, combining qualitative and quantitative techniques. These include literature reviews as well as empirical data collected through interviews, focus group discussions, and questionnaires. The authors of these chapters obtained the necessary ethical approvals, ensured confidentiality and anonymity, and secured informed consent from all participants.

Following this introduction, the first chapter by Agber Thaddeus Igbalumun and Isaac Mutelo discusses the existence of child rights from the perspective of African culture. The chapter notes that the notion of 'child rights' in traditional African societies remains contentious. Is the notion of child rights foreign to Africa or a mere product of globalisation and late modernity? Do child rights constitute the ontology of the African people, which is rooted in the dignity of the human person? By reconciling differing perspectives, the chapter offers an intermediary approach to the understanding of child rights in traditional African Societies based on the concept of 'personhood' (Kaime, 2005:224). The analysis leads to an insightful perspective on the rights of children in traditional African societies.

The second chapter by Joyline Gwara and Isaac Mutelo explores the intricate relationship between culture and children's rights in Africa. The authors propose a philosophical framework that reformulates the debate surrounding children's welfare through the lens of African philosophy. The chapter evaluates African traditional practices and beliefs and how they shape the understanding of childhood and children's rights. Harnessing concepts such as communitarianism, respect for human dignity, and community responsibility, the chapter advocates for a holistic approach that appreciates cultural heritage while simultaneously promoting children's rights. The chapter concludes by recommending ways in which African cultural values can be integrated with present-day child rights frameworks.

The third chapter by Michelle Brotherton analyses the normative content of selected rights in the African Children's Charter with a focus on the right to health. The author notes that the African Children's Charter provides for children's right to health in the same wording as the African Charter but elaborates with several measures to be considered in seeking to realise this right. The Charter stipulates that the state shall protect the family unit and 'shall take care of its physical health and moral well-being'. So, in addition to providing for the right to health, the African Children's Charter holds the State responsible for the physical health of the family unit. Subsequently, in the African Children's Charter, parents are deemed responsible for the health of the child within the family unit. This is arguably an example of a uniquely context-sensitive provision that reflects the values held in African communities, families, and cultures (Lloyd, 2002). The chapter thus examines how the African Children's Charter departs from the Children's Rights Charter and draws deductions about the normative content of the right to health. By examining the measures provided in the African Children's Charter, the chapter establishes that the normative content of children's right to health in Africa can be contextualised to challenges and problems unique to Africa.

In chapter four, Esther Musengi offers an analysis of the source of rights for learners with special educational needs in Africa. The author notes that the source of human rights is contentious, as human needs, human capabilities, and morality are common for establishing human rights (Bay, 1982). The contention becomes complex when the rights of special populations, such as children with disabilities, are considered, because as minors, they are unable to participate in the establishment of their rights and due to the limitations imposed on them by their disabilities. Many of them are also not able to exercise their rights, thereby leading to abuse. This framework is critical for deciphering emerging educational trends from special education to inclusive education.

By unpacking the sources that inform rights for learners with disabilities, policy and practice interventions become clearer. The chapter notes that when the foundational source of rights is understood, educational strategies and operational activities can be meaningfully aligned for the benefit of this special population (Ribet, 2011). At the strategic level, understanding the paradigmatic source of rights is critical in unpacking educational models that range from moral, medical, social, and rights-based. In this way, the intentional and unintended consequences of operationalising educational models within particular paradigms can be fully understood. The chapter proffers interventions that are appropriate for the intended source of rights. The chapter utilises Czech jurist Karel Vasak's generations of rights to discuss the rights to education of children with disabilities as enshrined in the African Charter on the Rights and Welfare of the Child. The focus, therefore, is on rethinking the source of rights for children with special educational needs in the context of universalist contestations in Africa.

The fifth chapter by Raymond Taruvinga analyses the challenges faced by Zimbabwean Child Labour Law enforcement agencies in the promotion of child rights and wellbeing. The author holds that although government agencies and other involved non-profit organisations have made organised efforts to eliminate the problem, significant numbers of Zimbabwean children are still engaged in undue labour. The chapter also explores the current child labour mitigation programs implemented by agencies and finds out what agency representatives suggested for improved performance. The analysis is grounded in the theory of performance, which offers components that determine the level of organisational performance. The chapter highlights a range of anti-child labour programs currently in place, their sufficiency, and the specific challenges faced by each target agency (Huntington, 2001).

In chapter six, Tapiwa Musasa discusses child rights and protection in Zimbabwe, with a focus on positive developments, gaps, and core drivers. The chapter notes that while conventions like the Convention on the Rights of the Child (CRC 1989), the African Charter on the Rights and Welfare of the Child (AFRWC 1990), and constitutions like the Zimbabwean constitution (2013), implementation remains a challenge due to traditional, religious and socio-economic challenges. The chapter unpacks the positive developments in Zimbabwe, as well as the gaps that need to be closed for comprehensive and effective child rights upholding and maximum child protection (Oti, 2017; Alderson, 2017). The findings indicate that the legal frameworks are mainly theoretical and they are applicable only in certain scenarios like rape cases and murder, while issues such as education, child marriages, and child labour continue to be affected by cultural values and religious beliefs, thus leaving children to suffer. The chapter recommends a multi-stakeholder approach, monitoring, and evaluation of policies and strategies at all levels so that issues affecting children are identified early enough and rectified. The chapter concludes by recommending the need for law enforcement agents to function without unjustified interference from politicians and other leaders so that the law effectively takes its course against child rights violators.

The seventh chapter by Chika Rita Ikeorji examines the role of social workers in promoting child rights in Africa. Children's rights are fundamental to their well-being, growth, and development, and ensuring their protection is of paramount importance. However, the chapter notes that numerous challenges persist in Africa, including poverty, armed conflict, child labour, and inadequate access to education and healthcare, which undermine the fulfilment of children's rights. Social work exists in society to help people resolve their social problems and enhance their social functioning. Using a multidisciplinary approach, the chapter argues that social workers play a vital role in addressing these challenges and advocating for the rights of children in Africa (Pink, Ferguson, and Kelly, et al. 2022).

Thus, the chapter examines social workers' multifaceted responsibilities and interventions to safeguard and promote child rights in Africa. It considers key areas where social workers make an impact by contributing to creating an environment that fosters the holistic development and well-being of children. The chapter notes the important role of social workers in cases where children encounter challenges such as child abuse, child labour, neglect, exploitation, lack of access to education, and poor healthcare. Social workers are responsible for sensitising communities and promoting behavioural change to eliminate harmful practices affecting children and collaborating with governmental and non-governmental organisations to advocate for policy reforms and the implementation of legislation that upholds child rights in Africa (Banks et al., 2021). The chapter recommends the need for comprehensive training programs, ongoing supervision, and supportive organisational structures to enhance social workers' knowledge and skills in child rights protection and advocacy.

The eighth chapter by Nokukhanya Ndhlovu and Tendai Chiguware discusses online child sexual abuse and exploitation in South Africa. The authors note that although noticeable progress has been made in the implementation of legal instruments such as the African Charter on the Rights and Welfare of the Child, children continue to be abused in Africa, with the highest incidences of child abuse worldwide (Nyasuguta, 2020). By analysing online child sexual exploitation and abuse concerning Africa, the chapter introduces the depth and dynamics of the issue in South Africa. The main objective of the chapter is to examine the different forms of online child sexual exploitation and abuse that children experience and the dynamics of online child sexual exploitation and abuse in Africa. The chapter recommends reshaping societal attitudes towards women and children, embracing Ubuntu's ideals of shared respect and protection.

In chapter nine, Willard Muntanga and Taruvinga Muzingili explore the challenge of child marriages in Zimbabwean rural communities. The author discusses how child marriages have become rampant in the Zambezi Valley communities as girl children get pregnant at the age of 13 years. In some cases, school children glide into marriages and engage in sexual relationships with married men in the community. The chapter notes that the driving forces for child marriages include poverty, lack of parental support, peer pressure, lack of exposure, and the growth of technology. Children who are forced into marriages in the rural areas often experience extreme poverty (Muntanga and Muzingili, 2019). The chapter locates the experiences and challenges faced by children in schools insofar as child marriages are concerned. The chapter concludes by offering suggestive measures and solutions to minimise the ultimate effects of child marriages in the Zambezi valley communities.

Following Willard Muntanga's discussion, chapter ten Francis Maushe, Wilberforce Kurevakwesu, Noel Garikai Muridzo, Etiya Edith Chigondo, and Albert Mashambanhaka continue to interrogate the issue of child marriages in Zimbabwe from the perspective of culture, girls' rights, and HIV and AIDS. The high prevalence of child marriages presents a threat to child protection and wellbeing. The author argues that key cultural practices that promote child marriages in Zimbabwe include cultural initiation practices (*Chinamwali*), sexual cleansing rituals, community pressure, and spiritual beliefs and religious practices. The consequences of child marriages include dropping out of school, poverty, intimate partner violence, birth-related complications, high exposure to HIV/AIDS and other Sexually Transmitted Infections (STIs), as well as stress and depression. The chapter recommends several interventions in an attempt to address child marriages. These include enforcement of laws to persecute perpetrators of child marriages, economic empowerment of young girls and women as well as the community, information dissemination about sexual health to rural girls and households, as well as engaging child rights and protection organisations (Kalamar, Lee-Rife and Hindin, 2016:1). The chapter also emphasises the need for grassroots leaders such as village heads, chiefs, and educational leaders to be trained so that they may easily identify potential victims of child marriages.

Chapter Eleven by Natalie Rutendo Simbini, Chikombe Takudzwa and Witness Chikoko focuses on access to services among the children in street situations in Zimbabwe's Harare Central Business District. The chapter adopts a child rights perspective to analyse and understand the realities of children. The chapter establishes that street children have limited access to essential services such as birth certificates, education, reproductive health services, and social protection services. The chapter concludes by lobbying and advocating for governments and other key stakeholders to improve the provision of services towards the children in street situations.

In chapter 12, Witness Chikoko discusses the challenge of child sexual abuse in Zimbabwe from the perspective of street children. Based on the empowerment theory, the author argues that street children face different dimensions or forms of child sexual abuse, including forced sex or rape, sodomy, multiple sexual partnerships, commercial sex work, early sexual debut, masturbation, intergenerational sex, ritual sex, bestiality, sexual poaching, oral sex, unprotected sex among others (Muridzo, 2017). The chapter concludes by lobbying and advocating for governments and other key stakeholders to increase their investments towards preventing and protecting street children from sexual abuse, violence, and exploitation.

The thirteenth chapter by Witness Chikoko examines the complex and/or multi-dimensional relationship between unintended pregnancies and substance abuse among adolescent street girls of Zimbabwe. The chapter establishes that some street girls have succumbed to unwanted pregnancies as a result of excessive substance abuse. Conversely, some of the girls became addicted to psychoactive substances as a result of the traumatic experiences associated with unwanted pregnancies. Some girls experience unwanted pregnancies as a result of using family planning tablets acquired on the streets, which might not work effectively. The use of substances and unwanted pregnancies demonstrate ambiguity of agency as well as self-destructive behaviours among children. Drawing from the child rights perspective, the complex relationship between unwanted pregnancies and substance abuse illustrates huge child rights violations prevalent on the streets. The chapter concludes by recommending that governments and other institutions, like nongovernmental organisations to provide more protection services targeting the street girls to reduce the risks associated with unwanted pregnancies and substance abuse.

The final chapter by George Olayeye Olatayo and Abimbola Christiana Ayegboyin considers the question of religion and the scourge of domestic servant syndrome in some Christian homes in Southwestern Nigeria. The chapter argues that while there is a decline in religious activities and practices in some parts of the world because of secularisation, in Nigeria, religion functions prominently in both private and social lives of the people. However, there is an increase in the social menace of domestic servant syndrome among Christian adherents in some communities and homes in the Southwestern parts of Nigeria. The chapter traces the history of child domestic workers in some Christian homes and its implications on society and national development.

In some cases, children who are involved in these activities are family servants who are subjected to long hours of domestic work at homes with major duties of looking after either children or the elderly. Some domestic servants are given inadequate care, love, and poor sleeping conditions with little or no remuneration for their services. The chapter focuses on reasons child domestic servants thrive in Nigerian Christian homes and highlights that if the scourge continues, there are social and spiritual threats to the future of Nigerian children who are engaging in domestic servant practices. The chapter advocates for social mechanisms, legislative backing, and a legal framework that can criminalise the practices of child labour in society. Such measures would encourage and preserve the child's right to act with unhindered access to fairness, justice, and equity.

References

Alderson, P 2017, *Children's rights: Best practice*, Available at: https://www.researchgate.net/publication/320466791_Children's_rights_best_practice [Accessed 2 June 2025].

Banks, S, Cai, T, De Jonge, E, Shears, J, Shum, M, Sobočan, AM, Strom, K, Truell, R, **Úriz**, MJ & Weinberg, M 2020, 'Practising ethically during COVID-19: Social work challenges and responses', *International Social Work*, vol. 63, no. 5, pp. 569–583.

Bay, C. 1982, 'Self-respect as a human right: Thoughts on the dialectics of wants and needs in the struggle for human community', *Human Rights Quarterly*, vol. 4, no. 1, pp. 53–75.

Chibwana, M.W.T. 2020, 'Evoking the principle of subsidiarity: Merit for a SADC Protocol for Children', *African Journal of Governance and Development*, vol. 9, no. 1, pp. 106–124.

Crosson-Tower, C. 1999, *Understanding child abuse and neglect*, 4th edn, Allyn and Bacon, Boston.

HeinOnline 2020, *Unpacking the history of American and international child rights*, Available at: https://home.heinonline.org/blog/2020/08/unpacking-the-history-of-american-and-international-child-rights/ [Accessed 12 September 2024].

Humanium n.d., *Geneva Declaration of the Rights of the Child, 1924 - Text*, Available at: https://www.humanium.org/en/text-2/ [Accessed 13 June 2025].

Huntington, S.P. 2001, *Political order in changing societies*, Yale University Press, New Haven.

Jimeno, R. 2020, 'The birth of children's rights between the First and Second World Wars: The historical events leading up to the Convention', *Miscellanea Historico-Iuridica*, vol. 19, no. 1, pp. 143–166.

Kaime, T. 2005, 'The Convention on the Rights of the Child and the cultural legitimacy of children's rights in Africa: Some reflections', *African Human Rights Journal*, vol. 5, pp. 221–238.

Kalamar, A.M., Lee-Rife, S. & Hindin, M. 2016, 'Interventions to prevent child marriage among young people in low and middle-income countries: A systematic review of the published and grey literature', *Journal of Adolescent Health*, vol. 59, no. 3, pp. 16–21.

Lloyd, A. 2002, 'A theoretical analysis of the reality of children's rights in Africa: An introduction to the African Charter on the Rights and Welfare of the Child', *African Human Rights Journal*, vol. 2, pp. 11–32.

Moreira, E. 2025, *The potential of the SADC Protocol on Gender and Development in advancing child protection*, Africa Legal Aid, Available at: https://www.africalegalaid.com/the-potential-of-the-sadc-protocol-on-gender-and-development-in-advancing-child-protection [Accessed 27 June 2025].

Muntanga, W. & Muzingili, T. 2019, 'The obscurity of early marriages in Binga rural district, Zimbabwe: Implications of the girl child', *Journal of Advances in Social Sciences and Humanities (JASH)*, vol. 5, no. 3, pp. 670–673.

Muridzo, N.G. 2017, *An exploration of the phenomenon of child sexual abuse in Zimbabwe*, Unpublished DPhil thesis, Department of Social Work, School of Human and Community Development, Faculty of Humanities, University of Witwatersrand, South Africa.

Nyasuguta, F. 2020, *Six types of sexual abuse that children face online*, Available at: https://www.the-star.co.ke/news/big-read/2020-07-16-six-types-of-sexual-abuse-that-children-face-online/ [Accessed 30 June 2023].

Office of the United Nations High Commissioner for Human Rights (OHCHR) n.d., *Background to the Convention*, Available at: https://www.ohchr.org/en/treaty-bodies/crc/background-convention [Accessed 2 March 2023].

Ofosu Oti, G. 2017, *Promoting and protecting children in Ghana*, Available at: https://www.ghanaweb.com/GhanaHomePage/features/Promoting-and-protecting-child-rights-in-ghana-534530 [Accessed 9 January 2023].

Pecora, P.J., Whittaker, J.K., Maluccio, A.N., Barth, R.P. & Plotnick, R.D. 1992, *The child welfare challenge: Policy, practice, and research*, Aldine de Gruyter, New York.

Pink, S., Ferguson, H. & Kelly, L. 2022, 'Digital social work: Conceptualising a hybrid anticipatory practice', *Qualitative Social Work*, vol. 21, no. 2, pp. 413–430.

Ribet, B. 2011, 'Emergent disability and the limits of equality: A critical reading of the UN Convention on the Rights of Persons with Disabilities', *Yale Human Rights & Development Law Journal*, vol. 14, pp. 155–210.

Save the Children Australia 2023, *Rights of the child*, Available at: https://www.savethechildren.org.au/our-stories/rights-of-the-child [Accessed 3 March 2025].

Sindayigaya, I. 2024, 'The African Charter on the Rights and Welfare of the Child, an instrument based on African socio-cultural realities: Truth or utopia?', *Open Journal of Social Sciences*, vol. 12, no. 2, pp. 510–532.

PART 1

Foundations and Frameworks of Children's Rights in Africa

Chapter One
The African Child as a Person: Child Rights in Traditional African Societies

Agber Igbalumun and Isaac Mutelo

Introduction

Children's rights are enshrined in international and regional legal instruments such as the United Nations Convention on the Rights of the Child (UNCRC) and the African Charter on the Rights and Welfare of the Child (ACRWC). However, when viewed from the perspective of traditional African societies, the notion of child rights is unclear. Does the notion of 'child rights' exist within traditional African cultures as it is understood and conceptualised in the Western liberal tradition? Responding to this question requires an analysis of the philosophical underpinnings of traditional African societies, particularly beliefs and rituals that are tied to personhood and the status of children within the community.

From the perspective of personhood, this chapter addresses the question of child rights, which remains contentious in traditional African societies. In some cases, the notion of child rights is seen as foreign to Africa, a mere product of globalisation and late modernity and an import from the West. By contrast, it has also been perceived as constituting the ontology of Africans, which is rooted in the inherent dignity and value of the human person. The attempt is to reconcile this discourse by analysing the concept of personhood in traditional African contexts by examining it across different regions of Africa. The chapter also analyses different perspectives of personhood in traditional African societies and how these influence the understanding and treatment of children. Understanding personhood will provide insight into the existence of child rights in traditional African societies in a way that is different from Western thought.

Understanding Child Rights

A child can be defined from different perspectives, including based on regional and international legal instruments. Although the transition from childhood to adulthood typically ranges from ages 15 to 21, the age at which one is most commonly recognised as an adult is 18. Article 1 of the Convention on the Rights of the Child (CRC) defines a child as 'every human being below the age of eighteen years unless under the law applicable to the child, majority is attained earlier'. This is in line with Article 2 of the African Charter on the Rights and Welfare of the Child, also known as the African Children's Charter, which considers a child to be any human being who is below eighteen years old. Unlike the Convention on the Rights of the Child, the African Charter on the Rights and Welfare of the Child does not allow exceptions based on national laws. In general, anyone who is above the age of eighteen is no longer a child but an adult.

Nevertheless, definitions of a child can also vary based on economic, social and cultural factors, as well as physical development, social status and responsibilities (Najeeb). In some African contexts, such as the Zulu people of South Africa, rites of passage are important in the process of transitioning from childhood to adulthood. They are rooted in the interactions between the living and the dead, the individual and the community and children and the elderly, thereby reinforcing harmonious co-existence (Drew, 2023). Child rights are certain entitlements which children, by virtue of being human, ought to benefit from. These entitlements are enshrined in the Convention on the Rights of Children (CRC), which was promulgated in 1989 following the United Nations Declaration on the Rights of Children (DRC), which was later adopted in 1959.

According to the CRC, children are entitled to special protection and care due to their vulnerability. The entitlements include the right to life, education, health, nationality, religion, parental or family care, to be protected from abuse, and not to participate in armed conflict (Doek, 2018). The Convention notes that all children, irrespective of their sex, race, religion, nationality, social origin, birth or other status, are to enjoy these rights. These rights were later contextualised by different regions or member states. For instance, the need to protect children and ensure that their rights are guaranteed, the African Charter on the Rights and Welfare of Children was adopted in 1990 and entered into force in 1999. The rights of children enshrined in this Charter are not essentially different from those enshrined in the Convention on the Rights of the Child.

However, these rights have been re-emphasised in an African context with sensitivity to African traditional practices. For example, Article 21 of the African Children's Charter emphasises protection against harmful social and cultural practices, such as discrimination on the grounds of sex and the prohibition of child marriage and the betrothal of boys and girls. The Charter also recognises the protection of children against apartheid and discrimination (Article 26). Children also have some responsibilities towards their family, society, state, and other legalised communities. These responsibilities include respect for their parents, elders, and superiors, and assisting them in times of need. They are required to serve their communities with their physical and intellectual capacities (Article 31). The African Children's Charter also emphasises that, irrespective of the rights children are entitled to, they also owe society certain responsibilities.

Conceptualising Traditional African Cultures

Traditional African societies can be regarded as the indigenous people of Africa with their cultural values. Cultural values, beliefs and customs distinguish every human society. The traditional African societies have certain values, beliefs and customs which distinguish them from other cultures, such as Western and Asian cultures. Cultural values include language, dress code, food, norms and other practices. Though cultural values vary from place to place, some of them are shared across Africa's diversity. Ogbujah Columbus (2014:209) notes that the cultural values which are shared throughout sub-Saharan Africa include a common understanding of communal living, respect for elders and authority, and time. Communal life is a peculiar characteristic of the African people and refers to the idea that no individual lives in isolation from the community to which they belong. In general, "traditional Africans share much of their life in common. They have communal farmlands, barns, trees, streams and markets for economic reasons. This accounts for why entire community members may distinguish themselves by their expertise in a specific skill or trade, as in wood carving, blacksmithing, etc" (Columbus, 2014:209).

Every individual derives his or her existence and identity from the community, and no individual can exist without the support of the community. As experienced in Africa, especially pre-colonial period, communitarianism stresses the centrality of community, togetherness, and cooperation. These values are essential for social structure, economic growth and political organisation in traditional African societies. The community and the individual in African ontology are mutually dependent. However, there is emphasis on the priority of the community to the individual, and this could be the distinguishing characteristic of African communism and the experience of community in other cultures. Another characteristic of traditional African societies is uncompromised respect for authority and elders. Elders in Africa are respected not by their material possessions or status but by their old age. This same respect is accorded to authoritative figures such as the kings or community chiefs, clan heads and the family heads. The understanding is that old age comes with wisdom, and whatever the elders say is likely to be respected. Elders are the custodians and the transmitters of the unwritten traditions that govern the affairs of human societies (Columbus, 2012:211). As custodians of the tradition, they are believed to be in communion with the ancestors with whom they derive their wisdom to govern the people in fairness and justice. On that basis, elders and traditional leaders are accorded an unrivalled respect in the traditional African societies.

Personhood in Traditional African Societies

The question of children's rights in African traditional societies should be approached with sensitivity and caution, given the diversity of cultural practices. To address this question, it is important to understand the fundamental basis for international legal instruments on the rights of children. According to Thoko Kaime, 'the fundamental value underlying the international bill of rights is the notion of the inherent dignity and integrity of every human being, whether child or adult' (2005:223). On that basis, dignity, which is inherent, rather than acquired, forms the bedrock of human rights. However, when applied to African traditional societies, this view raises intricate questions about the status of children. Are children considered complete human beings from birth, or is personhood a gradual process of becoming? One view contexts that in African thought, personhood is not only simply an inherent quality but is cultivated and attained through gradual communal integration (Musana, 2018). Mbiti suggests that 'the individual does not and cannot exist alone except corporately' (1969:108). This perspective emphasises the role of the community in shaping children and suggests that personhood is a process of 'becoming' a social being through learning and embodying communal values and customs.

Children are 'citizens-in-waiting', with potential for full personhood when they exhibit social and moral qualities (Ndofirepi and Shumba, 2014). If personhood is partly acquired, does the concept of inherent dignity fully apply to children in traditional African contexts? Does it imply that children are not persons or complete human beings with inherent dignity, but rather persons on the way to acquiring dignity? In general, the emphasis on communalism does not equate to a denial of children's worth or rights, and traditional African societies often have indigenous mechanisms for protecting children and ensuring their welfare. The notion of Ubuntu (personhood), which emphasises interconnectedness and accountability towards others, underlines the role of the community in raising and caring for children. The understanding of personhood in African ontology differs from the Western understanding of personhood as shown in the works of Aristotle, René Descartes, and John Locke. Such scholars understand personhood as the ability to reason, think and be conscious of one's actions over time.

However, those standards do not necessarily account for personhood in the African conception of persons, at least in most cultures. The concept of personhood is understood differently by the African people. For instance, Wiredu (1987:160-161) notes that the Akan people of Ghana believe that a person is a composite of three essential elements, namely, *nipadua* (body), *okra* (life-giving body), and *sunsum* (that which gives the person his or her personality). The *okra* is the innermost self, the essence of a person, the embodiment and the transmitter of the individual's destiny, and the spark of the supreme being in humanity (1987:161). The second component of a person, *sunsum*, refers to 'that which is responsible for the total effect communicated by an individual's personality' (Wiredu, 1987:162). The quality of *sunsum* is its ability to perish after death. Some of the attributes of *sunsum* include courage, gentleness, jealousy, forcefulness, and dignity. For him, these qualities are psychological, not sensible or physical (Gyeke, 1995:91).

Sunsum can leave the body when the person is asleep and later return to the body at will. The third component of a person, which is *nipadua* or body, is composed of the flesh, blood, and bones. This component is believed to be the material component of human beings. For the Akan culture, the three components, *okra*, *sunsum*, and *nipadua*, are what constitute a person. Understanding the three components that constitute a human being entails that among the Akan people, even unborn children are regarded as persons to a greater extent since they embody some of the core components that make someone a person. In some cultures, such as the Yoruba people of Nigeria and the Zulu of South Africa, personhood is somewhat linked to the naming of the child. A child is often considered a full person when they have been formally given a name which confers spiritual recognition, social identity and communal integration. Among the Zulu people of South Africa, a ceremony called *imbeleko* is conducted to:

> introduce the baby to the ancestors and to thank them and ask them to protect it. For imbeleko a goat must be slaughtered as a sacrifice to the ancestors (a goat is always slaughtered for a feast that involves talking to the ancestors), and the family elder responsible for talking to the ancestors will call the baby by its name when presenting it to the ancestors at the same time the goat is being slaughtered. Zulus usually carry more than one name; it can be several names given by members of the extended family. Names usually denote the family's expectations and encouragement for a baby; some reflect the family's experiences or how they relate to others in their community, sometimes they tell about the time/how the weather was like when the person was born, and so on (African Studies Center).

Before the name is given, an infant is regarded as being in transition to personhood. In some African cultures, the naming ritual enabled the child to be formally included socially and spiritually into an ethnic group, clan and family. The naming of children is a practice that is also common in other African societies. The ceremony often falls under the rite of passage—a transition from one stage of life to another. The naming ceremony welcomes the child into the family, making him or her part of the community. Among the Yoruba people of Nigeria, the naming ceremony is typically performed on the eighth day after the child's birth and is seen as a rite that integrates the child, making him or her a member of the family (Kanu 2019:33). Similarly, the Akamba people of Kenya name their children on the third day after birth. The ritual concludes when the father places an iron necklace on the child's neck on the fourth day to signify the child as a full human being who has transitioned from the spirit world (Mbiti 1969:156). These cases indicate the link between the notion of personhood and the naming of a child in Africa.

The understanding implies that personhood is fully realised when a child has been given a name, thereby being integrated into the community socially and spiritually. Thus, when a child has not been assigned a name, he or she remains in the process of becoming. On that basis, the concept of personhood is partly, though not fully, socially constructed. Since the child may be named anytime between the day of birth and the tenth day, depending on the culture, does this then compromise the notion of personhood and identity? For example, if the child is named on the eighth day, does it mean that he or she cannot be regarded as a complete person before the eighth day? The understanding is that the naming ceremony is perceived as an incorporating ceremony where a child is welcomed into the human family, and not necessarily as a rite that makes a child a complete person. The fact that naming rituals are done almost as soon as a child is born indicates the urgency of incorporating the child into the community.

Some African cultures, such as the Chewa people of Malawi and the Shona of Zimbabwe, hold that a child becomes a complete person when he or she can engage in reasoning, social norms, and moral conduct (Kaphagawani, 2004:339). On that basis, a child is born with the full potential to be a person and becomes a full person gradually as he or she develops the capacity for moral judgment, rational thought, social responsibility and communal participation. Nevertheless, African societies do not regard rational behaviour, moral reasoning, and social responsibility as sufficient criteria for personhood, although such aspects remain crucial, as discussed. Some African cultures trace personhood from the moment of conception. Mbiti observes that the understanding of family in the African traditional sense not only refers to the community of living people but also to the dead and unborn children (Mbiti, 1969:139–140). The inclusion of unborn children as part of the family in traditional African societies is crucial, as they represent the hope for the continuity of the family. To avoid the extinction of the family, African parents in most African cultures consider childbearing as a way of ensuring the continuity of the family.

The Akan people of Ghana believe that the unborn child is already regarded as a member of the community and family since the child's existentiality is based on blood relations (Owusu-Gyamfi, 2019; Hinduism Today, 1996). The emphasis is on the interconnectedness between the living, the dead and the unborn, which reflects the importance of lineage and the cyclical nature of human life. Due to the emphasis on lineage, which guarantees family and clan continuity, children are perceived as vital in carrying on the family traditions, customs and name. Among African cultures such as the Bemba people of Zambia and the Igbo people of Nigeria, children are highly valued and marriage is primarily seen as a means of procreation to the extent that a family without a child is deemed incomplete (Isidienu, 2015:119).

The viewpoint reaffirms the notion of ontological personalism, which provides an appealing foundation for understanding personhood in Africa. Ontological personalism emphasises that persons are essentially irreducible realities whose value and dignity stem from their very essence or being rather than social roles or functions. From this perspective, all human beings are human persons, and the intrinsic quality that makes one a full person begins at conception and is present throughout the life of an individual (Sullivan, 2003:10). Infants are thus neither potential persons nor 'half persons' but complete persons by their very nature. As Dennis Sullivan put it, 'there is no such thing as a potential person or a human non-person' (2003:10). Ontological personalism is based on the premise that "a human being is a substance. A substance is a distinct unity of essence that exists ontologically before any of its parts" (Sullivan, 2003:10). This view dates back to thinkers such as Aristotle and Thomas Aquinas, who discussed the notion of a being as a substance of a particular kind. For such thinkers, substance is understood as something that does not change in essence. For example, the substance present at the moment of conception is the same as that which remains throughout a person's life. This unchanging substance is equivalent to the inherent dignity or essence of every human being. If conception marks the beginning of personhood endowed with inherent dignity, then the idea of acquired personhood becomes questionable, as even children possess inherent dignity just like any other person.

Towards an Understanding of Child Rights in Traditional African Societies

The emphasis on the interconnectedness of the unborn, living and dead within the community, as well as marriage and lineage in some African cultures, suggests a recognition of the child's potential and belonging even before birth (Owusu-Gyamfi, 2019). If the unborn children are part of the human family, then it means that all children are part of this family. Moreover, children have the same essence or dignity as adults, given that what makes an adult a person is the same stuff that makes a child a person. Thus, if adults have certain entitlements or rights in traditional African societies, then children, too, should have rights. Since dignity is inherent and not acquired, it necessitates that children also have dignity. According to Kaime, 'in Africa, traditional value systems recognise human dignity and integrity of the individual as fundamental values. The concept of human dignity entails that all humans, by being human, are entitled to humanity, respect and dignity' (2005:224). Koime maintains that the principles of dignity are manifest in the traditional African societies through their responsibility to provide for the security and survival needs of their members.

Regarding children, Koime observes that human rights in Africa manifest themselves through the recognition that children are a valuable part of society (2005:224). In most traditional societies, children are seen as the future and the seedlings that ensure their continuity. Children are protected and nurtured for the survival of the family and community. Traditionally, grandparents are often excited to see their grandchildren, partly because they feel secure about the continuity of their family lines. When a child is born, the entire family and clan celebrate, but when a child dies, everyone is saddened. These subtle manifestations point to the fact that inherent dignity and value have always been ascribed to children in traditional African societies. While the notion of child rights is new, the way Africans have traditionally treated children shows that children have always been granted certain 'rights' as part of an African ontology.

Children in traditional African societies have the right to life, protection, nurture, and to belong to a human community.

African traditional culture understands the intrinsic worth and value of children and protects them. Koime observes that, 'African cultures recognise children as a special, precarious and fragile stage of the human being which requires special protection. This protection is translated into the traditional responsibility to provide for the security and survival needs of children and ensure their physical and psychological well-being' (2005:225). The fundamental goal of the traditional society is the survival and development of children. On that basis, the concept of 'child rights' has been implied in the way children have been protected and honoured in African traditional societies. However, the understanding that children have always been accorded certain rights in African societies is based on the view that African communitarianism puts the community before the individual. Relating this understanding to individual rights or entitlements, it insinuates that the rights or entitlements of the community are placed before those of the individual, that is, the child in this case. The individual is on the verge of losing his or her rights or entitlements once they conflict with those of the community.

The understanding that the community is before the individual partly entails that individual autonomy has little or no place in African communitarianism. However, what is evident in African societies is that 'the individual and the community are not radically opposed in the sense of priority but engaged in a contemporaneous formation' (Eze 2008:386). Both the individual and the community are important, such that they complement each other. At the same time, the individual can exist even when there is no community, but the community cannot exist without the individuals that form such a community. While this does not discredit the role of community in the formation of an individual, it emphasises the importance of individuality in any communal discourse. The community is fundamental to the social formation of an individual, where individuals become aware of their social duties and privileges towards themselves and others. When an individual suffers, it is the whole group that suffers (Mbiti, 1969:141).

The community's sole responsibility is for the preservation and protection of its members. According to Mbiti, 'whatever happens to the individual happens to the whole group, and whatever happens to the whole group happens to the individual. The individual can only say: "I am, because we are; and since we are, therefore I am'" (1969:141). Since the community and the individual are mutually dependent, there is no conflict between the rights of the community and those of the individual. In promoting the rights of the community, the individual's rights will be promoted since the two are not radically opposed but mutually dependent. The community cannot compromise the rights of the individual for its rights, but if at all it does, it will be for the common good of all the individuals that make up that community. This, therefore, means that the rights of everyone, including children, in traditional societies are important and have to be protected for the sustainability of the community.

Conclusion

African traditional societies have always regarded children as being imbued with dignity and inherent value. The emphasis on the interconnectedness between the unborn, living and the dead, as well as the importance of marriage, childbearing and family lineage, is crucial in understanding the place of children in Africa. Although the notion of 'child rights' is relatively new, some traditional African societies always had naming rituals, celebrated the birth of children and gradually integrated children into the community socially, spiritually, culturally and politically. From the perspective of African communitarianism, the issue of individual rights versus community rights becomes crucial, especially when one considers whether individuals have rights, considering the priority of the community over the individual. However, the individual and the community are not opposed to each other since they are mutually dependent. If the community attempts to compromise the individual's rights, it risks indirectly compromising its rights. For instance, if the community does not guarantee individuals the right to life, then there will be no continuity of its members, and it will become extinct. African societies have cherished and protected the lives of their members, irrespective of their age. While the notion that child rights are relatively new, Africans have always regarded children as having inherent value and dignity, and this has ensured that they are protected and safeguarded.

References

African Studies Centre n.d., *Zulu Names*, University of Pennsylvania. Available at: https://www.africa.upenn.edu/afl/zulunames.htm [Accessed 30 June 2025].

African Union 1979, *African Charter on the Rights and Welfare of the Child*, African Union.

ACRWC 1990, *African Charter on the Rights and Welfare of the Child*. Available at: https://au.int/sites/default/files/treaties/36804-treaty-african_charter_on_rights_welfare_of_the_child.pdf [Accessed 6 August 2024].

Drew, C. 2023, *25 Rite of Passage Examples*, Helpful Professor. Available at: https://helpfulprofessor.com/rite-of-passage-examples/ [Accessed 5 August 2024].

Doek, J.E. 2018, 'The Human Rights of Children: An Introduction', in Kilkelly, U. & Liefaard, T. (eds), *International Human Rights of Children*, Springer, Singapore. Available at: https://doi.org/10.1007/978-981-10-3182-3_1-1 [Accessed 7 August 2024].

Eze, M.O. 2008, 'What is African Communitarianism? Against Consensus as a Regulative Ideal', *South African Journal of Philosophy*, vol. 27, no. 4, pp. 386–399.

Gyekye, K. 1995, *An Essay on African Philosophical Thought: The Akan Conceptual Scheme*, Temple University Press.

Hinduism Today 1996, 'An Akan Queen Speaks', *Hinduism Today*, March. Available at: https://www.hinduismtoday.com/magazine/march-1996/1996-03-an-akan-queen-speaks/ [Accessed 30 June 2025].

Isidienu, I.C. 2015, 'The Family as the Bedrock of Igbo Traditional Society', *Journal of Modern European Languages and Literatures*, vol. 4, pp. 119–128. Available at: http://www.jmel.com.ng/index.php/jmel/article/view/57 [Accessed 30 June 2025].

Kaime, T. 2005, 'The Convention on the Rights of the Child and the Cultural Legitimacy of Children's Rights in Africa: Some Reflections', *African Human Rights Journal*, vol. 5, pp. 221–238.

Kanu, I.A. 2019, 'An Igwebuike Approach to the Study of African Traditional Naming Ceremony and Baptism', *International Journal of Religion and Human Relations*, vol. 11, no. 1, pp. 25–52.

Kaphagawani, D.N. 2004, 'African Conception of a Person: A Critical Survey', in Wiredu, K. (ed.) *A Companion to African Philosophy*, Blackwell Publishing Ltd.

Mbiti, J.S. 1969, *African Religion and Philosophy*, Anchor Books.

Musana, P. 2018, 'The African Concept of Personhood and its Relevance to Respect for Human Life and Dignity in Africa and the Global Context', *African Study Monographs*, Suppl. 56, pp. 21–32.

Najeeb, R. n.d., *A Universal Definition of What it Means to Be a "Child"*, UNICEF. Available at: https://www.unicef.org/sudan/stories/universal-definition-what-it-means-be-child [Accessed 3 August 2024].

Ndofirepi, A.P. & Shumba, A. 2014, 'Conceptions of "Child" among Traditional Africans: A Philosophical Purview', *Journal of Human Ecology*, vol. 45, no. 3, pp. 233–242.

Ogbujah, C. 2014, 'African Cultural Values and Inter-communal Relations: The Case with Nigeria', *International Institute for Science, Technology and Education*, vol. 4, no. 24, pp. 208–217.

Owusu-Gyamfi, C. 2019, 'Onipa: The Human Being and the Being of Human Among the Akan People of West Africa. Towards an African Theological Anthropology', *Trinity Postgraduate Review*, vol. 18, no. 1, pp. 74–94.

Sullivan, D.M. 2003, 'The Conception View of Personhood: A Review', *Ethics and Medicine*, vol. 19, no. 1, pp. 11–33.

United Nations n.d., *Convention on the Rights of the Child, Treaty Series*, vol. 1577, p. 3.

Wiredu, K. 1987, 'The Concept of Mind with Particular Reference to the Language and Thought of the Akans', in Floistad, G. (ed.), *Contemporary Philosophy: A New Survey*, vol. 5: *African Philosophy*, Dordrecht: Nijhoff.

Chapter Two
Reimagining Children's Rights in Africa: An African Philosophical Approach

Joyline Gwara and Isaac Mutelo

Abstract

There is an intricate relationship between culture and children's rights in Africa. This chapter proposes a philosophical framework that reformulates the debate surrounding children's welfare through the lens of African philosophy. The question concerns how best the rights of children can be examined from the perspective of African Philosophy. This is accomplished through a critical evaluation of traditional practices and beliefs and how they shape the understanding of childhood in relation to children's rights. Harnessing concepts such as communitarianism, respect for human dignity, and community responsibility, the chapter advocates for a holistic approach that respects cultural heritage while simultaneously promoting children's rights. The chapter aims to identify ways in which African cultural values can be integrated with present-day child rights frameworks.

Key words: Culture, African values, children's rights, cultural practices, dignity.

Introduction

Africa, being a home of diverse cultures, presents a rich yet sophisticated landscape that needs to be explored in an attempt to understand children's rights on the continent. In analysing African culture and values, one cannot assume or claim that Africa is homogeneous. Africa has diverse cultures, with different languages and different understandings of events and concepts. However, the chapter promptly argues that, while Africa is composed of diverse societies with different customs, languages, and traditions, there are fundamental similarities. These underlying common cultural elements justify the discussion on African culture as a unified entity. These elements include social values, religion, morals, political values, economics, and aesthetic values. At the core of these ties is religion. According to Mbiti (1969:3), the African is 'in all things religious' and 'religion is in their (Africans') whole system of being'. There is unity in diversity, whereby common threads that weave together African societies bind them together to form a vibrant African culture.

Legal frameworks such as the United Nations Convention on the Rights of the Child argued for a reconsideration of how children's rights are construed and applied in different cultural contexts. The chapter argues for the reframing of children's rights through the viewpoint of African philosophy, particularly emphasising Afro-communitarianism and the respect for human dignity. These cultural values cultivate community support, collective care or interconnectedness, foster educational values, ethical responsibilities, and offer children a robust sense of belonging and identity. These enhance social harmony and safeguard the well-being of children through collective obligations. However, the chapter also notes that some cultural practices pose challenges to the realisation of children's rights in Africa. Practices such as child labour, early child marriages, rites of passage, female genital mutilation, and corporal punishment, amongst others. These cultural practices reflect deeper societal problems, such as gender inequality and economic problems. They have a negative bearing on the physical and emotional welfare of the child. In addition, they hinder children's access to education, hence violating their rights.

It is imperative to analyse the dual nature of African cultural practices and beliefs concerning children's rights. This chapter explores ways in which African culture resonates with children's rights. Having clarified key concepts, this chapter examines African cultural values in line with the rights of children. The chapter emphasises the need to preserve beneficial cultural practices while addressing those that are harmful to children's well-being.

Culture and African Culture

There are several definitions of the concept of culture. The first scholar to have coined the term culture, Edward B. Taylor (1871), defined it as that complex whole which includes knowledge, belief, art, morals, laws, customs or any other capabilities and habits acquired by man as a member of society. From Taylor's definition, it is clear that culture encompasses everything that people learn and share as members of a society, which in turn influences their thoughts, behaviours, and interactions. In support of Taylor's definition, Gyekye (as cited in Machingura and Gwara, 2022:144) understands the word culture in a comprehensive sense to encompass the entire life of a people: their morals, religious beliefs, social structures, political and educational system, and other products of their creative spirits.

Other scholars such as Bello (1991:189) defined culture as 'the totality of the way of life evolved by a people in their attempts to meet the challenge of living in their environment, which gives order and meaning to their social, political, economic, aesthetics and religious norms thus distinguishing a people from their neighbours'. Culture is the entirety of a people's way of life, which is shaped by their environment and evolves. Culture differentiates one community from another, providing a unique identity that guides human behaviour in a specific context. It provides a group of people with various unique aspects, such as ways of greeting, ways of dressing, music and dance, social norms, and important life events like birth, marriage, and death. The cultural norms and values are passed on from generation to generation:

> *The child just grows into and within the cultural heritage of his people. He imbibes it. Culture, in traditional society, is not taught; it is caught. The child observes, imbibes and mimics the actions of his elders and siblings. He watches the naming ceremonies, religious services, marriage rituals, and funeral obsequies. He witnesses the coronation of a king or chief, the annual yam festival, the annual dance and acrobatic displays of guilds and age groups or his relations in the activities. The child in a traditional society cannot escape their cultural and physical environments.* (Fafunwa,1974:48).

Fafunwa's comment demonstrates that in traditional societies, children acquire culture through observation, imitation and participation. These are not formally taught, but rather, children absorb their cultural heritage from their society through watching and engaging with elders at various communal events. Lindsey (as cited in Machingura and Gwara, 2022:144) buttresses this point by highlighting that it is through socialisation that culture is passed on from generation to generation. Thus, children grow naturally into their culture and internalise it, making it an integral part of their identity and worldview.

Having analysed the notion of culture, it is important to define 'African culture.' African culture is a rich and diverse complex mixture of traditions, customs, and values that have been influenced by the history, geography and people of the continent. It plays a significant role in shaping the identities of the people on the continent. African culture is not a monolithic entity, but rather a broad ethnicity comprising distinct sub-communities that resist simplistic labels (Burness, 2023). The rich and diverse African culture varies not only from one country to another, but within each country as well. The culture of each ethnic group centres on family and can be found in each group's art, music and oral literature (Victoria Falls Guide, 2025).

Though it is diverse, African culture has similarities that pertain to the importance of morals, respect for culture, and reverence for elders, amongst others. It places a great emphasis on communalism and collectivism. African culture has been defined by Ezedike (2009:455) as:

> ... the total of shared attitudinal inclinations and capabilities, art, beliefs, moral codes and practices that characterise Africans. It can be conceived as a continuous, cumulative reservoir containing both material and non-material elements that are socially transmitted from one generation to another. African culture, therefore, refers to the whole of African heritage.

African culture embodies the comprehensive and multifaceted nature of African existence, embracing all its dimensions and manifestations. However, it has evolved over the years. Burness (2023) notes that African culture has been influenced by other continents, showing a willingness to adapt to the ever-changing modern world, whilst still cherishing its roots. It has adapted to modernity in various ways while maintaining its unique identity, traditions, and values (Burness, 2023). Changes brought about by urbanisation and globalisation have an impact on the African traditional ways of life. This has led to the emergence of new cultural forms and expressions. Clarke (as cited in Musya, 2023:2) argues that 'African culture was not static or frozen in time, but rather dynamic, creative and ever-changing'. Despite the changes, several key elements have remained central to African identity. These include oral traditions, such as storytelling, music, and dance, which have been used to transmit cultural heritage.

Children's Rights

Human rights are the fundamental rights and freedoms that belong to every single one of us, anywhere in the world (Amnesty International UK, 2025). They are inherent to all human beings regardless of race, sex, nationality, ethnicity, language, religion, or any other status. The key basic qualities of human rights are universal, inalienable, indivisible and interdependent. Thus, children's rights are human rights that apply especially. Article 1 of the United Nations Convention on the Rights of the Child defines a child as 'all people under 18 years of age'. Children and young people have the same general human rights as adults and also specific rights that recognise their special needs. Children are neither the property of their parents nor are they helpless objects of charity. They are human beings and are the subject of their rights (Singh and Bharti, 2021:220). Elias (as cited in Peña and Sánchez Cárdena, 2015:3) highlights that the rights of children protect the life, freedom, and development of minors. He further argues that these rights are a language used to enable their development in favourable conditions. He notes that the theory of rights states that any society that is deemed democratic must protect individuals and give them the possibility of achieving their personal life projects. Therefore, the language of rights has been used throughout history to facilitate the attainment of equality, promotion of fairness, social welfare and the protection such as children who deserve to be protected, until they can avoid the threats posed by modern society.

To protect the rights of children in Africa, the African Children's Charter was implemented. The fact that each region has its own unique human rights problems or priorities necessitated the need for the African Children's Charter. The UN General Assembly affirmed the value of regional agreements to promote and protect human rights, as regional treaties are best placed to consider and resolve their own human rights situations, whilst upholding culture, traditions and histories unique to the region (Lloyd, 2002:14). There are certain rights which need to be protected in Western countries, which may not necessarily apply to African countries. A case in point is the right of children to know their exact origin, if conceived through in vitro fertilisation, is of less importance in Africa than in Europe. Africa may be more concerned with a provision for the protection of the child against regimes practising discrimination and for the prohibition of negative prejudicial regional and cultural practices (Lloyd, 2002:14).

African Cultural Values and Children's Rights

African cultural values play an important role in shaping perspectives on children's rights. The understanding of the individual as embroiled in a web of relations within the society allows for the development of an environment that upholds children's rights. Afro-communitarianism and respect for human dignity are important in the understanding of child rights in Africa.

Afro-Communitarianism and Children's Rights

At the core of African communitarianism lies its emphasis on the importance of the community, shared collective responsibility, interconnectedness, and respect for human dignity. African communitarianism centres on the relationship that exists between the individual and the community. An individual is understood as owing his or her existence to the existence of others. In this view, the idea of community is central in the African understanding of relations. Thus, an individual's identity is defined in terms of the individual's relationship with the community. Thus, the concept of social relations becomes relevant and of paramount importance in the African worldview. Africans generally believe that when a person is born, he or she is born into the world of the visible and enters an already established community.

According to Tempels (1959:29), created beings for the Bantu preserve a bond with one another, an intimate ontological relationship. For him, the world of forces was held together like a spider's web of which no single thread could be caused to vibrate without shaking the whole network. In tandem, Mbiti (1969) has argued that the individual is simply part of a whole. The role of the community becomes that of making, creating or producing the individual who depends on the corporate group. After birth, the child must go through rites of incorporation so that he or she becomes fully integrated into the entire society:

> Only in terms of other people does the individual become conscious of his being, his duties, his privileges and responsibilities towards himself and other people. When he suffers, he does not suffer alone but with the corporate group; when he rejoices, he rejoices not alone but with his kinsmen, his neighbours and his relatives, whether dead or living. When he gets married, he is not alone, nor does the wife belong to him alone. So, also, the children to the corporate body of kinsmen, even if they bear only their father's name. Whatever happens to the individual happens to the whole group, and whatever happens to the whole group happens to the individual. The individual can only say: 'I am because we are; and since we are, therefore I am'. This is a cardinal point in the understanding of the African view of man (Mbiti, 1969:108-109).

These collective values are encapsulated in *ubuntu*, which is the view that *umuntu ngumuntu ngabantu* (a person is a person through others). Metz (2010:93) conceives of *ubuntu* as a kind of dignity a human being has by their capacity for communal relations. He further notes that dignity is a superlative non-instrumental value devoid of social construction. It is typical of individual members of the same species and does not vary based on one's status. Ikuenobe goes beyond Metz's understanding of dignity by arguing that it transcends having the capacity for harmonious relationships and is constituted by ensuring this harmony. Molefe (2020:814) provides his understanding of dignity as a capacity of showing moral sympathy towards the lives and conditions of others. This African understanding of human dignity underscores the intrinsic value of all members of society, including children. Every child has inherent worth. Children are therefore seen as valuable members of the community who are not merely dependents. Where child dignity is respected, children are provided with an equitable environment that fosters active engagement in their societies, advocating for their rights and needs. Since individuals are not isolated beings, but rather are part of a broad social fabric. The interdependence of the individuals brings about a sense of communal responsibility, which is key for upholding the rights of children. In other words, adults have a role of nurturing, protecting, and advocating for the well-being of the child.

In most African societies, an individual has to be incorporated into a society where they will then achieve personhood. Personhood is something that individuals can fail to achieve (Menkiti, 1984:172). Personhood is something which has to be achieved and is not given simply because one is born of human seed (Menkiti, 1984:172). Full personhood is not perceived as simply given at the very beginning of one's life, but is attained after one is well along in society, which indicates straightaway that the older an individual gets, the more they become a person. Ifeanyi Anthony Menkiti notes that many languages, English included, refer to children and newborns as 'its'. His point is that one can use the word 'it' only when referring to children and newborns, but cannot use it regarding older people (Menkiti, 1984:173). Menkiti further argues that in the African context, there is a relative absence of ritualised grief when the death of a young person occurs, whereas with the death of an older person, the burial ceremony becomes more elaborate and the grief more ritualised, indicating a significant difference in the conferral of ontological status.

Menkiti's work can be understood as suggesting that individuals derive their identity and rights from the community. While this view echoes the importance of social interconnectedness, it tends to undermine the rights of children. His views overlook the specific rights of children as unique individuals. The fact that he does not see children and newborns as persons is problematic. His argument can simply be used to justify the perpetuation of harmful traditional practices in the name of social cohesion, hence violating the rights of children.

In disregarding Menkiti's reasoning on the use of 'it' regarding children, contrasted with the fact that one cannot refer to adults using the same pronoun. For Matolino, the first problem with Menkiti's argument is his attempt to ground the normative difference between babies and adults in African thinking, through his alleged evidence of the usage of the English word 'it' as an indicator of the ontological difference between babies and adults (Matolino, 2001:28). He further argues that the most curious thing about this supposed normative significance of 'it' in African thinking is that the normative significance fails to find expression in any African language, including Menkiti's own Igbo. According to Matolino, the normative function of 'it' would have carried more weight had Menkiti (1984:28) shown that there is such a word in his language which does the normative work of showing the ontological difference between the young and the old. He also argues that Menkiti's attempt at using the word 'it' from the English language in the way he does as evidence for his conclusion betrays either a selective use of the word or a serious misunderstanding of how the word operates in the English language.

Gyekye also found Menkiti's view to be problematic. Unlike Menkiti, who views children as not yet persons, Gyekye argues that children will mature into exercising moral values 'in the fullness of time' as they engage various individual and corporate ethical boundaries in their life—not just because they pass from one status to another (Bell, 2002:62). According to Gyekye (1997:59-62), Menkiti's radical communitarianism fails to give adequate recognition to the individual's creativeness and inventiveness, and it fails to give individuals due regard for their human rights.

For Gyekye (1996:36), the idea of communitarianism emphasises activity and the success of the wider society, not necessarily to the detriment of the individual member of society. Thus, African cultures generally recognise that the naturally social human being also has individuality, personal will, and an identity that must be exercised. He argues that the view that the almighty presence of the community crushes the individual in traditional African societies is not the whole truth (Gyekye, 1996:36). The individual can re-evaluate existing communal values, which is key to the fact that the community does not wholly engulf the individual. The individual can wriggle out of it. Thus, the capacity of self-assertion which the individual can exercise presupposes, and derives from, the autonomous nature of the person (Gyekye and Wiredu, 1992:112).

Gyekye's views are significant for upholding the rights of children. Children have a right to be heard. Gyekye's acknowledgement of children possessing individuality is key to upholding the rights of children to expression and participation in decisions affecting their lives. His argument that children are moral agencies in potency fosters the view that they will mature into morally responsible individuals. Thus, environments that promote this growth must be provided for children to uphold their rights. His emphasis on personal will supports children's rights to make choices and assert their preferences. Though children are part of a community, they have individual needs and rights. These include the right to education, healthcare, and protection from harm.

Thus, communitarianism, through its emphasis on community, interconnectedness, respect for human dignity and collective responsibility, upholds children's rights. The fact that children are integral members of the community, the community, in turn, has to create an environment in which the well-being of children is nurtured and protected. The famous African adage "it takes a village to raise a child" (Simona, 2024) is indicative of the fact that extended families and communities must nurture children. This shared responsibility fosters the rights of children to protection and education as the whole community works together to realise them.

Cultural Practices that Violate Children's Rights

From the ongoing discussion, it is apparent that African cultural values such as Afro-communitarianism and respect for human dignity help foster children's rights. However, it is noticeable that certain cultural practices are detrimental to children's rights. It is thus important to examine cultural practices that violate children's rights. These practices include female genital mutilation, rites of passage, child marriages, child labour, and corporal punishment.

Child labour has been defined as work performed by children who are too young for the task in the sense that by performing it they unduly reduce their present economic welfare or their future income-earning capabilities either by shrinking their future external choice set or reducing their productive capabilities (Andvig, 2000:4). The International Labour Organization and the United Nations Children's Fund (2021) notes that child labour is higher for boys than for girls, though it is common for both sexes. The statistics also show a high number of child labourers in rural areas as compared to urban areas. The report shows that nearly one-third of 5 to 11-year-olds in child labour are in hazardous work that directly endangers their health, safety, and moral development (2021). This is happening in Africa despite the call by the Convention on the 'Rights of the Child' to protect the child from economic exploitation and from performing any work that is likely to be hazardous (Assefa, 2000:3).

In developing countries, one in three girls is married by age 18 and one in nine by age fifteen. Child marriages have devastating lifelong consequences. Less likely to complete primary and secondary school, more likely to experience unwanted pregnancies, more likely to experience violence and more likely to remain poor (African Union, 2015:5). In many African countries, patriarchal attitudes towards women and girls are perpetuated by cultural and religious norms, not only rendering girls more vulnerable to child marriage but also actively promoting it. For instance, in the Kivu region of the DRC, great importance is placed on a girl's virginity before marriage. After the wedding day (whether a traditional or civil marriage), the groom's family is supposed to give a gift to the bride's mother if she is a virgin. The absence of a gift is a grave dishonour and a sign that the mother did not raise her daughter properly.

Hence, the sooner a girl is married, the higher the chances of getting a gift and the lower the chances that dishonour will befall the family (Centre for Human Rights, 2018:7). This is closely associated with Female Genital Mutilation (FGM), which involves partial or total removal of the external female genitalia, or other injury to the female genital organs for non-medical reasons (WHO, 2025). It is mostly carried out on young girls between infancy and age 15. Most of those who support female genital mutilation believe it maintains cleanliness, increases a girl's chances of marriage, protects her virginity, and discourages 'female promiscuity', thus preserving the family honour (The Conversations, 2024). The World Health Organisation (2015) reports that more than 230 million girls and women alive today have undergone female genital mutilation (FGM) in thirty countries in Africa, the Middle East and Asia where FGM is practised.

In Ghana, Benin, Togo, and Yorubaland in Nigeria, the system of *trokosi* is prevalent. This is whereby young virgin girls, usually between the ages of six and eight years, are sacrificed to the gods, as a form of reparation for the crimes committed by their relatives (Asomah:2015). The priests, who are the custodians of the shrines of the gods, begin to have sexual intercourse with the girls as soon as they become teenagers. All these practices and beliefs violate children's rights.

Conclusion

The chapter explored the relationship between African cultural values and children's rights in view of African philosophy. With the changes in time, it is important to address the challenges of upholding traditional beliefs while ensuring that the rights of children are respected and protected. The balancing has to take into consideration both cultural heritage and the principles in international human rights frameworks. As highlighted above, African cultural values place great emphasis on community, respect for human dignity, and interdependence. Through *Ubuntu*, Afro-communitarianism can help us uphold children's rights. However, other cultural practices such as child labour, child marriages, and female genital mutilation are detrimental to children's rights. It is imperative that all stakeholders sift through African cultural values and uphold those that respect children's rights and discard those that are detrimental to children's rights.

References

African Union. 2015, *Campaign to end Child Marriage in Africa: The Effects of Traditional and Religious Practices of Child Marriage on Africa's Socio-Economic Development. A Review of Research, Reports and Toolkits from Africa*, Available at: https://au.int [Accessed 12 April 2023].

Amnesty International UK. 2025, *What are human rights?*, Available at: https://www.amnesty.org.uk/what-are-human-rights [Accessed 15 March 2023].

Andvig, J.C. 2000, *An Essay on Child Labour in Sub-Saharan Africa – A Bargaining Approach*, Oslo: Norsk Utenrikspolitisk Institutt (Norwegian Institute).

Asomah, Y. 2015, 'Cultural rights versus human rights: A critical analysis of the trokosi practice in Ghana and the role of civil society', *African Human Rights Law Journal*, vol. 15, no. 1, pp. 129–149. Available at: http://dx.doi.org/10.17159/1996-2096/2015/v15n1a6 [Accessed 5 April 2023].

Assefa, A., *The incident of child labour in Africa with empirical evidence from rural Ethiopia*, ZEF Discussion Papers on Development Policy, No.32, Bonn: University of Bonn, Centre for Development Research (ZEF).

Bell, R.H. 2002, *Understanding African Philosophy: A Cross-Cultural Approach to Classical and Contemporary Issues*, London: Routledge.

Bello, S. 1991, *Culture and Decision Making in Nigeria*, Lagos: National Council for Arts and Culture.

Burness, B. 2023, *Exploring the Five Characteristics of African Culture*, Available at: https://mukangoafrica.co.za/what-are-the-five-characteristics-of-african-culture [Accessed 25 April 2023].

Centre for Human Rights. 2018, *A Report on Child Marriage in Africa*, Available at: https://www.chr.up.ac.za [Accessed 15 April 2023].

Children's Rights Alliance. 2013, *Summary of the UN Convention on the Rights of the Child*, Available at: https://childrensrights.ie/wp-content/uploads/2023/04/SummaryUNCRC.pdf [Accessed 20 March 2023].

Fafunwa, A.B. 1974, *History of Education in Nigeria*, London: George Allen and Unwin.

Gyekye, K. 1996, *African Cultural Values: An Introduction*, Philadelphia: Sankofa Publishing Company.

Gyekye, K. & Wiredu, K. (eds.) 1992, 'Person and Community in African Thought', in *Person and Community: Ghanaian Philosophical Studies*, Washington, D.C: The Council for Research in Values and Philosophy.

Lloyd, A. 2002, 'A theoretical analysis of the reality of children's rights in Africa: An introduction to the African Charter on the Rights and Welfare of the Child', *African Human Rights Law Journal*, pp. 11–32.

Machingura, F. & Gwara, J. 2022, 'Cultures, Women, and the Apostolic Faith Mission in Zimbabwe', in Chitando, E., Chirongoma, S. & Biri, K. (eds.), *Women and Religion in Zimbabwe: Strides and Struggles*, Lanham: Lexington Books.

Matolino, B. 2001, 'The (Mal) Function of "It" in Ifeanyi Menkiti's Normative Account of Person', *African Studies Quarterly*, vol. 12, no. 4, pp. 23–27.

Mbiti, J.S. 1969, *African Religions and Philosophy*, London: Heinemann.

Menkiti, I. 1984, 'Person and Community in African Traditional Thought', in Wright, R.A. (ed.), *African Philosophy: An Introduction*, Lanham: University Press of America, pp. 171–181.

Metz, T. 2010, 'Human dignity, capital punishment and an African moral theory', *Journal of Human Rights*, vol. 9, pp. 81–99.

Molefe, M. 2020, *African personhood and applied ethics*, Makhanda, South Africa: NISC Pty Limited.

Musya, J.K. 2023, *Building Bridges: The Role of African Culture in Promoting Peace and Unity*, Nairobi: The Kairos Book Publishers.

Simona. 2024, *It Takes A Village To Raise A Child – Its Relevance In Modern Times*, Available at: https://mamiina.co.uk/it-takes-a-village-to-raise-a-child [Accessed 18 April 2023].

Singh, H. & Bharti, J. 2021, 'Child Rights and Human Rights: Review', *EPRA International Journal of Multidisciplinary Research (IJMR)*, vol. 7, no. 12, pp. 220–224.

Taylor, E.B. 1871, *Primitive Culture: Researches into the Development of Mythology, Philosophy, Religion, Language, Art and Custom*, 2nd ed., London: John Murray.

Tempels, P. 1959, *Bantu Philosophy*, Paris: Presence Africaine.

The Conversation. 2024, *Female genital mutilation is on the rise in Africa: disturbing new trends in driving up the numbers*, Available at: https://theconversation.com/female-genital-mutilation-is-on-the-rise-in-africa-disturbing-new-trends-are-driving-up-the-numbers-227175 [Accessed 20 April 2023].

United Nations. n.d., *Peace, dignity, and equality on a healthy planet*, Available at: https://www.un.org/en/global-issues/human-rights [Accessed 12 April 2023].

Victoria Falls Guide. 2025, *African Culture*, Available at: https://www.victoriafalls-guide.net/african-culture.html [Accessed 15 March 2023].

WHO. 2025, *Female Genital Mutilation*, Available at: https://www.who.int/news-room/fact-sheets/detail/female-genital-mutilation [Accessed 14 March 2023].

Chapter Three
Normative Content of Selected Rights in the African Children's Charter: The Right to Health

Michelle Brotherton

Introduction

> 'Noting with concern that the situation of most African Children, remains critical due to the unique factors of their socio-economic, cultural, traditional and developmental circumstances, natural disasters, armed conflicts, exploitation and hunger, and on account of the child's physical and mental immaturity he/she needs special safeguards and care' (Preamble, African Charter for the Rights and Welfare of the Child)

The African Charter on the Rights and Welfare of the Child ('African Children's Charter') provides for children's right to health in the same wording as the African Charter on Human and Peoples' Rights ('African Charter') but elaborates with a list of measures to be taken in seeking to realise this right. The African Children's Charter was enacted to reflect the rights of the child in the African context. Similarly, the International Children's Rights Charter outlines the measures to be taken by States parties to fully realise the right to health for children. It emphasises primary health care, recognising it as an effective means to give effect to the right to health. The African Children's Charter does not replace the International Children's Rights Charter but adds to it, addressing issues that are more prevalent in Africa specifically. Such as HIV/AIDS, harmful cultural practices, environmental factors unique to Africa, and rural access to health care services. Like the African Charter, the context-sensitive framework of the regional system allows for appropriate provisions to be made regarding the right to health that is reflective of the issues faced and adequately addresses the problems and challenges to effectively realise children's right to health in Africa.

The African Charter departs from other international law instruments and stipulates that the state shall protect the family unit and, per article 10(1), 'shall take care of its physical and moral health'. So, in addition to providing for the right to health, the African Charter holds the state responsible for the physical health of the family unit. Subsequently, in the African Children's Charter, parents are deemed responsible for the health of the child within the family unit. This is arguably an example of and uniquely context-sensitive provision that reflects the values held in African communities, families, and cultures. The African Children's Charter provides a list of measures to be achieved and arguably goes further than the African Charter with, for example, providing explicitly for preventative care. The African Children's Charter also addresses issues and challenges faced in Africa, in particular, such as nutritional issues and access to safe drinking water.

In looking at how the African Children's Charter departs from the International Children's Rights Charter and also the African Charter, certain deductions about the normative content of the right to health of children can be made. This chapter considers the normative content of children's right to health in the African context as provided for by the African Children's Charter. Through examining the measures provided for in Article 14 of the African Children's Charter, the normative content of children's right to health in Africa can be contextualised to challenges and problems unique to Africa. Additionally, this chapter will then consider problems and issues pertaining to children's right to health that are unique or specific to Africa, including issues such as female genital mutilation, child marriage, nutritional concerns, safe drinking water, and rural access to health care services.

Regional and International Instruments Pertaining to the Rights of the Child

Although the primary focus of this chapter pertains to the African Children's Charter, it is necessary to consider relevant provisions in other instruments which inform the normative content of the right as provided for in the African Children's Charter. Some of these provisions have influenced the African Children's Charter, and some have influenced the interpretation thereof. Some also provide means by which to address issues not provided for or considered in the African Children's Charter. Article 24 of the Convention of the Rights of the Child provides that:

> States Parties recognise the right of the child to the enjoyment of the highest attainable standard of health and the facilitation of the treatment of illness and rehabilitation of health. State Parties shall strive to ensure that no child is deprived of his or her right of access to such healthcare services.

The accompanying obligations in article 24(3) read: 'States Parties shall take all effective and appropriate measures with a view to abolishing traditional practices prejudicial to the health of children.' The African Charter on Human and Peoples' Rights also has important provisions. Article 16 of the African Charter provides for the right to the 'best attainable state of physical and mental health'. Article 16(2) places the obligation on States Parties to the Charter to 'take the necessary measures to protect the health of their people and to ensure that they receive medical attention when they are sick'. These provisions do not solely pertain to adults but all people, including children and thus this provision should be read with the relevant provisions in the African Children's Charter and should inform both the normative content and the State Party obligations. The African Charter, in Article 1, commits to recognising the rights, duties, and freedoms of people and undertakes to 'adopt legislative and other measures to give effect to them'.

Another important instrument is the African Youth Charter, which was adopted in Banjul, The Gambia, on 2 July 2006 and entered into force on 8 August 2009. Like the African Children's Charter, the African Youth Charter emphasises the family unit. Article 8 provides for the protection of the family, including the prohibition of child marriage. An interesting instrument, the African Youth Charter provides for some aspects of children's health rights which are not addressed in any other instruments. For example, it addresses issues such as youth participation, national youth policies, education and skills development, and even youth employment, *inter alia*. It also explicitly addresses health rights in Article 16, wherein a range of measures to be taken by member states to ensure the right to health are emphasised. Among these (but not limited to), which are somewhat particular to the African context, include the need to ensure access to medical care in rural areas, to involve youth in determining their reproductive health needs, to provide access to reproductive healthcare services and contraceptives, to institute programmes about African health pandemics such as HIV/AIDS, tuberculosis, and malaria and to prevent unsafe abortions.

The African Charter on the Rights and Welfare of the Child

The African Children's Charter was adopted by the Organisation of African Unity on 11 July 1990 and came into force on 29 November 1999. As of 2024, 50 African Union members had ratified the African Children's Charter; five have not. These five include Morocco, the Sahrawi Arab Democratic Republic, South Sudan, and Tunisia. Three countries have ratified the Charter but have entered reservations, namely Egypt, Mauritania, and Sudan, but none of these reservations pertain particularly to issues of health (African Charter on the Rights and Welfare of the Child, 1990). Article 14(2) of the African Children's Charter sets out what states need to address to achieve children's right to health as guaranteed by the African Children's Charter:

a) Reduce infant and child mortality rates;
b) to ensure the provision of necessary medical assistance and healthcare to all children, with the emphasis on the development of primary healthcare;
c) to ensure the provision of adequate nutrition and safe drinking water;
d) to combat disease and malnutrition within the framework of primary healthcare through the application of appropriate technology;
e) to ensure appropriate healthcare for expectant and nursing mothers;
f) to develop preventative healthcare and family life education, and provision of services;
g) to integrate basic health service programmes in national development plans;
h) To ensure that all sectors of society, in particular parents, children, community leaders, and community workers, are informed and supported in the use of basic knowledge of child health and nutrition, the advantages of breastfeeding, hygiene and environmental sanitation and the prevention of domestic and other accidents;

i) *to ensure the meaningful participation of non-governmental organisations, local communities and the beneficiary population in the planning and management of basic service programmes for children;*
j) *to support through technical and financial means, the mobilisation of local community resources in the development of primary healthcare for children.*

As laid out above, article 14(2) of the African Children's Charter provides for comprehensive measures that states need to take to ensure that the right to health of children is realised. Among these provisions, some reflect uniquely African considerations, problems, and challenges. Article 14(2)(c), for example, addressing nutrition and safe drinking water, is arguably a provision necessary mostly in developing nations and places at risk of famine or malnutrition, or where drinking water is scarce, such as in many African countries. Thus, the explicit inclusion of this reflects that the context in which this aspect of the right to health of children must be realised has been considered. Article 14(2)(f) provides for the development of preventative healthcare but arguably goes further than the African Charter by including family life education regarding preventative health care. This, again, reflects values unique to African communities where emphasis is placed on the family and community as a unit as opposed to an individualistic approach to healthcare provision. Similarly, Article 14(2)(h) emphasises that all sectors of society, including parents and the community, are to be informed of the necessary information to assist in realising children's right to health, such as information on breastfeeding, hygiene, nutrition, environmental sanitation, and the prevention of accidents. This, especially when read with the emphasis the African Children's Charter places on the family unit, reflects the communitarian spirit which is contextually necessary to consider when seeking to realise children's right to health in Africa.

The rights in the African Children's Charter are interrelated and interdependent. Article 4 pertains to the best interests of the child and provides that in 'all actions concerning the child undertaken by any person or authority, the best interests of the child shall be the primary consideration'. Article 5 pertains to the survival and development of the child, and Article 5(2) provides that 'States Parties to the present Charter shall ensure, to the maximum extent possible, the survival, protection and development of the child'. The latter's link to the African Children's Charter's guarantee of children's right to health is evident, pertaining to the survival, protection, and development of the child. Health rights are pivotal to the survival, protection, and development of children.

Like the African Charter, the African Children's Charter commits to recognising the rights, freedoms, and duties of children and commits to undertake necessary steps and to 'adopt legislative or other measures'. Specifically, of concern when considering issues pertaining to Africa in particular, article 1(3) provides that 'Any custom, tradition, cultural or religious practice that is inconsistent with the rights, duties and obligations contained in the present Charter shall, to the extent of such inconsistency, be discouraged'. Article 21 of the African Children's Charter provides specifically for protection against harmful social and cultural practices. State Parties are tasked to eliminate harmful social and cultural practices affecting the 'welfare, dignity, normal growth and development of the child'. In particular, State Parties are to eliminate 'those customs and practices prejudicial to the health or life of the child' and also 'those customs and practices discriminatory to the child on the grounds of sex or other status'. Article 21 also prohibits child marriage, which has health implication as will be discussion further below.

The Normative Content of the Right to Health of Children in Africa

The African Children's Charter:

> [C]harges that the concept of rights and welfare of the child should be inspired and characterised by the virtues of African cultural heritage, historical background and the values of the African civilisation. In other words, the Charter requires that the rights and welfare of the child, which are derived from universal sources, must be alive to the reality of African children. (Kaine, 2009:121)

Having considered the specific provisions providing for and relating to children's right to health in Africa, and in particular those provided for in the African Children's Charter, it is now possible to consider the normative content of the right and what it entails, beyond even the scope provided for in article 14(2) of the African

Children's Charter. The overview of provisions allows one to consider what the right to health of children means in the African context and, therefore, how it can be realised and protected. The World Health Organisation notes that health is not merely the absence of illness or disease (World Health Organisation, 2022). The very reason that there are human rights instruments, both international, regional, and national, providing for the protection of children's rights is that children are vulnerable. This vulnerability requires special protection (Palm, 2017).

Children are vulnerable both physically and mentally, both of which have health rights implications. Their vulnerability also places them at greater risk of certain ailments and health complications. The World Health Organisation holds that children should be able to grow, develop and reach their full potential as well as live in conditions conducive to attaining the highest standard of health (Palm, 2017; Constitution of the World Health Organisation). Generally, children's rights provisions address the age and developmental discrepancy between adults and children and therefore, age and developmentally appropriate needs need to be considered and addressed. A means through which to do this is legislation and age-specific services (Bou-Said, 2022). Importantly, children's health rights need to include pre- and post-natal healthcare too (Palm, 2017). Contextualising children's health rights in Africa is necessary because 'African children are inheritors and keepers of African Cultural Heritage' (Kaine, 2009). It is thus within this context that children's health rights need to be considered and what the right to health of children, within this context, entails.

The World Health Organisation provides that the right to health must be enjoyed without discrimination on the grounds of age. A core principle of the right to health, as recognised by the World Health Organisation, is non-discrimination, and thus, children cannot be discriminated against when considering health rights. Special provision needs to be made for children in order not to discriminate against them based on age (World Health Organisation, 2022). The World Health Organisation has adopted what is known as the AAAQ framework (World Health Organisation, 2022). This holds that healthcare must be available, accessible, acceptable, and of quality. Accessibility in particular refers to non-discrimination, physical accessibility, financial accessibility, and information accessibility. Acceptability refers to having respect for medical ethics, being culturally appropriate (of specific importance in the African context), and being sensitive to gender. Quality refers to healthcare or medicines being safe, effective, people-centred, timely, equitable, integrated, and efficient. A resolution of the African Commission echoes this approach of the World Health Organisation. The African Commission passed a resolution in 2008, the Resolution on Access to Health and Needed Medicines in Africa. This resolution incorporates some of the more internationally recognised frameworks of human rights, as it:

> *To guarantee the full scope of access to needed medicines, including: The availability in sufficient quantities of needed medicines, including existing medicines and the development of new medicines needed for the highest attainable level of health; the accessibility of needed medicines to everyone without discrimination, including physical accessibility of needed medicines to all; economic accessibility (affordability) of needed medicines to all; information accessibility about the availability and efficacy of medicines; the acceptability of medicine supplies, being respectful of cultural norms and medical ethics; the quality of medicine supplies, ensuring that available medicines are safe, effective and medically appropriate.*

As apparent above, African regional authorities have recognised the international standards and guidelines pertaining to the normative content of the right, without discarding the particulars of the African context. The Abuja Declaration on HIV/AIDS, Tuberculosis and other related Infectious Diseases of 2001 aspires that every child survives to have a healthy childhood (Aspiration 4). The aims for the year 2040 include the commitment that no child dies a preventable death, that mother-to-child-transmission of HIV is eliminated, that anti-retroviral treatment is provided for all children living with HIV, that every child is vaccinated against vaccine-preventable diseases, to curb malaria and other preventable diseases, to ensure the availability of nutritional supplements; to provide child education on HIV, to promote exclusive breastfeeding, to reduce maternal mortality; and that all children are to have access to health care services. The fundamental normative content of the health rights of children needs to be considered within the African context for them to be realised. As Sillah and Chibanda (2013:50) put it:

> *The African Charter of the Rights and Welfare of the Child was designed to serve as a blueprint for the observance of children's rights by every African country. The African Charter became the epitome of what children's rights ought to be taking into consideration that the child, due to the needs of his physical and mental development, requires particular care about health, physical, mental, moral and social development, and requires legal protection in conditions of freedom, dignity, and security.*

This is arguably why the African Children's Charter is said to offer a higher level of protection than the Children's Rights Charter (Lloyd, 2002). The Children's Rights Charter arguably has a Western bias, in particular because there was very little input from African countries in the drafting of the Children's Rights Charter (Lloyd, 2002). The African Children's Charter puts children's health rights into the African cultural context, which is arguably necessary to guarantee these rights. Thus, in considering the normative content of children's health rights, it is helpful to do so against the backdrop of some points made in the preamble of the African Children's Charter. In particular, the preamble notes:

> *Taking into consideration the virtues of their cultural heritage, historical background and the values of the African civilisation, which should inspire and characterise their reflection on the concept of the rights and welfare of the child.*

In light of such considerations, the normative content of children's health rights needs to be interpreted to be fully realised in Africa.

Children's Health Rights Issues Specific to the African Context

Ekundayo (2015) maintains that the "lack of enjoyment of the right to health has had a disproportionate effect on the poor and other vulnerable or disadvantaged children in Africa. This is as a result of poverty, underdevelopment, and corruption, which are prevalent on the continent." As reflected by Ekundayo, some issues are quintessential to the African context, and it is within this context that health rights need to be considered. It is important to now consider key issues particular to the African continent, issues that affect African people because of the context in which they live. These are also not the only health rights issues prevalent in Africa, just ones that have been chosen to be highlighted, given the discussions above. Each will be considered briefly as a health rights issue and considering the health implications of the issue, as well as possible provisions that have been made to address these issues.

Rural Access to Healthcare Services

Rural access to healthcare services is a problem that is certainly not unique to Africa, but is prevalent in Africa. Many parts of African society live in rural settings. Physical access to some of these places is difficult, making the accessibility of healthcare an issue. For example, emergency healthcare services struggle to access rural parts of South Africa because the roads are in disarray, or in some parts, there are only footpaths to the settlements or villages. This issue of physical accessibility to healthcare services also means that people struggle to access necessary medicines and often fail to keep up to date with chronic medication because of the effort it takes to get to a healthcare facility. Such issues, in turn, perpetuate ill health in such rural areas. The African Youth Charter recognises this in article 8 in providing that there needs to be access to healthcare services for persons living in rural areas. Similarly, information accessibility is an issue in rural communities where health education is not prevalent or perhaps not available in the local language. Efforts need to be made to ensure that people living in rural settings are given adequate opportunities to participate in their health rights. Given the number of rural communities in Africa, this is an issue which arguably needs more attention, especially as it pertains to health and accessibility of health. It does not help to have the resources if people cannot access them.

Malnutrition

According to the World Health Organisation (2023), malnutrition refers to "deficiencies or excesses in nutrient intake, imbalance of essential nutrients or impaired nutrient utilisation." Whilst malnutrition covers lack of nutrition as well as issues such as overweight and obesity, in Africa, the prevalent issue is undernutrition. Undernutrition results in stunting, underweight, wasting, and micronutrient deficiencies. Wasting is common in Africa in areas where children lack adequate access to nutrient-rich foods. The World Health Organisation defines wasting as "low weight-for-height" and warns that wasting in children puts them at greater risk of death if not treated. Another issue prevalent in Africa is stunting. Stunting is defined by the World Health Organisation as low height for age. Stunting occurs because of chronic undernutrition and is 'usually associated with poverty, poor maternal health and nutrition, frequent illness and/or inappropriate feeding and care in early life' (World Health Organisation, 2023). Article 14(2)(c) of the African Children's Charter makes provision for the need to address the nutrition of children. Considering Article 5 of the African Children's Charter, which provides for the development and survival of the child, it is evident that the provision of adequate nutrition was contemplated in the drafting of these documents as it pertains to the African context.

Environmental Health

Reducing environmental risks could prevent one in four child deaths. Over 1.7 million child deaths in children under the age of five were attributable to the environment (World Health Organisation, 2018). These include deaths from diseases such as respiratory infections, diarrhoea, neonatal conditions, malaria, and injuries. Environmental risks impact the health and development of children from conception into adulthood. Addressing issues such as pollution, water pollution, and air pollution can significantly impact children's health and the realisation of their health rights. Of major concern in Africa specifically is the issue of safe drinking water, as well as the state of the water in which children play or bathe. The African Children's Charter considers this in Article 14(2)(c). According to UNICEF (2019), 'only 5 per cent of children in Africa live in areas where air pollution is reliably measured at ground-level'. This means that the other ninety-four per cent of children are living in conditions where the air pollution cannot be measured reliably.

Air pollution is particularly harmful to babies and young children as it can be harmful to the development of their lungs. As UNICEF Executive Director Henrietta Fore has noted that 'Air pollution is a silent killer of children. And in Africa especially, we know the problem is severe, we just don't know how severe'. Water is another environmental health concern. For example, only about twenty-five per cent of the African population enjoys access to piped drinking water supplies, according to UNICEF (2013). This illustrates a problem faced by rural communities that has health impacts on water, hygiene, and sanitation. UNICEF (2021) estimates that one in five children globally does not have enough water to meet their daily needs. Areas of extreme water vulnerability include many Southern African countries.

Female Genital Mutilation

The African Children's Charter disallows any harmful cultural practices. One of these is arguably female genital mutilation. According to the World Health Organisation and the Pan American Health Organisation (2012), female genital mutilation 'comprises all procedures that involve partial or total removal of the external female genitalia, or other injury to the female genital organs for non-medical reasons'. Whilst there are different reasons for this practice, a common reason is that it is believed to ensure that the female adheres to social norms such as sexual restraint and femininity. Unfortunately, this practice is prevalent in Africa. Female genital mutilation has absolutely no health benefits. It is a harmful cultural practice with both short-term and long-term health risks. These include, but are not limited to, pain, excessive bleeding, sepsis, need for surgery, urinary problems, poor quality of sexual life, infertility, chronic pain, keloids, and psychological consequences.

As the World Health Organisation and the Pan American Health Organisation (2012) point out, 'the practice reflects deep-rooted inequality between the sexes and constitutes an extreme form of discrimination against women. Female genital mutilation is nearly always carried out on minors and is therefore a violation of the right of the child'. The African Children's Charter, in addressing harmful cultural practices as well as non-discrimination, provides a tool by which to potentially address this issue from a rights-based perspective. Article 1(3) of the African Children's Charter provides for discouraging any custom, tradition or practice that is inconsistent with the rights provided for in the African Children's Charter. Female genital mutilation is certainly a harmful practice that impedes the health rights of girls and young women.

Child Marriage

Child marriage amounts to a health rights issue because of its outcomes. Child Marriage is when women or girls are married before the age of 18, and often involves issues of consent. Both physical and mental consequences impact the health rights of the child subject to child marriage. Article 21 of the African Children's Charter protects harmful practices and explicitly prohibits child marriage. UNICEF (2022) estimates that of the girls and women alive today, over 650 million were married before their eighteenth birthday. Half of these reside in Eastern and Southern Africa. It is commonly held that girls who marry at a young age are more vulnerable to intimate partner violence and sexual abuse, both of which carry physical and mental health consequences. Whilst this is a global issue, more child marriages take place in sub-Saharan Africa and South Asia. The health consequences are explained by Flavia Bustreo, M.D., Assistant Director-General for Family, Women's and Children's Health at the World Health Organisation (2013):

> Complications of pregnancy and childbirth are the leading cause of death in young women ages 15-19. Young girls who marry later and delay pregnancy beyond their adolescence have more chances to stay healthier, to better their education and build a better life for themselves and their families.

Child marriage is not in the best interest of the child, as contemplated in Article 4 of the African Children's Charter, and additionally can carry health risks both physically and mentally. Article 1(3) of the African Children's Charter discourages practices inconsistent with the rights in the charter, read with the explicit prohibition against child marriage, and does not condone child marriage as an acceptable practice.

Conclusion

Understanding the circumstances in which children's health rights exist is essential for the attainment of the rights. Health rights in particular require a context-sensitive approach as they are so interlinked and intertwined with other rights. Considering children's health rights without considering the circumstances in which they 'exist' is fruitless. Care needs to be taken to understand the particularities of the context in which these rights exist. Without such an approach, one is arguably left with rights that cannot be applied or realised. The African Children's Charter seeks to provide a more context-sensitive approach to children's rights in Africa than what is entailed in the Children's Rights Charter. The African context is unique, with unique problems and issues stemming from contextual issues specific to the African continent. A blanket approach to children's health rights, therefore, cannot work when faced with specific challenges which were not considered in the drafting of the Children's Rights Charter. The African Children's Charter particularly provides more context-sensitive provisions pertaining to the health rights of children.

This is important as the health challenges faced by children in Africa are not always the same as elsewhere. When read with other documents which are particular to the African context, a greater understanding of the normative content of children's right to health can be attained. Details on the health needs and issues faced by children in Africa are exemplified when a context-sensitive approach is adopted. This Chapter has sought to highlight the different provisions providing for children's health rights in Africa and examined the context-sensitive approach taken in drafting these provisions. Additionally, these provisions cannot be read in a vacuum but must be considered together to gain a better understanding of the provisions made for children's health rights in Africa.

References

Abuja Declaration on HIV/AIDS, Tuberculosis and Other Related Infectious Diseases 2001, *OAU/SPS/ABUJA/3*, Organisation of African Unity, Abuja, Nigeria, 24–27 April. Available from: https://www.veritaszim.net/node/2370 [Accessed 10 August 2023].

African Charter on Human and Peoples' Rights 1981, (adopted 27 June 1981, entered into force 21 October 1986) *1520 UNTS 217*.

African Charter on the Rights and Welfare of the Child 1990, *OAU Doc. CAB/LEG/24.9/49* (adopted 11 July 1990, entered into force 29 November 1999).

African Commission on Human and Peoples' Rights 2010, *Principles and Guidelines on the Implementation of Economic, Social and Cultural Rights in the African Charter on Human and Peoples' Rights*. Available from: https://achpr.au.int/index.php/en/node/871 [Accessed 10 September 2023].

African Committee of Experts on the Rights and Welfare of the Child, 2016, *Africa's Agenda for Children 2040: Fostering an Africa Fit for Children.* Available from: https://www.refworld.org/policy/legalguidance/acerwc/2016/en/113891 [Accessed 1 August 2023].

African Youth Charter 2006 (adopted in Banjul, The Gambia on 2 July 2006, entered into force 8 August 2009). Available from: https://www.pulp.up.ac.za/images/edocman/legal-compilations/compendium/African%20Youth%20Charter%202006_2009.pdf [Accessed 1 August 2023].

Bou-Said, H. 2022, *Report on Human Rights Violations faced by Children of African Descendants,* International Human Rights Council, HRCOUNCIL/GEME/2020/68.

Constitution of the World Health Organisation 1946, (adopted June 1946, entered into force 7 April 1948). Available from: https://www.who.int/about/governance/constitution [Accessed 10 July 2023].

Convention on the Rights of the Child 1989, (adopted 20 November 1989, entered into force 2 September 1990) *1577 UNTS 3.* Available from: https://www.ohchr.org/en/instruments-mechanisms/instruments/convention-rights-child [Accessed 10 August 2023].

Ekundayo, O. 2015, 'Does the African Charter on the Rights and Welfare of the Child only underline the repeated Convention on the Rights of the Child provisions? Examining the similarities and differences between the ACRWC and the CRC, *International Journal of Humanities and Social Science,* vol. 5, no. 7, pp. 143–158.

Kaine, T. 2009, 'The foundations of rights in the African Charter on the Rights and Welfare of the Child: A historical and philosophical account', *African Journal of Legal Studies,* pp. 120–136.

Lloyd, A. 2002, 'A theoretical analysis of the reality of children's rights in Africa: An introduction to the African Charter on the Rights and Welfare of the Child', *African Human Rights Journal,* vol. 2, pp. 11–32.

Palm, W., Hernandez-Quevedo, C., Klasa, K. & van Ginneken, E. 2017, *Implementation of the Right to Health Care under the UN Convention on the Rights of the Child,* European Observatory on Health Systems and Policies. Available from: https://eurohealthobservatory.who.int/publications/m/implementation-of-the-right-to-health-care-under-the-un-convention-on-the-rights-of-the-child [Accessed 5 March 2023].

Sillah, R.M. & Chibanda, T.W. 2013, 'Assessing the African Charter on the Rights and Welfare of the Child as a blueprint towards the attainment of children's rights in Africa', *IOSR Journal of Humanities and Social Sciences,* vol. 11, no. 2, pp. 50–55.

UNICEF 2019, *Only 6 per cent of children in Africa live in areas where air pollution is reliably measured at the ground level*. Available from: https://www.unicef.org/press-releases/only-6-per-cent-children-africa-live-areas-where-air-pollution-reliably-measured-ground [Accessed 6 June 2023].

UNICEF 2021, *One in five children globally does not have enough water to meet their everyday needs*. Available from: https://www.unicef.org/press-releases/one-five-children-globally-does-not-have-enough-water-meet-their-everyday-needs [Accessed 10 August 2023].

UNICEF 2022, *Child Marriage in Eastern and Southern Africa*. Available from: https://www.unicef.org/resources/child-marriage-in-eastern-and-southern-africa-a-statistical-oveview-and-reflections-on-ending-the-practice [Accessed 10 August 2023].

World Health Organisation (WHO) 1978, *Declaration of Alma-Ata International Conference on Primary Health Care*, Alma-Ata, USSR, 6–12 September. Available from: https://www.globalfamilydoctor.com/site/DefaultSite/filesystem/documents/starfield/declaration_almaata.pdf [Accessed 10 August 2023].

World Health Organisation (WHO) 2005, *International Health Regulations*, 3rd ed., Geneva (adopted 2005, entered into force 15 June 2007).

World Health Organisation (WHO) 2013, *Child Marriages: 39,000 every day*. Available from: https://www.who.int/news/item/07-03-2013-child-marriages-39-000-every-day-more-than-140-million-girls-will-marry-between-2011-and-2020 [Accessed 10 August 2023].

World Health Organisation (WHO), 2018, *Environmental Health*. Available from: https://www.who.int/news-room/fact-sheets/detail/climate-change-heat-and-health [Accessed 10 June 2023].

World Health Organisation (WHO) 2022, *Human Rights*. Available from: https://www.who.int/news-room/fact-sheets/detail/human-rights-and-health [Accessed 3 June 2023].

World Health Organisation (WHO) 2023, *Malnutrition*. Available from: https://www.who.int/news-room/fact-sheets/detail/malnutrition [Accessed 10 August 2023].

World Health Organisation (WHO) & Pan American Health Organisation (PAHO), 2012, *Female Genital Mutilation*. Available from: https://www.who.int/publications/i/item/WHO-RHR-12.43 [Accessed 1 July 2023].

Chapter Four
Rethinking the Source of Rights for Learners with Special Educational Needs in Africa

Esther Musengi

Introduction

The inherent human value and dignity should guarantee one's protection and safety in society. Human rights are rights held simply by being human, implying equality, inalienability, and universality. This inherent link between humanity and rights means that all individuals possess the same fundamental rights (Donnelly, 2013). Based on this understanding of rights, this chapter utilises the United Nations Convention on the Rights of People with Disabilities (CRPD) to argue that restricting the source of such rights only to special educational needs violates the indivisibility of rights for learners with disabilities. Since the source of human rights is contentious, as human needs, human capabilities, and morality are common aspects for establishing human rights (Bay, 1982), focusing on just one source potentially violates the civil, political, economic and social rights of learners with disabilities. The narrow focus on 'needs' results in a one-sided educational thrust that has strong potential to translate into lifelong discrimination because human rights are arguably the most significant political force shaping the life experience of people with disability (Perlin, 2013). The chapter, therefore, examines human rights theory, tracing its historical evolution. It also discusses the development of human rights in the United Nations and their indivisible application in the CRPD within the cultural context of the southern Africa region, aspiring to attain the United Nations Sustainable Development Goals (SDGs).

Conceptual Analysis of the Notion of Human Rights

From the perspective of an analytical theory of human rights, a 'right' relates to two central moral and political senses; that is, rectitude and entitlement. In the sense of rectitude, the emphasis is on the right thing to do, or something being right (or wrong), while in the sense of entitlement, reference is made to being owed or belonging to one in particular (Dworkin, 1977; Donnelly, 2013). If one is threatened or denied, right-holders are authorised to make special claims that ordinarily outweigh utility, social policy, and other moral or political grounds for action (Donnelly, 2013). Both rectitude and entitlement link right and obligation in systematically different ways. Claims of rectitude, such as 'That's wrong,' 'That's not right,' or 'You really ought to do that,' focus on a standard of conduct and draw attention to the duty-bearer's obligation under that standard. By contrast, claims of entitlement focus on the right-holder and draw the duty-bearer's attention to the right-holder's special title to enjoy her right. Donnelly (2013) argues that rights in this sense are thus 'subjective' as they focus on the subject who holds them rather than an 'objective' standard to be followed or state of affairs to be realised.

Rights are not reducible to the correlative duties of those against whom they are held, even though failure to discharge one's obligations results in violating standards of rectitude and harming another, thereby making the violator subject to special remedial claims and sanctions. Conversely, having a right is not reducible to enjoying a benefit because right-holders are not passive beneficiaries of duty-bearers' obligations. Right-holders are actively in charge of the relationship, as suggested by the language of 'exercising' rights. In exercising their rights, right-holders may assert their right to service by pressing claims against duty-bearers, choose not to pursue the matter, or even excuse duty-bearers, largely at the right-holders' discretion. Donnelly (2013) notes that rights empower, not just benefit, those who hold them and violations of rights are a particular kind of injustice with a distinctive force and remedial logic.

Human rights are at once a utopian ideal and a realistic practice for implementing that ideal. One might say, in effect, 'Treat a person like a human being and you'll get a human being.' One might also, by enumerating a list of human rights, say, in effect, 'Here's how you treat someone as a human being'. Human rights thus can be seen as a self-fulfilling moral prophecy: 'Treat people like human beings and you will get truly human beings.' The forward-looking moral vision of human nature provides the basis for the social changes implicit in claims of human rights. If the underlying vision of human nature is within the limits of 'natural' possibility, and if the derivation of a list of rights is sound, then implementing those rights will make real that previously ideal nature (Donnelly, 2013).

Human rights claims characteristically seek to challenge or change existing institutions, practices, or norms, especially legal practices. This is in tandem with Charlton (1998), who argues that the political-economic and cultural dimensions of everyday life are the root of oppression for people with disabilities. It follows, therefore, that human rights most often seek to establish or bring about more effective enforcement of parallel 'lower' rights. Bagenstos (2009) gives the example of claims of a human right to everyday health care in the United States, which typically aim to create a legal right to health care. To the extent that such claims are politically effective, the need to make them in the future will be reduced or eliminated; the human rights claim will be replaced by a claim of ordinary legal rights. On this basis, a set of human rights can thus be seen as a standard of political legitimacy. The Universal Declaration of Human Rights, for example, presents itself as a standard of achievement for all peoples and all nations. To the extent that governments protect human rights, they are legitimate. This protection should not be a monopoly of the government, as Toledo (2013) points out. She argues that a central element in every democratic agenda in the twenty-first century is the sharing of power between the state and civil society.

Human rights authorise and empower citizens to act to vindicate their rights, to insist that these standards be realised, and to struggle to create a world in which they enjoy the objects of their rights. However, Fleischer and Zames (2011) note that despite the passage of legislation such as the Americans with Disabilities Act (ADA), people with disabilities reported that it has not been fully enforced; the barriers they face remain primarily attitudinal. Additionally, there is a growing backlash against disability rights and the ADA. This is despite what Heyer (2015) calls the U.S. disability community's self-awareness of its leadership position in the international disability community – a leadership position that misleads Ribet (2011) to view the CRPD as an internationalisation of the United States disability law framework. To address such challenges, Lang, Kett, Groce and Trani

(2011) argue that disabled people have to generate the commitment from civil society and government. Therefore, even though human right claims express not merely aspirations, suggestions, requests, or laudable ideas, but rights-based demands for change, the change may need to go well beyond legislation.

Substantive Theories of Human Rights and the Source of Human Rights

Popular sources for establishing human rights are human needs, human capabilities and morality (Bay, 1982). Green's (1981) position that a basic human need logically gives rise to a right is consistent with Maslow (1970), who argued that it is legitimate and fruitful to regard instinctoid basic needs as rights. However, human needs are an obscure and controversial source of rights, as science reveals a list of empirically validated needs that will not generate anything even approaching an adequate list of human rights. Even a key proponent of a needs theory of human rights (Bay, 1982; 1977) admitted that it is premature to speak of any empirically established needs beyond sustenance and safety. Human instinctoid tendencies, strong as they are, are far weaker than cultural forces.

In place of human needs, the idea of 'human capabilities' has become increasingly popular in recent discussions of human rights (Sen, 2005; Nussbaum, 2003; 1997). There certainly are important links between rights and capabilities. Human capabilities may be somewhat less contentious than human needs, but appeals to capabilities largely restate, rather than resolve, the problem of providing a source for human rights. Leading proponents such as Sen (2005) simply do not present capabilities as a ground for human rights. Human rights and human capabilities have something of a common motivation, but they differ in many distinct ways, and so he argues that they go well with each other, so long as no attempt is made to subsume either entirely within the other. Nussbaum (2003) is a proponent of defining the securing of rights in terms of capabilities, a proposal which Donnelly (2013) argues is a way of operationalising the enjoyment of human rights, not grounding their substance. Vizard (2007) also argues for defining capabilities in terms of human rights. However, many internationally recognised human rights simply are not fundamentally matters of capabilities. Many political rights cannot be adequately analysed within the capability approach. Human rights are fundamentally about human dignity, not human capabilities— although it is plausible to see human capabilities as also rooted in human dignity, although derived from it by different means (Donnelly, 2013).

The source of human rights is humanity's moral nature, which is only loosely linked to scientifically ascertainable needs and not adequately captured by the idea of human capabilities. The human needs or nature that ground human rights is a prescriptive moral account of human possibility. The scientist's human nature says that beyond this, we cannot go. The moral nature that grounds human rights says that beneath this, we must not permit ourselves to fall. Human rights are needed not for life but for a life of dignity, a life worthy of a human being. A right to something implies that people who enjoy that right will live richer and more fully human lives. This notion is aligned with developing or realising human capabilities, but it goes well beyond capabilities. Conversely, those unable to enjoy human rights will, to that extent, not merely see their capabilities diminished, they will be estranged from their moral nature.

The scientist's human nature sets the natural outer limits of human possibility, but human potential is widely variable. Society plays a central role in selecting which potential or capabilities will be realised. Donnelly (2013) argues that these days this selection is significantly shaped by the practice of human rights, which are rooted in a substantive vision of man's moral nature. Human rights set the limits and requirements of social, especially state action, but that action, guided by human rights, plays a major role in realising human nature. When human rights claims bring legal and political practice into line with their demands, they create the type of person posited in the underlying moral vision. Just as an individual's nature or character arises from the interaction of natural endowment, social and environmental influences, and individual action, human beings create their essential nature through social action on themselves. Human rights provide both a substantive model and a set of practices to realise this work of self-creation.

Human nature is a social project rather than a pre-social given, as exemplified by Marx and Burke's theories (Donnelly, 1985), clearly indicating that such a conception is not tied to any particular political perspective. Human rights theories and documents point beyond actual conditions of existence—beyond the "real" in the sense of what has already been realised—to the possible, which is viewed as a deeper human moral reality (Donnelly, 2013). Human rights are therefore less about the way people are than about what they might become. They are about moral rather than natural or juridical persons. The Universal Declaration of Human Rights, for example, tells us little about life in many countries. And where it does, that is in large measure because the rights enumerated in the Universal Declaration of Human Rights have shaped society in their image. Where theory and practice converge, it is largely because the posited rights have helped to construct society and human beings in their image. Where they diverge, claims of human rights point to the need to bring (legal and political) practice into line with (moral) theory. The Universal Declaration, like any list of human rights, specifies minimum conditions for a dignified life, a life worthy of a human being. Even wealthy and powerful countries regularly fall far short of these requirements. As Donnelly (2013) observed, though, this is precisely when, and perhaps even why, having human rights is so important: they demand, as a matter of entitlement (rights), the social changes required to realise the underlying moral vision of human nature.

From a substantive perspective, human rights theory is linked to a theory of human nature to defend a particular set of human rights. However, because a few issues in moral or political philosophy are more contentious or intractable than theories of human nature, there are many well-developed and widely accepted philosophical anthropologies. For example, Aristotle's zoon politikon; Karl Marx's "human natural being" who distinguishes himself by producing his own material life; John Stuart Mill's pleasure-seeking, progressive being; Immanuel Kant's rational being governed by an objective moral law; and feminist theories that begin by questioning the gendered conceptions of "man" in these and most other accounts (Donnelly, 2013). There are a few moral issues, though, where discussion typically proves less conclusive. Philosophical anthropologies are good starting points for substantive theories of human rights to justify arrays of competing and contradictory lists of human rights clamouring for either philosophical or political attention.

The contentious and intractable nature of theories of human nature is possibly one reason why the disability rights movement is dissatisfied with contemporary theorising on disability rights. This is supported by Bagenstos's (2009) observation that it is fallacious to speak of "the" disability rights movement, as if there were a single organisation with unified goals and tactics, as no social movement is a unitary actor. Social movements are collections of people who feel various affiliations, a variety of motivations, a range of different disabilities, different life experiences, and different ideological perspectives. Theorising about disability rights is, therefore, viewed as inadequate because of the various, conflicting affiliations of disabled people. Charlton (1998) posits that the scant attempts to theorise the conditions of everyday life for people with disabilities are either incomplete or fundamentally flawed as a result of the medicalisation and depoliticisation of disability and consequent failure to account for the vast majority of people with disabilities who live in the Third World.

Bickenbach (2009) also points out that progressive realisation of rights and situational sensitivity of difference avert the conflict between universalism of rights and cultural sensitivity, as this happens only if these positions are expressed in extreme form. Indeed, given resource and other constraints, the realisation of human rights will always be a matter of political negotiation, and a social commitment to equality demands that transparent, fully-informed and fully-participatory procedures, respectful of difference. In support, Goodhart (2003) abhors the preoccupation with cultural relativism versus universalism, which he argues crowds out most other theoretical questions in the field of human rights theory.

Further to the contentions in rights theorising, Freeman (2004) weighs in with the argument that theorists and practitioners usually wrongly assume that the concept of human rights is secular and that this takes priority over other values. He observes that these assumptions are controversial for those who approach human rights from the perspective of religious beliefs. Notwithstanding the varied, contentious, and intractable theories of human nature, there is a remarkable international normative consensus on the list of rights contained in the Universal Declaration and the 1966 International Human Rights Covenants (the International Covenant on Economic, Social and Cultural Rights and the International Covenant on Civil and Political Rights). Although it may sound perverse, Donnelly (2013) suggests that the non-substantive nature of analytic theories of rights is one of their great attractions, as there are great dangers in tying one's analysis of human rights to any particular theory of human nature. Analytical accounts of human rights are compatible with many theories of human nature and are thus available to provide relatively neutral theoretical insight and guidance across or within a considerable range of positions.

The Universal Declaration of Human Rights

Human rights date back to the recognition of certain limited religious rights for some Christian minorities in the Peace of Westphalia (1648), which brought the Thirty Years' War to an end and is usually seen, with the benefit of hindsight, as an early precursor of the idea of international human rights. In the nineteenth century, international campaigns against the slave trade and slavery had clear overtones of what in contemporary times is being called human rights advocacy (Morsink, 1999). After World War I, workers' rights and minority rights were addressed by the newly created International Labour Organisation and the League of Nations. Nonetheless, before World War II, the very term 'human rights' was largely absent from international discourse. For example, it is not mentioned in the Covenant of the League of Nations, which is usually seen as an expression of the 'idealism' of the immediate post–World War I era.

With the creation of the United Nations in 1945, which took place in the shadow of not only an unusually vicious global war but also of the Holocaust, the idea of all human beings having equal, extensive and inalienable rights and states having rights or obligations began to take centre stage. The preamble of the United Nations Charter lists as two of the four principal objectives of the organization 'to reaffirm faith in fundamental human rights, in the dignity and worth of the human person, in the equal rights of men and women and of nations large and small' and 'to promote social progress and better standards of life in larger freedom.' Similarly, Article 1 lists as one of the four purposes of the United Nations "to achieve international co-operation in solving international problems of an economic, social, cultural, or humanitarian character, and in promoting and encouraging respect for human rights and fundamental freedoms for all without distinction as to race, sex, language, or religion."

In 1946, the newly created United Nations Commission on Human Rights quickly began to define these abstract statements of post-war optimism and goodwill. The original commission was composed of eighteen elected members, generally representative of the then 51 members of the United Nations. It drafted an authoritative statement of international human rights norms and a statement of principles, adopted as the Universal Declaration of Human Rights by the UN General Assembly on December 10, 1948. This resolution of the UN General Assembly is not itself directly binding in international law but is given force by the 1966 International Human Rights Covenants—the International Covenant on Economic, Social and Cultural Rights (ICESCR) and the International Covenant on Civil and Political Rights (ICCPR) (Donnelly, 2013). The Universal Declaration, however, is unquestionably the foundational document of international human rights law as it establishes the basic parameters of the meaning of 'human rights' in contemporary times.

The Universal Declaration and the Covenants, together known as the International Bill of Human Rights, proclaim a short but substantial list of human rights which have five structural features (Donnelly, 2013). First, human rights are rooted in a conception of human dignity. Second, universal entitlements are the mechanism for implementing such values as non-discrimination and an adequate standard of living. Third, all the rights in the Universal Declaration and the Covenants, except the right of peoples to self-determination, are rights of individuals, not corporate entities. Fourth, internationally recognised human rights are treated as an interdependent and indivisible whole, rather than a menu from which one may freely select or choose not to select. The most controversial aspect of this feature is the equal status of economic, social, and cultural rights. Fifth, although these are universal rights, held equally by all human beings everywhere, states have near-exclusive responsibility to implement them for their own nationals.

The United Nations' Convention on the Rights of Persons with Disabilities (CRPD)

Until recently, the dominant medical and charity models viewed disability as a problem localised with the individual, thereby reinforcing the perception that they were broken people whose only hope for normalcy lies with medical or rehabilitation experts who might repair them (Lord, 2009). However, because the medical and charity models stem from the false assumptions of the able-bodied majority, they are being discarded in favour of approaches that reflect the experience of persons with disabilities themselves. A shift has occurred in which people with disabilities are now generally recognised as rights-holders based on equal opportunities. In the fight to protect rights in every aspect of life, including the lives of people with disabilities, the human rights-based approach is rapidly replacing the charity-based one, at least in the discourse, to overcome the shortcomings and to change the paradigm of any intervention, at least in theory (Katsui, 2008). Harpur (2012) considers the United Nations' Convention on the Rights of Persons with Disabilities (CRPD) as having created a dynamic new disability rights paradigm that empowers disability people's organisations and creates a new paradigm for disability scholars. He observes that despite receiving nominal protection under general human rights conventions, persons with disabilities have had many of their human rights denied to them. The CRPD goes further than merely re-stating rights as it has a transformative vision (Lord and Stein, 2008). It creates a new rights discourse, empowers civil society and renders human rights more obtainable for persons with disabilities.

The CRPD is the first binding international treaty to specifically protect the rights of the world's population of people with disabilities (Kanter, 2007. The CRPD calls on participating governments to change their country's laws as necessary to comply with the terms of the Convention to protect the rights of their citizens with disabilities. The scope and coverage of the Convention are unprecedented as it recognises unequivocally the right of people with disabilities to dignity, to live in the community, to exercise their legal capacity, and to ensure their full and equal enjoyment of rights recognised in the Convention. Kayess and French (2008) laud the Convention as a landmark document in the struggle to reframe the needs and concerns of persons with disability in terms of human rights. They regard the CRPD as having finally empowered the world's largest minority to claim their rights and to participate in international and national affairs on an equal basis with others who have achieved specific treaty recognition and protection.

The Convention is crucial because, in general terms, two positions on disability usually inform the crafting of legislative frameworks for disability rights. The first position is that disability is both a cause and consequence of poverty, as poverty and disability reinforce each other, contributing to increased vulnerability and exclusion (Trani and Loebe, 2012; Chataika, 2019). However, Chataika, Berghs, Mateta and Shava (2015) argue for the second position, which asserts that people with disabilities are not just vulnerable victims, and may not identify themselves as disabled, or even live in poverty. Both positions converge on the need to mainstream disability in the economy. Mainstreaming disability is important because people with disabilities constitute about 15% of the world's population, which makes them the world's largest minority group (WHO and World Bank, 2011) and therefore, the biggest issue in international development (Chataika, 2019). People with disabilities are the biggest issue in development, as evidenced by their being mentioned under five of the United Nations' 17 Sustainable Development Goals (SDGs). They are mentioned under SDG 4 on education, SDG 8 on growth and employment, SDG 10 on inequality, and SDG 11 on accessibility of human settlements. This focus is not accidental, as people with disability have the potential to contribute significantly to human prosperity.

Not surprisingly therefore, according to Berghs (2020), the United Nations Convention for People with Disabilities (CRPD) (United Nations, 2006) gives expression to how poverty and development are linked to disability, which can be addressed by changing attitudes, removing barriers and strengthening assurances of protection of rights in every aspect of life. According to De Beco (2019), the CRPD, as a foundational disability protocol, has blurred the distinction between civil and political rights, on the one hand, and economic and social rights, on the other. The CRPD gives expression to how poverty and development are linked to disability, which can, however, be addressed by changing attitudes, removing barriers and giving assurances of protection of rights in every aspect of life (Berghs et al., 2020). Mladenov (2013) argues that for the Convention to be effective, disabled people's collectives should be recognised and admitted as important stakeholders in the community of interpretation that gives the CRPD its meaning.

The CRPD in the Southern African Cultural Context

Tradition shows differences in the way in which the body and physical characteristics are given value and meaning in different cultures. African traditions continue to change as more and more people become exposed to non-traditional ways of life as a result of globalisation, urbanisation and colonialism. Most babies in modern Africa are now delivered in hospitals by nurses trained as midwives, and infanticide is now a crime. Charlton (1998) illustrated this by noting that a facial scar is considered a deformity in much of Western culture but is considered a badge of honour by the Dahomey of Africa, a pre-colonial kingdom in West Africa, located in what is now Benin. This concurs with the assertion by Devlieger (1998a) that Western bio-medical definitions of impairment are not universal, and Stone (2001), who said that perceptions of the body and mind vary across cultures and also change over time. Overall, this suggests that the value given to physical characteristics influences traditional attitudes towards disability. It is noteworthy that, from the social perspective, disability is a social construct, not an objective condition (Armstrong & Barton, 1999; Trent, 1994), which implies that the social context helps define disability and related concepts. Anyone attempting to universalise the category 'disability' runs into conceptual problems, because such definitions take into account the social and cultural contexts (Tugstaad and White, 1995)

In this context, where there appears to be no cross-cultural carry-over of such a construct from Western to African countries, Devlieger (1998a) argued that a term such as 'disability' does not have ready equivalents even in some European languages such as French. He pointed out that the practice of grouping people in a recognisable category as 'disabled' could be traced back to the histories and cultural contexts of specific Western societies. Devlieger (1998a, p. 53) pointed out that the establishment of colonial languages brought with it much of the disability-related terminology translated into local African languages, with the term for physical disability usually becoming generic by acquiring broader meanings which incorporate people with a variety of impairments. It is conceivable, therefore, that the colonial importation of disability-related terminology disrupted the pre-colonial traditional harmony existing between many categories of disabled persons and non-disabled society because the traditional view of personhood is amenable to diversity.

Ubuntu, the traditional African view of personhood, denies that persons can be defined by focusing on this or that particular physical or psychological characteristic of the lone individual (Menkiti, 2007). Rather than focusing on hearing, seeing or lack of these abilities, a person is defined by reference to the environing community. As Mbiti (1969) notes, the African view of the person can be summed up in the statement: 'I am because we are, and since we are, therefore I am.' Based on this African dictum, as far as Africans are concerned, the reality of the communal world takes precedence over the reality of individual life histories (Menkiti, 2007). In Africa, it is in rootedness in an ongoing human community that the individual comes to see himself as a person, and it is by first knowing this community as a stubborn perduring fact of the psychophysical world that the individual also comes to know himself as a durable, more or less permanent, fact of this world. In the African dictum 'I am because we are', the 'we' referred to here is not an additive 'we' but a thoroughly fused collective 'we' (Menkiti, 2007). It is a collectivity in the truest sense in which there is assumed to be an organic dimension to the relationship between the component individuals. This contrasts with the Western understanding of community, where there is a non-organic bringing together of atomic individuals into a unit more akin to an association than to a community.

The primacy of community in Africa is consistent with the international disability protocol that links disability with development, the CRPD. Not surprisingly, therefore, the CRPD has been hugely influential in southern Africa despite criticisms of its implementation in this region. As noted by Quinn and Degener (2002), the core problem of putting the values of the CRPD into practice stems largely from the relative invisibility of people with disabilities in the past and that they tended to be viewed as objects rather than subjects in their own right. This meant that the legal protections normally associated with the rule of law were either not applied or were severely curtailed. Perceiving them as subjects rather than objects entails giving them access to the full benefits of basic freedoms that most people take for granted and doing so in a way that is respectful and accommodating of their differences.

Conclusion: Moving Beyond 'Needs'

The foregoing discussion suggests that entitlement as a basis for rights may be closely associated with needs, deficits and the medical model that spawned 'Special Needs Education', special schools and integration for learners with disabilities. Entitlement focuses on the right-holders' special title to enjoy their rights, which is subjective as they may or may not exercise this right. This contrasts with a rectitude basis for rights, which enables an 'objective' standard to be followed and a desired state of affairs to be realised. From the rectitude point of view, rights are not reducible to the correlative duties of those against whom they are held, and also learners with disabilities whose rights may be threatened or denied would have the right to make special claims that ordinarily outweigh utility, social policy, and other moral or political grounds for action. In the rectitude view, learners' right to education is not reducible to the enjoyment of a benefit because, as right-holders, learners with disabilities are not passive beneficiaries of duty-bearers' obligations. As right-holders, they should be actively in charge of the relationship, exercising their human rights that are at once a utopian ideal and a realistic practice for implementing that ideal. The active exercise of their rights is based on a forward-looking moral vision of human nature that becomes a self-fulfilling moral prophecy. This forward-looking moral vision of human nature provides the basis for the implicit claims to human rights that learners with disabilities have through inclusive educational interventions. Inclusive educational interventions characteristically seek to challenge existing institutions, practices and norms in order to facilitate full participation of all members of society.

The moral nature that grounds human rights sets the inclusive standard as the minimum beneath which learners with disabilities must not permit themselves to fall. The learners have the right not just for life, but for a life of dignity, a life worthy of a human being who participates fully in society. The right to a life of dignity implies that learners with disabilities will live richer and more fully human lives. This notion is aligned with developing human capabilities but goes well beyond capabilities as it recognises that society plays a central role in selecting which widely variable capabilities will be realised. Human rights authorise and empower learners with disabilities to act to vindicate their rights, to insist that certain standards be realised, and to struggle to create a world in which they enjoy the objects of their rights. The status quo is that these learners' rights are violated as shown by research findings that learners with disabilities are more prone to abuse than their non-disabled peers (Sobsey, 1994; Dale and Fellows, 1999; Sullivan and Knutson, 2000a, 2000b) especially those who live in what Marchant (2001) calls extra-familial situations such as residential schools (Westcott and Cross, 1996; Sobsey, 2003).

Determining the breach of disabled children's rights is complicated by studies that show that what is and is not child abuse varies from culture to culture, although there may be common ground across societies (O'Brien & Lau, 1995; Shakeshaft & Cohan, 1995; Shumba, 2007). For example, when children's needs such as food, affection and protection are not fulfilled by adults, then the children are said to be abused as they may not become properly oriented in the world. However, the extent and manner in which these needs are fulfilled will vary between families and from culture to culture. In this light, a common understanding of what constitutes abuse at a residential institution, which is a 'melting pot' of cultures, may be difficult to arrive at, as one person's abuse may be another's acceptable provision of children's needs. Therefore, some caregivers and educators may not be aware that what they do to children or what is done to their children is abuse, while others may construe well-intentioned actions as abuse.

In light of these contextual observations, it becomes evident that restricting the source of children with disabilities' rights only to special educational needs violates the indivisibility of their rights, as it relegates them to a deficiency focus. The deficiency focus itself is prone to lowered standards and abuse in the various settings where children with disabilities are supposed to be served. The source of human rights for learners with disabilities has to take a broader view, which includes their human capabilities and the morality associated with serving them. The broader focus has a stronger potential to translate into lifelong empowerment that enables learners with disabilities to act to vindicate their rights, to insist that certain standards be realised, and to struggle to create a world in which they enjoy the objects of their rights.

References

Armstrong, F. & Barton, L. (eds.) 1999, *Disability, Human Rights and Education: Cross-Cultural Perspectives*, Open University Press.

Bagenstos, S.R. 2009, *Law and the Contradictions of the Disability Rights Movement*, Yale University Press.

Bay, C. 1977, 'Human Needs and Political Education', in R. Fitzgerald (ed.), *Human Needs and Politics*, Pergamon Press.

Bay, C. 1982, 'Self-Respect as a Human Right: Thoughts on the Dialectics of Wants and Needs in the Struggle for Human Community', *Human Rights Quarterly*, vol. 4, no. 1, pp. 53–75.

Beghs, M., Chataika, T., El-Lahib, Y. & Dube, K. 2020, 'Introducing Disability Activism', in M. Beghs, T. Chataika, Y. El-Lahib & K. Dube (eds.), *The Routledge Handbook of Disability Activism*, Routledge.

Bickenbach, J.E. 2009, 'Disability, Culture and the UN Convention', *Disability and Rehabilitation*, vol. 31, no. 14, pp. 1111–1124.

Charlton, J.I. 1998, *Nothing About Us, Without Us: Disability Empowerment and Oppression*, University of California Press.

Chataika, T. 2019, 'Introduction: Critical Connections and Gaps in Disability and Development', in T. Chataika (ed.), *The Routledge Handbook of Disability in Southern Africa*, Routledge.

Chataika, T., Berghs, M., Mateta, A. & Shava, K. 2015, 'From Whose Perspective Anyway? – The Quest for African Disability Rights, in A. de Waal (ed.), *Advocacy in Conflict: Critical Perspectives on Transnational Activism*, Zed Books.

Chimedza, R. 2008, 'Disability and Inclusive Education in Zimbabwe', in L. Barton & F. Armstrong (eds.), *Policy, Experience and Change: Cross Cultural Reflections on Inclusive Education*, vol. 4, Springer, pp. 123–132.

Dale, P. & Fellows, R. 1999, 'Independent Child Protection Assessments: Incorporating a Therapeutic Focus from an Integrated Service Context', *Child Abuse Review*, vol. 8, no. 1, pp. 4–14.

De Beco, G. 2019, 'The Indivisibility of Human Rights and the Convention on the Rights of Persons with Disabilities', *International and Comparative Law Quarterly*, vol. 68, pp. 141–160.

Devlieger, P.J. 1998, 'Physical "Disability" in Bantu Languages: Understanding the Relativity of Classification and Meaning', *International Journal of Rehabilitation Research*, vol. 21, pp. 63–70.

Donnelly, J. 1985, *The Concept of Human Rights*, St. Martin's Press, New York; Macmillan, London.

Donnelly, J. 2013, *Universal Human Rights in Theory and Practice*, Cornell University Press, Ithaca and London.

Dworkin, R. 1977, *Taking Rights Seriously*, Harvard University Press, Cambridge, Mass.

Fleischer, D.Z. & Zames, F. 2011, *The Disability Rights Movement: From Charity to Confrontation*, Temple University Press.

Freeman, M. 2004, 'The Problem of Secularism in Human Rights Theory', *Human Rights Quarterly*, vol. 26, no. 2, pp. 375–400.

Goodhart, M.E. 2003, 'Origins and Universality in the Human Rights Debates: Cultural Essentialism and the Challenge of Globalisation', *Human Rights Quarterly*, vol. 25, no. 4, pp. 935–964.

Green, R.H. 1981, 'Basic Human Rights/Needs: Some Problems of Categorical Translation and Unification', *Review of the International Commission of Jurists*, vol. 27, pp. 53–58.

Harpur, P. 2012, 'Embracing the new disability rights paradigm: The importance of the Convention on the Rights of Persons with Disabilities', *Disability & Society*, vol. 27, no. 1, pp. 1–14.

Heyer, K. 2015, *Rights Enabled: The Disability Revolution from the US to Germany and Japan to the United Nations*, University of Michigan Press, Michigan.

Kanter, A.S. 2007, 'The Promise and Challenge of the United Nations Convention on the Rights of Persons with Disabilities', *Syracuse Journal of International Law and Commerce*, vol. 34, no. 2, pp. 287–321.

Katsui, H. 2008, *Downside of the Human Rights-Based Approach to Disability in Development*, Working Paper 2/2008, Institute of Development Studies, University of Helsinki.

Kayess, R. & French, P. 2008, 'Out of Darkness into Light? Introducing the Convention on the Rights of Persons with Disabilities', *Human Rights Law Review*, vol. 8, no. 1, pp. 1–34.

Lang, R., Kett, M., Groce, N. & Trani, J-F. 2011, 'Implementing the United Nations Convention on the Rights of Persons with Disabilities: Principles, Implications, Practice and Limitations', *ALTER: European Journal of Disability Research*, vol. 5, pp. 206–220.

Lord, J.E. 2009, 'Disability Rights and the Human Rights Mainstream: Reluctant Gate-Crashers?', in B. Clifford (ed.), *The International Struggle for New Human Rights*, University of Pennsylvania Press.

Lord, J.E. & Stein, M.A. 2008, 'The Domestic Incorporation of Human Rights Law and the United Nations Convention on the Rights of Persons with Disabilities', *Faculty Publications*, Paper 665. Available from: [https://scholarship.law.wm.edu/facpubs/665] [Accessed 10 August 2023].

Marchant, R. 2001, *Bridging the Gap: Child Protection Work with Children with Multiple Disabilities*, Marcus.

Maslow, A. 1970, *Motivation and Personality*, Harper and Row.

Mbiti, J. 1969, *African Religions and Philosophies*, Doubleday and Company.

Menkiti, I.A. 2007, 'On the Normative Conception of a Person', in K. Wiredu (ed.), *A Companion to African Philosophy*, Heinemann, pp. 324–331.

Mladenov, T. 2013, 'The UN Convention on the Rights of Persons with Disabilities and its Interpretation', *ALTER: European Journal of Disability Research*, vol. 7, pp. 69–82.

Morsink, J. 1999, *The Universal Declaration of Human Rights: Origins, Drafting, and Intent*, University of Pennsylvania Press, Philadelphia.

Nussbaum, M.C. 1997, 'Capabilities and Human Rights', *Fordham Law Review*, vol. 66, pp. 273–300.

Nussbaum, M.C. 2003, 'Capabilities as Fundamental Entitlements: Sen and Social Justice', *Feminist Economics*, vol 9, no. 2–3, pp. 33–59.

Perlin, M.L. 2013, 'Human Rights Law for Persons with Disabilities in Asia and the Pacific: The Need for a Disability Rights Tribunal', *Journal of Policy and Practice in Intellectual Disabilities*, vol. 10, no. 2, pp. 96–98.

Quinn, G. & Degener, T. 2002, *The Current Use and Future Potential of the United Nations Human Rights Instruments in the Context of Disability*, Human Rights and Disability Series.

Ribet, B. 2011, 'Emergent Disability and the Limits of Equality: A Critical Reading of the UN Convention on the Rights of Persons with Disabilities', *Yale Human Rights & Development Law Journal*, vol. 14, pp. 155–210.

Sen, A. 2005, 'Human Rights and Capabilities', *Journal of Human Development*, vol. 6, no. 2, pp. 151–166.

Shakeshaft, C. & Cohan, A. 1995, 'Sexual Abuse of Students by School Staff Personnel', *Phi Delta Kappan*, vol. 76, no. 7, pp. 513–520.

Sobsey, D. 2003, 'Exceptionality, Education, and Maltreatment', *Exceptionality*, vol. 10, no. 1, pp. 29–46.

Sobsey, R. 1994, *Violence and Abuse in the Lives of People with Disabilities: The End of Silent Acceptance?*, Paul H. Brookes Publishing.

Stone, E. 2001, 'A Complicated Struggle: Disability, Survival and Social Change', in M. Priestley (ed.), *Disability and the Life Course: Global Perspectives*, Cambridge University Press.

Sullivan, P.M. & Knutson, J.F. 2000, 'Maltreatment and Disabilities: A Population-Based Epidemiological Study', *Child Abuse & Neglect*, vol. 24, pp. 1257–1273. Toledo, P.M. 2013, 'At the UN . . . The South Also Exists, in M. Sabatello & M. Schulze (eds.), *Human Rights and Disability Advocacy*, University of Pennsylvania Press.

Trani, J.F. & Loeb, M. 2012, 'Poverty and Disability: A Vicious Cycle? Evidence from Afghanistan and Zambia, *Journal of International Development*, vol. 24 (S1), pp. S19–S52.

Trent, J.W. 1994, *Inventing the Feeble Mind: A History of Mental Retardation in the United States*, University of California Press.

United Nations. 2006, *Convention on the Rights of Persons with Disabilities*. Available from: http://www.un.org/disabilities/default.asp?navid=12&pid=150 [Accessed 10 August 2023].

Vizard, P. 2007, 'Specifying and Justifying a Basic Capability Set: Should the International Human Rights Framework Be Given a More Direct Role?', *Oxford Development Studies*, vol. 35, no. 3, pp. 225–250.

Westcott, H. & Cross, M. 1996, *Towards Ending the Abuse of Disabled Children*, Venture Press.

World Health Organisation [WHO] & the World Bank. 2011, *World Report on Disability*, WHO.

PART 2

Legal and Policy Dimensions of Child Protection

Chapter Five
Understanding the Challenges Faced by Zimbabwean Child Labour Law Enforcement Agencies

Raymond Taruvinga

Introduction

This chapter draws attention to the problem area of child labour in Zimbabwe. It details the historical background and distinct socio-economic characteristics which increase the labour vulnerability of children while reducing the competence of target agencies. The chapter offers insights into the unique challenges faced by anti-child labour agencies as a way of enabling the development of feasible solutions to the child labour problem in Zimbabwe. The nature of current child labour mitigation programs in the country, which helps to ascertain their adequacy, is examined. It is based on the perceptions of senior agency officials on the most appropriate solutions to the encountered challenges. Having assessed the problem regionally and locally, the chapter formulates practical recommendations which respond particularly to the Zimbabwean situation.

Background to the Problem of Child Labour in Zimbabwe

The Government of Zimbabwe established institutional mechanisms for the enforcement of laws and regulations on child labour, including its worst forms such as child trafficking, sexual exploitation and exposure to extremely hazardous work sites; this task force comprises two agencies namely, the Department of Child Welfare and Probation Services and the Department of Labour Administration. Although Zimbabwe commendably ratified most key international convention on the elimination of child labour, such as the (International Labour Organization (ILO) Convention on Minimum Age of Employment (1973), ILO Convention on the Worst Forms of Child Labour (2000),

United Nations Convention on the Rights of the Child (UN CRC, 1989), UN CRC Optional Protocol on Armed Conflict (2000), UN CRC Optional Protocol on the Sale of Children and Child Prostitution (2000) and the Palermo Protocol on Trafficking in Persons(2000), the status of labouring children in the country has worsened.

Statistical evidence of the deteriorating condition of child labour is revealed by the 2011 national child labour survey conducted by the Government of Zimbabwe, which discovered that 41.91% of Zimbabwean children aged five to seventeen and 37.11% of children aged five to fourteen are engaged in economic activity (ZIMSTAT, 2012). Of children five to fourteen years of age engaged in economic activity, 95.6% work in agriculture, forestry and fishing. These workplaces, by ILO standards, constitute the worst forms of child labour because they can result in loss of life. In addition to that, approximately 100,000 of the country's 1.3 million orphans survive on their own in child-headed households. Given that Zimbabwe has ratified most legal instruments to ensure the protection of children from undue labour, the problem remains critical. Law enforcement agencies have not contained the problem adequately; it is therefore necessary to explore the challenges facing such agencies in implementing their mandate, and that is the gist of this research.

The Theory of Performance and Its Relevance

The Theory of Performance (ToP), developed by thinkers such as Elger (2007), informed the analysis of findings for this chapter and will consequently be employed as an organising framework for the discussion of findings in this chapter. The theory of performance develops and relates six foundational concepts to form a framework that can be used to explain performance as well as performance improvements. These comprise context, level of knowledge, level of skills, personal factors, fixed factors and level of identity. The problem is the ineffective performance of child labour law enforcement agencies in Zimbabwe. The theory of performance states that performance is a gradual process. Elger (2007) refers to it as a 'journey'. A performer's location in the journey is their 'level of performance'. Each level characterises the quality of a performance. For example, Elger (2007) notes that as an academic department improves its performance level, the department members can produce more effective student learning, more effective research and a more effective culture. An alternative illustration is a manager advancing his or her level of performance; he or she can organise people and resources more effectively to get higher-quality results in a short time. As an agency's level of performance progresses gradually, its ability to yield desired results increases.

The theory of performance maintains that performers advance through stages; thus, the effectiveness of performance can be characterised in levels, with an organisation performing on level three being better than one on level two. As an indication of progress or lack of it, Elger (2007) developed attributes of high performance, namely quality, capacity, capability, cost effectiveness, skills, knowledge, identity and motivation. Increases in quality mean results produced by the performer are more effective in meeting or exceeding the expectations of stakeholders. A rise in performer capability entails the ability to tackle more challenging performances or projects. Cost effectiveness means that as a performer progresses in level, their amount of effort or financial resources to produce a result goes down. Increased capacity involves the ability to generate more throughput. An increase in skills results in the ability to set goals, persist and maintain a positive outlook increase in breadth of application and effectiveness. Another indication of a performer's level is knowledge; both depth and breadth of knowledge increase for a high-performing agency. Lastly, identity and motivation mean individuals develop a greater sense of who they are as professionals; organisations develop their essence.

According to Elger (2007), the performance of a system depends on the components of the system and the interactions between these components. Similarly, the level of performance of an individual or an organisation depends on six components: context, level of knowledge, level of skills, personal factors, fixed factors and level of identity. Elger (2007) explains each component, together with exemplars to illustrate the utility of each component. The first is the context of performance. This component includes variables associated with the situation in which the individual or the organisation operates. For example, the performance of an academic department is coupled with the organisational effectiveness of the host college. This component relates to the environmental circumstances associated with the performance. Personal factors include variables associated with the personal situation of an individual as a performer. For example, a student's performance is impacted by the quality of his or her home environment. This component involves the life situations with may affect performers. The level of knowledge involves facts, information, concepts, theories or principles acquired by a person or a group through experience or education. For example, knowledge on the relationship between various dynamics in a field of interest knowledge derived from human experience, can be communicated or recognised.

Another component proposed by Elger (2007) is the level of skills. Skills describe specific actions used by individuals, groups or organisations in multiple types of performances. For example, goal setting, observation, persistence and making assumptions; according to Elger (2007), skills inform action and action is relevant in a broad range of performance contexts. The fifth component which influences performance is the level of identity. As an organisation matures, it develops its mission, its way of doing business and its uniqueness. For example, a research team evolves itself into a performance organisation. The level of identity is associated with maturation in a discipline or culture internalised by an individual or organisation, whereby the organisation takes on a shared identity. Lastly, fixed factors make up a component which includes variables unique to an individual that cannot be altered. For example, a performer whose domain is psychomotor performance, genetic factors may have an impact on his or her level of performance.

Several challenges are deterring Zimbabwean child labour law enforcement agencies from achieving the desired results. This alludes to the need for an explanation for the current performances of these agencies, and as reflected in the above discussion, the theory of performance by Elger (2007) covers the length and breadth of that. The theory of performance informs learning in non-traditional contexts like organisations. Any agency has an internal system which affects its performance or ability to bring about intended results; this theory is responsive to that because the gist of the theory of performance is an explanation of how six distinct components interact holistically to affect the performance of an entity. One of the intended outcomes and the ultimate purpose of this research is to find a way of improving the performance of anti-child labour agencies in Zimbabwe and which can relate to the three axioms offered by Elger (2007) for the improvement of both individual and organisational performance. This, therefore, means, this theory is applicable, not only as a lens through which the challenges faced by anti-child labour agencies can be analysed, but as a guide for the provision of performance improvement plans. Lastly, Elger's (2007) elements of performance discussed above were used to guide the interview schedule construction, particularly the set of questions designed to explore the specific agency challenges.

Contextual and Organisational Challenges

Several factors affect agency performance in an attempt to eliminate child labour. The challenges are organised into two broad categories in accordance with the guiding theory frame. These categories are contextual challenges which are specific to the field of operation, as well as internal factors which are more specific to internal agency dynamics. Below is a tabular presentation of participant profiles.

Personnel Inadequacies

All three agencies – the Coalition Against Child Labour in Zimbabwe, the Department of Child Welfare and Probation Services and the Department of Labour – expressed a challenge regarding their personnel from two perspectives. Firstly, there is a lack of relevant skills among the available staff designated for specific roles, and secondly, there is a shortage of members of staff or understaffing. Conversing with the principal labour officer at the Department of Labour, it was apparent that the department had become a 'training ground' for private companies that recruit government-trained labour inspectors by offering better salary packages. Labour officers are the principal employees responsible for the execution of the Department of Labour's primary programs and most fundamental departmental activities. As the officer stated, the training of labour officers is carried out in-house with the use of government manuals and resources. Labour officers are trained and knowledgeable on the relevant national law regulating Zimbabwean labour practices. In addition, labour officers are responsible for labour inspections, which form the basis of the child labour detection process. They are also the ones who determine, under the law, if the work any particular child is exposed to is within acceptable limits or classified as exploitative labour.

Name of Agency	Respondent's Position	Code	Key Duties
Coalition Against Child Labour in Zimbabwe.	Projects manager	Participant A	• Manage all agency programs. • Represent the agency at the District Child Protection Committee. • Seek donor funding for the agency.
	Assistant project manager	Participant B	• Deputise the project manager. • Supervise junior agency volunteers. • Implement programs at the ward level.
Department of Child Welfare and Probation Services.	District Child Welfare Officer	Participant C	• Managing all child welfare programs. • Overseeing government grants. • Supervising all district staff members.
	Social Welfare Assistance Officer	Participant D	• Deputising the district child welfare officer. • Managing social welfare assistance schemes. • Working with community workers.
Department of Labour.	Principal Labour Officer	Participant E	• Supervising district labour administration. • Coordinating all anti-child labour agencies. • Liaise with potential donors.
	Labour officer	Participant F	• Deputising principal labour officer. • Settling labour disputes. • Conducting labour inspections.

The recruitment freeze by the government is another cause for understaffing, given the overwhelming number of cases handled annually. The ILO (2014) also bemoans how labour ministry inspectorates are already overstretched, especially in developing economies with vast informal sectors which need constant inspections. This can be partly regarded as a government problem, but this deterring challenge of personnel inadequacies was also the subject of discussion with the nongovernmental organisation. The project manager at the Coalition Against Child Labour in Zimbabwe made comments alluding to this challenge, stating that donor funding remains scarce and unpredictable, thereby forcing his agency to downsize to cut back on expenditure. This leaves the NGO no option but to rely on a pool of volunteers whose availability and consistency are not reliable.

Considering the state of affairs on a similar matter with the Department of Child Welfare and Probation Services, there is a massive shortage of child case workers per ward. These are community-based child care workers who are better positioned to detect child labour cases faster than office-based personnel. Child labour incidents are recorded in the community; therefore, the Department of Child Welfare and Probation Services, as the principal government department for safeguarding the rights of children, should have as many trained child care workers on the ground as possible. Literature concurs with this major staffing challenge, many state nations significantly reduce their ability to curb the prevalence of child labour in their countries because the agencies tasked with the responsibility of combating child labour are more often than not, highly understaffed (PSA, 2021); and the available members of staff, mostly in sub-Saharan government agencies may not be specifically trained for the intricate nature of child rights protection matters (Huntington, 2001). The performance of agencies is hindered by the two discussed components of Elger's (2007) Theory of Performance. Elger (2007) maintains that the level of skills and the level of knowledge within an organisation are directly proportional to its level of performance.

Role of Traditional Values

Although child labour law is enforceable by law, the cooperation of target communities would make the eradication of the problem faster and less complicated. Officials made harmonious comments on the need to win community cooperation in the struggle against child labour, as it is as much their struggle as it is the government's. One official noted that other government efforts, such as the fight against malaria or HIV within communities, have recorded faster progress because communities involved demonstrated instant readiness to cooperate, but unfortunately, that is not the case with the more complicated matter of child labour. Lack of cooperation by communities was identified as one major challenge faced by anti-child labour agencies. Almost all responses pointed to the traditional values and beliefs of the indigenous people of Zimbabwe as the root cause of this lack of cooperation among community members. The initial notion to understand is that child rights are deduced from the broad context of human rights themselves, and on that note, it becomes necessary to realise that Africa has a more conservative rather than liberal approach to child rights. Chakarisa (2010) states that the African Charter on the Rights and Welfare of the Child imposes certain responsibilities on the child towards his or her family.

The value of cattle in the Shona and Shangani tribes (dominant tribes in rural Zimbabwe) supersedes any form of logic, justifying the negativity of child labour on child welfare. Speaking to the project manager at the Coalition Against Child Labour in Zimbabwe, the author noted the interviewee's concerns that the customary one cow per annum payment for child labour was much more valuable to parents of child labourers compared to the long-term potential of sending them to school. The officer noted that:

> *For you to understand the intensity of the matter, first, you need to understand that the Shangani people, who are the most populous in the rural wards of this district, value cattle above all forms of wealth; it probably has some sort of symbolic value to them. (Respondent A)*

The respondent stated that labouring children are paid in the form of cattle in most cases in the rural wards of the district, since cattle are a valuable asset and symbol of wealth to the indigenous people of Zimbabwe. It is challenging for the agency to neutralise the values held by the adult members of the community about the importance of livestock over child wellbeing. Reiterating the same sentiments, the principal labour officer at the Department of Labour stated that it raised no alarm to the communities in question to find full-time cattle herders of school-going age. The principal labour officer went on to explain that, because the elders endorse it, it is difficult for the government and the private organisations to neutralise this belief system.

The social welfare assistance officer at the Department of Child Welfare and Probation Services brought to attention that the values of local people, which fuel child labour, go beyond just the importance of cattle as a material gain. The position of the child in the African family setting was raised by this official; he argued that a child's entry into the labour market was left to the discretion of parents. Once parental consent is granted, it becomes acceptable. This is reflective of the observations put forward by Abdullah (2022) that social norms position the family as the predominant context for child labour practices. Generational customs, such as parents regarding their children as a source of labour, take time to moderate through sensitisation, evoking the law on a community under such circumstances without conversation, forces that community to become closed and even more resistant to positive change.

In some cases, religion negatively influences community perceptions of child labour. Several officials expressed concern over some religious sects within the communities whose beliefs perpetuate child labour and resistance against its eradication. A volunteer for the Coalition Against Child Labour in Zimbabwe stated that girls are often prematurely married off to assume adult labour responsibilities as they try to fend for themselves in polygamous homes where they face financial neglect. The vulnerability of women and girls has always been a common phenomenon in African societies. In this case, it is not exclusively a matter of custom; there is an additional force which is equally, if not more difficult to combat, which is religion. The issue of child marriages, commonly resulting from the giving away of girls aged below sixteen to older men, is closely related to patriarchy. Both dynamics of religion and patriarchy are embedded in community culture and way of life for generations, while the fight against child labour is a relatively very young and new cause; its introduction to communities in Zimbabwe is met with accounts of adamant resistance. An anti-child labour agency in Europe or North America may not consider community traditions such as child marriages or patriarchy as a major problem. This matter is localised in sub-Saharan Africa. In this instance, even if the agencies in question were operating with no internal problems, their performance would still be less than desired because of external forces which arise from the context of their operations.

Insufficient Program Funding

Third-world governments have attributed the staggered progress on their anti-child labour efforts to a lack of sufficient funds. Bonnet (2001) argues that third world governments have scaled down budget allocations to sectors which directly affect the welfare of children, namely education, health and social protection. Donback (2022) also identifies a lack of political will in investing substantially towards the elimination of child labour on a global scale. The first presentation is on the comments issued by representative officials of the nongovernmental agency because of its uniqueness, especially on this particular challenge from the other two, which are government agencies.

The project manager at the Coalition Against Child Labour in Zimbabwe, who by job description manages the entirety of this agency's programs, expressed concern over this challenge, noting that the disbursal of funds from the donor community changed from annual to quarterly. He further explained how this inconvenienced the smooth application of programs. He stated that when the agency got funding on an annual basis, it made program planning and budgeting less complicated for management because they would plan for the whole year without hindrances. Now that funding comes quarterly, with uncertainty, management is experiencing constant budget deficits, and he said it creates gaps in the program's monitoring process, which are difficult to consolidate. He went on to add that the current funding cycle of three years was too short to see child labour cases through from identification to rehabilitation. When funding is terminated prematurely, the agency cannot afford to maintain sufficient monitoring, thereby exposing rescued children to possible relapse. As far as the effects on program coverage are concerned, this organisation's volunteer elaborated that operations were restricted to a single ward in the entire district of Chiredzi due to funding challenges.

Challenges in adequately funding programs proved to be more acute with the two government anti-child labour agencies. Conversing with the district child welfare officer revealed that education assistance, though indirect, was the government's major child labour rescue programme. Unfortunately, the District Child Welfare Officer explained that the funding allocated by the government for its major anti-child labour program is 23% of the required amount for it to be implemented at full capacity. This means the number of vulnerable children who need to access education to evade labour increases. The lesser the funds, the more selective the eligibility criteria become. The district child protection officer further mentioned that, although assistance on access to education is the major tool, the government has other programs mentioned earlier, like the cash transfers made to households in an attempt to raise their incomes, but recently the funds to that program have been severely reduced. The dangerous effects of this are that if the government fails to raise the household incomes of families in question, they may withdraw their children from school, though their fees are paid by the government, to work and secure the immediate survival needs of the household.

The social welfare assistance officer at this agency focused more on the effects of insufficient funds on the grassroots structures. He expressed his observations that the continual functionality of child protection committees in communities relies on funds from the district office, which are currently constrained, which means they miss their scheduled quarterly meetings to report on the state of child welfare in their communities. Responding to probes on how lack of programs funding has affected the achievement of the department's ultimate goal with regards to child labour, the principal labour officer stated that his office could not afford to conduct regular spot check inspections and ambush visits to suspected worksites especially in the informal sector where children are likely to be exploited, he lamented that his fellow officers were glued to chairs because they last had a functional vehicle at the district office 15 years ago.

Unattractiveness: Proposed Alternative to Child Labour

Agencies' anti-child labour programs and the gist and ultimate aim of the programs, both by government and the nongovernmental sector, are to offer formal education as an alternative to child labour. This alternative appears unattractive to both parents and the labouring children themselves; formal education as an option has proven incapable of luring target groups. A volunteer for the Coalition Against Child Labour in Zimbabwe stated that the physical state of rural schools left little to be desired by parents and child labourers alike. Under these circumstances, the argument is that children no longer find the school setting and conditions any better than those offered at employment sites. Besides having to endure harsh temperatures and learning in open spaces, there is a lack of material incentive to continue with education. The principal labour officer argued that the promise of education guaranteeing a future suspect was an abstract concept to target communities. The ILO (2014) also reports on the undesirability of re-entry into formal education for rescued children, especially those who spend over three years in the labour market.

Deducing from the conversation, the officials themselves seemed to be caught in a dilemma of having to accept the impractical requirements they are asking of parents, given the situation in Zimbabwe, at the same time, do their jobs as they are obliged by the law. The anti-child labour task force in Zimbabwe can no longer present schooling as a viable option, thereby matching arguments on the growing unattractiveness of formal education in Zimbabwe made by Robson (2000). This problem stems from two causes: the first is the government's inability to constantly renovate rural school infrastructures, especially in areas of new human settlement. This is a funding problem, which is why it is discussed in a subsection under program funds insufficiency. The second cause to why the schooling alternative is no longer selling is the acute rate of unemployment in Zimbabwe. In the past decade, the ordinary parent realised that formally educating a child may not yield returns in the long run, thereby making it a bad investment. That situation presents a challenge to child labour enforcement agencies.

Corruption

One of the major challenges regards the detrimental effects of corruption on child labour mitigation programs. Due to corruption in some instances, government resources are wasted on undeserving children who get enlisted for aid at the expense of deserving children from poor households who are at risk of child labour. Community-based selection bodies for education assistance omitted deserving children from their listing. Government involves community members as a way of ensuring popular participation, secondly because community members are most aware of vulnerable children within their communities. Unfortunately, corrupt members are partial in their selection, and poor children end up failing to attain the help necessary for them to escape child labour. Rehabilitation programs set by the coalition against child labour as a nongovernmental agency have faced their share of corruption hurdles. The project manager stated that resources may be unveiled in adequate amounts, but if they are spent on undeserving children, the prevalence of child labour will remain high. He reported that:

> *When we ask community child protection committees and community traditional leaders to present to us children engaged in child labour so that we can rehabilitate them, we often get children who have never laboured, and it is difficult for us to identify them (Respondent A).*

When asked to explain why the agency found it difficult to audit the authenticity of proposed beneficiaries, the official mentioned that if they did that, it would seem to undermine the decisions made by the community leaders and grassroots committees who are the gatekeepers to the target communities. Accepting their suggestions, though lacking in transparency at times, ensures maximum cooperation from them; in other words, these are agency-community politics. Corruption at all levels of society is a grave problem in Zimbabwe. According to Transparency International, the 2014 corruption perception index rates Zimbabwe 156th out of 175 countries. The extremity of the corruption situation, particularly in Zimbabwean society, qualifies it to be regarded as a contextual problem deterring agency performance.

Corruption as a deterring factor affecting agency performance in Zimbabwe confirms literature on the effects of corruption on Asia agencies, as Asia is a child labour hotspot. The review of literature on Asian corruption revealed that it is the anti-child labour agencies which have corrupt members who often tip child employers of planned police raids in advance (Moran, 1993). More recently, Miyashita et al (2021) discuss how government bureaucrats take bribes from businesses which employ children. However, the kind of corruption in Zimbabwe is more aligned with the previously discussed arguments made by Suvarchala (2001), who states that basic poverty alleviation programs offered by sub-Saharan African Governments underperform because they are corruption-ridden. Access to poverty-alleviating aid in Zimbabwe is sometimes not determined by transparent means, and that slows down agencies' progress on child labour reduction.

HIV/AIDS and Child Labour in Zimbabwe

All three agencies concurred on the additional challenge presented by HIV and AIDS for African anti-child labour agencies. The pandemic has increased the number of labour vulnerabilities to children as well as reduced the caregivers' or parents' capability to keep children in school. The various typical scenarios demonstrating the impact of the disease on Zimbabwean society and ultimately child labour, as they were reported by interviewed officials, are to be discussed under this section. Dialoguing with the district child welfare officer at the Department of Child Welfare and Probation Services, it was evident that this agency was particularly concerned with the boom in numbers of labour-vulnerable children. Commenting on the matter, he stated that:

> *The number of orphans in the country is just too high for any developing country to cushion . . . The National AIDS council has a record of over a million orphans countrywide, and almost fifty thousand child-headed households (Respondent C)*

The district child welfare officer at the Department of Child Welfare and Probation Services explained how the figures have grown to surpass any average agency's capability to contain the problem. Despite the steady progress in the reduction of AIDS related deaths globally, the pandemic remains a major driver of child labour (ITUC, 2012). Scholars like Bhalotra (2003) have argued that the bulk of orphans globally are sub-Saharan African children who then face the highest probability of entering labour markets due to the decline in altruism of extended family caregivers.

The nongovernmental Coalition Against Child Labour in Zimbabwe's projects manager emphasised that rehabilitating a working child who is head of household by sending him or her back to school is impractical because, in some cases, the extended family members who can be traced for that child are often in abject poverty. HIV/AIDS as a driver of child labour has been more detrimental to the realisation of agency goals in Zimbabwe than in neighbouring countries in the region. Anti-child labour agencies in Sub-Saharan Africa, Asia and South America, where the population is predominantly Arabic and Hispanic, the rate of HIV/AIDS is significantly lower than that of sub-Saharan Africa and their performance is not affected by HIV/AIDS as a major challenge. Therefore, it can be concluded that the capacity of Zimbabwean agencies is reduced by a problem which arises solely from the context in which they are performing, which is an HIV/AIDS infected region.

Clients' 'Donor Syndrome'

The Clients' 'Donor Syndrome' challenge is peculiar to the operations of NGOs such as the Coalition Against Child Labour in Zimbabwe, a donor-funded nongovernmental agency. A volunteer for this agency expressed concern over how the target community is reluctant to take ownership of anti-child labour programs being implemented in their villages. In his view, communities have complete reliance on the agency to facilitate and implement every program and the retards progress. He noted that:

> *You seldom find community members taking initiative to ensure the survival of projects. Originally, we planned to make exemplary cases, for example, erecting a few blocks at a remote school, with the hope that parents from other schools would take up the effort, but they have remained dormant, expecting us to refurbish every rural school in the wards (Respondent B)*

The project manager also confirmed that target communities have misconceptions about donor agencies having vast amounts of financial resources to the point they some even view the fight against child labour are the agency's obligation, although the programs are intended to benefit them and their children. They explained that some projects could be more successful if the effort were collaborative. The project's manager reported that some capable parents may intentionally leave all obligations to the agency, including purchasing uniforms, stationery and paying fees. That situation is what officials from this agency termed as 'donor syndrome', and they regarded it as a challenge affecting maximum community initiative and reducing the potential for faster child labour reduction. If that is understood by the communities, then they can make an effort to meet the agency halfway in creating child labour-free zones.

High Child Labourer Mobility

The rescue process for a child labourer involves three basic steps, which are detection, rehabilitation and monitoring. The stages of this process have to be completed to ensure a sustainable rescue of a child from undue labour. The interviewed volunteer at the Coalition against Child Labour noted that this process is often interfered with by the abrupt relocation of beneficiaries. He stated that:

> *Continuous monitoring is based on the assumption that the child will be at a known and constant residence, but many times we have cases of children relocating to live with different family members in different cities, making them out of reach and at risk of quitting school and making re-entry into labour (Respondent B).*

Many children who are agency beneficiaries are orphans, and often the extended families take turns to care for them, which results in them rotating among family members who, in most cases, live outside the agency's geographic areas of operation. In such instances, children who had been going to school under the sponsorship of the agency, as well as the private tutelage while living with guardians within the agency's area of operations, will suddenly cease to receive such support, and the risk of them sliding back into child labour is high.

The ILO (2010) points out the labour vulnerabilities of children who migrate across borders, and Zimbabwean children were reported to migrate beyond the country's borders to seek employment, the main destination being South Africa. Officials from the Department of Labour voiced this concern, noting that the country's proximity to South Africa is a fuelling factor. The principal labour officer argued that South Africa has been the main labour destination for many migrant workers in the sub-Saharan region and beyond, but Zimbabwe, being very close to South Africa, more Zimbabwean workers are bound to migrate there and among them, children under eighteen years of age and some even under sixteen. He stated that:

> *Chiredzi district is in the southern part of Zimbabwe, making it even closer to South Africa. Children easily migrate there illegally, where they find themselves in exploitative labour arrangements. Once they cross the border, they are out of our jurisdiction, but they are still Zimbabwean children engaged in child labour, and that makes them our concern (Respondent E).*

Expressing similar concerns, the project manager at the Coalition Against Child Labour in Zimbabwe stated that drought spells, which hit the country in the past five agricultural seasons, are forcing rural residents, including children, to seek alternative means of living outside their subsistence farming. That increases the rate at which children illegally migrate to South African farms and high labour zones. Chiredzi, the location of this research, is an even drier region where subsistence agriculture, on which rural populations rely on has been underperforming for years, leaving people with minimal survival options. This problem, however, is not restricted to Chiredzi but the entire southern region of the country. The principal labour officer explained that there have been attempts by the department to rehabilitate trans-border migrant workers, including children, though the program lost viability due to logistical costs.

Conclusion

Agency challenges are both internal and external. Internal challenges comprise agency inadequacies resulting from various causes, including acute budget constraints and skills shortages. External agency challenges are reported to be added difficulties emanating from the context in which Zimbabwean agencies operate, these include society attitudes and inflated numbers of child labourers. Most of the challenges affecting agencies are contextual. There are several factors, mostly peculiar to Zimbabwe, emanating from the target communities like poverty and HIV, which present aggravated challenges from Zimbabwean agencies. The internal factors affecting agencies, particularly government agencies, seem to stem from resource shortages.

The most significant responses revealing the nature of challenges affecting agency performance concur and confirm the elements listed by Elger (2007) as the major determinants of organisational performance in his theory of performance. Components such as the level of skills and knowledge, which Elger (2007) stated to affect agency performance, proved to bear the same effect on Zimbabwean anti-child labour agencies as revealed by officials representing the agencies. The most important determinant of agency performance, bearing the most influence on the low performance of Zimbabwean agencies, is the context of performance, thereby confirming the validity of Elger's theory on agency performance. It is also worth noting at this point that, as Elger suggested, an agency whose components of performance are high tends to realise higher performance, which is why the non-governmental agency appeared to be the agency with a relatively higher achievement rate. Deducing from responses on officials' recommendations, the nongovernmental agency, compared to the government agencies, seems to have officials who engage in constant reflective practice, allowing them to implement corrective measures more swiftly, resulting in notably higher performance levels. That practice confirms Elger's arguments on the positive effect of reflective practice on agency performance.

References

Abdullah, A., Huynh, C.R.I., Emery, C.R. & Jordan, L.P. 2022, *Social norms and family child labour: A systematic literature review*, Available at: https://pubmed.ncbi.nlm.nih.gov/35409766/ [Accessed 18 August 2023].

Bhalotra, S. 2003, *Child labour in Africa*, Available at: www.oecd-ilibrary.org [Accessed 7 July 2023].

Bonnet, M. 1993, *Child labour in Africa*, Available at: www.heinonlinebackup.com [Accessed 10 June 2023].

Chakarisa, T.C. 2010, *The application of international law on child labour in an African context*, Available at: www.ahrlj.up.ac.za [Accessed 10 July 2023].

Donback, N. 2022, *How NGOs and governments can address the growing child labour crisis*, Available at: https://www.devex.com/news/how-ngos-and-governments-can-address-the-growing-child-labor-crisis-102478 [Accessed 19 August 2023].

Elger, D. 2007, *Theory of performance*, Available at: www.webpages.uidaho.edu [Accessed 30 March 2023].

Huntington, S.P. 2001, *Political order in changing societies*, Yale University Press, New Haven.

International Labour Organisation 2010, *Facts on child labour*, Available at: www.ILO.org [Accessed 2 March 2023].

International Trade Union Confederation 2012, *AIDS remains a cause of child labour despite progress*, Available at: https://www.ituc-csi.org/aids-remains-a-cause-of-child [Accessed 19 August 2023].

Miyashita, T., Okada, K. & Takakura, K. 2021, *Child labour, corruption, and development*, Available at: https://ideas.repec.org/p/osk/wpaper/2020.html [Accessed 19 August 2023].

Moran, M. 1993, *Ending exploitative child labour practices*, Available at: digitalcommons.pace.edu [Accessed 12 June 2023].

Public Service Association 2021, *Understaffed and under pressure*, Available at: https://issuu.com/cpsu/docs/20370_review_magazine_february_2021_web_version/s/11893864 [Accessed 19 August 2023].

Robson, E. 2000, *Invisible careers: Young people in Zimbabwe's home-based health care*, Available at: http://onlinelibrary.wiley.com [Accessed 18 May 2023].

Suvarchala, G. 2001, *Legislation to combat child labour: An international perspective*, Available at: onlinelibrary.wiley.com [Accessed 6 June 2023].

Zimbabwe National Statistics Agency 2012, *Census 2012 preliminary report*, Available at: www.zimstat.co.zw [Accessed 7 September 2023].

Chapter Six
Child Rights and Child Protection in Zimbabwe: Counting the Gains, Exploring the Gaps and Drivers

Tapiwa Musasa

Introduction

The violation of the rights of children is partly rooted in a historical perception that views children not as autonomous individuals, but merely as dependents. The label of 'dependents' often reduces children to burdens rather than recognising them as valuable members of society. Such perception does not reflect the dignity, care, and protection that children deserve. This chapter maintains that referring to children as dependents undermines their humanity and strips away the warmth, love, and respect owed to them as equal members of the human family. Thinkers such as Thomas Aquinas have emphasised the need to treat children with the same dignity and respect by virtue of being human. On that basis, adults should take responsibility for children with affection and dignity. The media is laden with reports of child rights violations in terms of rape, child sexual exploitation, child marriages, child ritual killings, and school dropouts, despite the existence of policies and laws meant to protect and uphold the rights of children. This is against the understanding that any adult becomes a duty bearer and is responsible for child safeguarding, protection, and care. All individuals are expected to unite towards the building of safe communities where children can be treated with dignity. However, in some cases, adults and leaders are also perpetrators of these child rights violations. This chapter is partly based on views from stakeholders on the effectiveness of the existing child rights policies and other legal frameworks in an attempt to explore the relationship between the modern child rights instruments, conventions, cultural and religious practices of child rights and protection. In addition, the chapter explores the gaps between the blueprints and the practical application of child protection efforts by examining the impacts of religion, culture, legislation, and the economic environment in Zimbabwe.

The State of Child Rights and Child Protection Globally

The major legal instruments on the rights of children include the international Convention on the Rights of the Child of 1989 (referred to as the "Convention" under this chapter), the African Charter on the Rights and Welfare of the Child of 1990 referred to as the "Charter" under this chapter), and the Zimbabwean Constitution of 2013 (referred to as the "Constitution" under this chapter). These instruments consider a child as any human being below the age of 18 years. The legal instruments emphasise key rights of children, including the right to education, the right to be protected from sexual exploitation, the right to be protected from child marriages and freedom from economic exploitation or child labour.

Upholding the rights of the child has always been met with challenges across the globe, based on the premise that child rights and protection issues remain contentious. In Argentina, for example, the Government ratified the Convention on the Rights of the Child in 1990, which enabled child rights to have constitutional status in 1994. Despite all these actions, the rights of children in the country continued to be violated, with children being used by rebel groups. According to Amnesty International (2002), those who fought against this were threatened or killed. According to Thum (2021), the Government of Argentina has made several positive strides in promoting the right to education for all children, with public education being universal and free for all children. However, the right to non-discrimination remains under threat in Argentina because children of minority groups do not have proper access to education, and some of them do not have proper documentation to enable them to start schooling. Child labour has increased due to poverty and the impacts of COVID-19, and child prostitution has also increased. Despite the existence of international policies and conventions, the right of the child continues to be violated, and many underlying factors need to be addressed and improved, including legislation.

India is also a signatory to the Convention, having ratified it in 1992. According to Save the Children (2020), child rights go beyond human rights because children are a special, vulnerable group that needs extra protection from adults; thus, legislation should be enforced effectively. One of the major challenges in child rights in India is child labour, although the Indian law now specifies that no child can work when he or she is below the age of fourteen. In addition, though the Prohibition of Child Marriages Act was passed in 2006 and implemented in 2007, child marriages continue. According to Mahajan (2016), child marriages are technically illegal in India. A law passed in 1929 to abolish child marriages could not stop the practice, and another one was passed in 2006. However, girls as young as eight years old continue to be married off by their parents and guardians due to poverty. This shows that while the law exists to ban child marriages, implementation remains a challenge.

According to Leech (2017), every child in Russia has the right to education as stated by the Russian Constitution and the country's obligation to international legal instruments. Despite the existence of laws, migrant children in Russia have been reported to be turned away from schools due to a lack of proof of residence. As a result, the Russian Federation was ranked as number 84 of 181 countries on the Kids Right Index in 2019, because of such incidences of discrimination against children based on who they are. This is against Article 2 of the Convention on the Rights of the Child, an indication that there is a gap between the law and the practical application of child rights laws and policies even in developed countries.

In Switzerland, the rights of children are strictly enforced in the best interests of the child (Humanium 2019). However, the country has one of the highest rates of children who commit suicide, and this has been attributed to easy access to lethal resources like firearms. This becomes a violation of the right to protection because adults are supposed to be protecting children. In addition, Children in Switzerland also constitute forty-five per cent of the people on social welfare assistance, and they are in the zero–seventeen years age group. These statistics indicate that most countries have cases of child rights violations, although there are differences between the developing and developed world. There is a need, therefore, to tighten the laws protecting children and enforce them in a way that is in the best interest of children as stated by the Convention on the Rights of the Child (CRC).

The State of Child Rights and Protection in Sub-Saharan Africa

Several countries in Sub-Saharan Africa ratified the Convention. Zimbabwe, Ghana, and Kenya, for example, ratified the Convention in 1990, while Zambia, Tanzania, Malawi, Nigeria and Ethiopia ratified the Convention in 1991. This indicates that most African countries are state parties in the fight against child rights violations by virtue of having ratified the Convention (UN 2012). However, several cases of child rights violations are found in Africa partly because of challenges like poverty, the absence of stiffer penalties for perpetrators, and religious and cultural beliefs that are prioritised over the rights of the child. According to Ofosu Oti (2017), the rights of children in Ghana are still violated because of many factors, including ignorance of the rights, weaker law enforcement mechanisms, and exclusion of children from participating in state institutions.

In Kenya, children have historically experienced abuse physically, sexually, and emotionally. The Government has made efforts to ratify the Convention and the Optional Protocol to the Convention so that laws can be strengthened. According to UNICEF (2019), several strategies have been put in place to protect the rights of children in Kenya. However, Chigiti (2012) notes that child labour is still rampant in Kenya, and children are forced to be engaged in armed conflict in the name of protecting the community and their livestock. This could be attributed to many factors, including poverty, ignorance, cultural practices, and exploitation. Efforts to curb economic exploitation have not yielded much as guided by the laws. This means more has to be done by the Government to match the dictates of the African Charter on the Rights and Welfare of the Child.

In Mozambique, the state of child rights is deteriorating. Due to poverty, the education system is substandard, and some inequalities persist based on geographical location, gender, and poverty (Humanium, 2020). The teacher-pupil ratio is also very high, with non-extensive teacher training programs. Thus, children drop out of school more frequently and throw themselves into more poverty and unemployment. Children end up engaging in child labour, which is rampant at twenty-two per cent. As reported by Human Rights Watch (2019), children with albinism have been discriminated against and are unable to access education, public health systems, and are sometimes rejected by their own families in Mozambique. Traditional beliefs in witchcraft once led to killings and kidnappings of children with albinism, grossly fueling the violation of the rights of children in Mozambique. The plight of children in Mozambique is worsened by natural disasters, which destroy livelihoods and increase incidences of vulnerability and poverty, escalating problems such as child marriages (forty-eight per cent of children are married before eighteen years), poor nutrition and health, teen pregnancy stigma, and disparities between urban and rural environments.

The Benefits of Upholding Children's Rights-Analysis of a Few Selected Rights

Upholding children's rights has benefits at the individual, family, community and national levels. While the provision of these rights includes enabling them to access basic needs, there are higher aims involved, which the child realises as they mature (Aderson, 2017). While the provision of these rights includes enabling them to access basic needs, there are higher aims involved, which the child realises as they mature (Aderson, 2017). Children have the right to health, to life, to protection and to special care and attention from their parents as well as from the community in which they live. Communities become important as they ensure that every child survives in a safe environment. As guided by the international and regional legal instruments, the national legislation guarantees such rights (Gradinarova, 2023).

The right to education is enshrined in Articles 28 and 29 of the Convention on the Rights of the Child (CRC), as well as Article 11 of the African Charter on the Rights and Welfare of the Child (ACRWC). This reaffirms every child's entitlement to free, compulsory, and quality education that fosters their full development and dignity. The right to education provides children the opportunity to learn equal rights, respect for peers and parents, as well as their responsibilities in families, communities and the nation at large. Their intellectual, mental and physical potential grows to the fullest as they get exposure to the world (Alderson, 2017). When parents offer children an opportunity to learn, they invest in their future so that they are well-prepared leaders for the future. According to Amoah and Asamoah (2022), an increase in the education of a mother increases the chances of survival of the children born, thereby indicating a positive correlation between maternal education and child survival.

Balaj, York and Sripada (2021) have observed a reduction in under-5 (children under the age of five) mortality of thirty-one per cent (ninety-five per cent CI 29.0–32.6) for children born to mothers with twelve years of education (completed secondary education) and 17.3% (15.0–18.8) for children born to fathers with twelve years of education, compared with those born to a parent with no education. A single additional year of schooling is, on average, associated with a reduction in under-five mortalities of 3.04% (2.82–3.23) for maternal education and 1.57% (1.35–1.72) for paternal education (Balaj et al, 2021). These statistics are an indication that education is crucial for child survival. When children are denied access to education, this increases the chances of child mortality.

The right to health and access to health services is affirmed in Article 24 of the Convention on the Rights of the Child (CRC) and Article 14 of the African Charter on the Rights and Welfare of the Child (ACRWC). This obliges member states to ensure that all children enjoy the highest standard of health and access to necessary medical services. Children must enjoy their right to health and access to health services. This ensures that children are competent enough to participate in any activity, to play with their peers and to lead an active life. Government policies, political decisions, wars and refugee crises are some of the factors which can negatively affect the right and access to health by children (Gradinarova, 2023). When families suffer, children also suffer; thus, the economic situation in a country, the political situation and the social standing of the family all affect the access to health for children. It is not possible to target the child only and exclude family members in the right to health because the same children are affected emotionally and psychologically when their family members are sick or unable to access health facilities due to financial constraints. According to Alderson (2017), the right to health encompasses all rights, since no right can be enjoyed when someone is sick. It is therefore critical to ensure that children, their families and communities access healthcare services.

The right to identity is enshrined in Articles 7 and 8 of the Convention on the Rights of the Child (CRC). It affirms every child's right to a name, nationality, and family relations, as well as the obligation of member states to preserve and, when necessary, re-establish these aspects of a child's identity. Children need to be registered immediately after birth so that they have an identity and a nationality. Parents who do not make an effort to register their children violate the rights of their children from a very tender age. According to Selim (2019), the same children will struggle to get access to formal educational institutions without these crucial documents. This legal proof of identity is a requirement, and can help protect children from violence, abuse and exploitation. Children are unable to prove their age, which puts them at a much higher risk of being forced into early marriage or the labour market, or recruited into the armed forces when they do not have birth certificates. In addition, the lack of identity documents for female children becomes a vicious cycle and can become a gender inequality issue. Later in life they may not be able to register their children in cases of divorce, teenage unwanted pregnancies, rape or incest, further aggravating gender inequality gaps (Selim, 2019). The factors contributing to low rates of child registration at birth include cost, culture and ethnicity, geographical location and level of education of the parents. Governments should therefore make efforts to eliminate these barriers to increase the number of children registered at birth in each nation.

The issue of child labour is addressed in Article 15 of the African Charter on the Rights and Welfare of the Child (ACRWC). The Article obligates member states to protect children from all forms of economic exploitation and work that is likely to be hazardous or interfere with their education, health, or development. The International Labour Organisation (ILO 2014) notes that while there are many child labourers globally, Sub-Saharan Africa continues to be the region with the highest incidence of child labour (twenty-one per cent of five–seventeen-year-olds, or 59 million). This indicates the need for more robust strategies to reduce the number of children who are working while underage. 'Child labour' is a narrower concept than "economically active children", excluding all those children aged twelve years and older who are working only a few hours a week in permitted light work and those aged fifteen years and above whose work is not classified as 'hazardous' (ILO 2014). When children are given light work which is aligned to their ages, they find time to play, associate, read, and explore the world to identify their talents through games and play. Child labour, therefore, becomes the greatest enemy for child development since some of the children do hazardous work, leading to injury and death. The ILO (2021) observes that for child labour to be eliminated, countries must work together to address the challenge.

Article 13 of the African Charter on the Rights and Welfare of the Child (ACRWC) emphasises the right of children with disabilities to special measures of protection, ensuring their dignity, self-reliance, and active participation in the community. The emphasis is on the need to include all children with disabilities in any plans outlined for children, as well as assist them to enjoy their rights just like any other child. Such children are often observed by society as having a problem that should not be prioritised. According to UNICEF (2018), children with disabilities are often placed in institutional care for the wrong reasons, sometimes missing in national statistics, excluded from mainstream educational institutions and placed in special schools as well as surrounded with myths and stigma. There is a need for inclusive education, which has been defined by UNICEF (2017) as an education system that includes all students, and welcomes and supports them to learn, whoever they are and whatever their abilities or requirements. This entails ensuring that teaching and the curriculum, school buildings, classrooms, play areas, transport and toilets are appropriate for all children at all levels. Inclusive education means all children learn together in the same schools. When special attention is given to children living with disabilities, these challenges can be reduced so that they also enjoy their rights just like every child. Focus should be made on systems, monitoring, partnerships, cultural change and support systems (UNICEF, 2017).

Progress on Child Rights and Child Protection in Zimbabwe

Zimbabwe ratified the Convention on the Rights of the Child (CRC) in 1990 and the African Charter on the Rights and Welfare of the Child (ACRWC) in 1995. Special Acts and policies developed by Zimbabwe to protect the rights of the child since 1980 include the Maintenance Act (Chapter 5:09), the Children's Act (Chapter 5:06), the Zimbabwe National Orphan Care Policy (1999), Section 70 of Criminal Law (Chapter 9:07, Chapter 9:23), Customary Law (Chapter 7:05), the Labour Act (Chapter 28:01) was updated in 2019, the Legal Age of Majority (LAMA 1982), Marriage Act (Chapter 5:11), Education Amendment Act (2020), Education Act (Chapter 25:04), The Constitution of Zimbabwe (2013) and the Children's Amendment Act No. 8 of 2023. However, despite the existence of these pieces of legislation and ratification of international conventions, child rights continue to be violated in Zimbabwe, showing a gap between theory and practice.

In 1996, Zimbabwe established the Victim Friendly Unit (VFU) through the Zimbabwe Republic Police (ZRP) to proactively and reactively assist sexually assaulted women and girls to gain confidence and give evidence in a friendly environment separated from the perpetrator. There have also been increased activities, roles and involvement of NGOs, Churches, Government Departments, and individuals in child welfare and child protection are positive and noticeable. The Roman Catholic Church has historically mobilised resources, including clothing, food, school fees, school uniforms, and stationery, among others, to benefit vulnerable children in and outside their churches. A member of the St Anne's Guild at the St Gerard's Parish in Harare noted that:

> As a guild, we request two orphaned or vulnerable children through St Vincent De Paul. Charity in the church. We usually start with them from grade 5 or Grade 6. We pay their school fees, we buy their uniforms and stationery, and we pay for their examination fees until they get to Advanced Level, then we get others. We are making an impact as a guild. This is a small number, but every child counts, and that makes a difference in the lives of those few children. This is our way of avoiding harsh judgment as Christians, as stated in Mathew 25:1. We are encouraging others to join us in upholding child rights.

Zimbabwe has also experienced an increase in organisations that assist children with basic needs provision. The table below shows key organisations that offer support for children's development and protection.

Organisation	Focus Areas
Girl Child Empowerment Zimbabwe	Marginalised girls with disabilities
Mavambo Trust	Healthcare for orphans.
Child Line Zimbabwe	Provides safe environments for all children.
Gadzamoyo Street Children Foundation	Provides survival skills and food handouts to destitute children.
Girl Child Network Zimbabwe	Promoting girls' empowerment, providing safehouses for girls in crisis.

Childcare Ministries	Feeding underprivileged schoolchildren.
Campaign for Female Education (CAMFED)	Support for girls to go to secondary school, covering needs including school fees, uniforms, sanitary wear, stationery, bicycles, boarding fees and disability aids.
Plan International Zimbabwe	Ensuring quality and inclusive education for all children, especially girls, skills training, and protection of children from violence and abuse.
Hope World Zimbabwe	Improving the well-being of orphans and vulnerable children.

Gaps and Causes of Child Rights Abuse in Zimbabwe

The first factor leading to the violation of the rights of children is child marriage. Religion and culture have fueled child marriages, which in turn have contributed to school dropouts, a rise in illiteracy rates amongst certain religious sectors, an increase in infant mortality, increased post-neonatal mortality, higher maternal mortality, and higher fecundity rates. These have contributed to a violation of the right to education, the right to life, and the right to health for the affected children, and the law is not effective against religious perpetrators. One participant noted that:

> The law tends to turn a blind eye on perpetrators of child marriages in the church. Men above 70 years of age are marrying, or better still raping 12-year-old girls in the name of a 'dream marriage' and nothing is done about it. The law enforcement agents claim that there will be no complaint and no basis for an arrest, which is very painful and defeats all efforts to promote children's rights.

The Children's Act has allowed children to marry at sixteen years (the age of consent) since its inception in 2001, and this gap has been taken advantage of by perpetrators of child marriages. By contrast, the Constitution of Zimbabwe, Chapter 4:78(1), allows only those who have attained the age of eighteen years to form a family, showing gaps between the two pieces of legislation. This gap has caused harm since perpetrators of child marriages took advantage of the age of consent stipulated by the Children's Act. However, the amendment of the Children's Act in May 2023 (Children's Amendment Act No 8 of 2023) brought necessary changes. A police officer noted that:

> *A gap existed in the definition of a child between the Constitution of Zimbabwe and the Children's Act. This gap did more harm as criminals took advantage of it. The new amendment act will go a long way in protecting young girls against child marriages, but still, there is a need to monitor strict enforcement of the laws protecting children.*

The second factor contributing to child rights violations is stigma and exclusion of children living with disabilities. Most societies do not accommodate children living with disabilities and other special conditions. In religious and traditional circles in Zimbabwe, a disabled child is treated as bad luck, punishment from God for sins committed, like infidelity, or a result of ritual ceremonies practised by the family. One key informant noted that:

> *I have a disabled child, and people are not very welcoming. They look at you like you have been cursed by God. When you enter the church with the child, people look at you from head to toe, from the door of the church until you sit down. Usually, no one wants to sit close to you, and as a result, you either hide the child from people or give the child away to orphanages to avoid shame and stigma from society.*

The statement shows that instead of being inclusive and receptive, the church can stigmatise and exclude children with disabilities, thereby limiting their ability to enjoy their rights. As the third factor, endemic poverty and persistent economic hardships in the country are contributing to child marriages, child labour, school dropouts, and child sexual exploitation. Lack of an enabling environment for economic growth, high unemployment rates have incapacitated some parents, leading to failure to provide for their children's basic needs, which they are expected to do by the law. As a result, the Social Welfare Department remains overwhelmed and cannot absorb all children in need. Child labour is increasing as children drop out of school to work for food and clothing in mines, farms and households as maids and gardeners. The fourth factor contributing to the violation of child rights is a Lack of knowledge of referral pathways and children's rights. Some children are still not aware of their rights. A law enforcement agent emphasised that:

> Many child abuse cases go unreported because some people do not know where to go. The Zimbabwe Republic Police is making efforts to raise awareness through campaigns so that anonymous tip-offs can be used to report such cases. Children are also urged to be taught to report abuse to any elderly person around them without fear. The role of parents and the school remains very key in educating the child on their rights.

The final factor contributing to the violation of the rights of children is the distance between schools in some rural areas. This has led to an increase in school dropouts. One parent said:

> In some rural areas like Gokwe North district, young children travel distances of more than twenty kilometres to the nearest school. Young children end up dropping out of school. Some are raped on the way to school or sexually exploited by senior male members of the community leading to unwanted early pregnancies, early marriages, and school dropouts.

State of Child Rights in Zimbabwe and the Way Forward

Child rights are critical, and children need to be protected not only because they are the future generation, but because they are equal human beings who deserve to be treated with respect and dignity by being born and are human. There are enough laws protecting the rights of the child in Zimbabwe, though the implementation of the laws leaves a lot to be desired. In some cases, the law enforcement agents overlook religious sects that perpetrate child marriages despite the provision of such laws in the constitution of Zimbabwe. A child cannot raise another child efficiently and effectively, that why child mortality is higher at these churches. The high child mortality rates are caused by poor hygiene, poor food handling procedures and general lack of knowledge on how to raise children. The bodies of these young children are not fully grown, so they die during childbirth. This should be treated as murder, but it seems no one even cares about these deaths. There is a need for more awareness campaigns, sensitisation, and sensitisation for the benefit of child protection and holistic development. This is in line with Oti (2017), who emphasises the need to educate children and everyone else on their rights for safe communities in which children can grow and develop without threats of ritual killings, rape, and kidnappings. Even if we consider the affected children to be a minority, the human rights instruments advocate for individual recognition for every child; thus, no child should be left behind.

In addition, some religious sects continue to promote the violation of the child's right to education, as some girls are married before completing primary and/or secondary education. This is against Article 28 of the Convention and Article 11 of the Charter. If children are allowed to complete their secondary education, they get a chance to grow physically and be able to handle childbirth complications, which are so high in religious sects practising child marriages. Letting the children attain at least secondary education promotes child survival and child development as more knowledge is gained in childcare and hygiene practices, thus reducing child neonatal figures (Balaj et al, 2021). There is life, survival, and development in stopping child marriages and encouraging both boys and girls to attain secondary and tertiary education. These ideas are supported by Amoah and Asamoah (2022), who observe a positive correlation between the mother's education and child survival. The boys also marry early, and they are trained as vendors of different wares before they complete their secondary education, a gross violation of children's rights. If the boys and girls are left to complete their secondary education, they will find time to enjoy their youth, make personal aspirations and achievements when they learn from others, as well as learning more about their rights, which they can also share with peers, parents, and guardians.

Some religious sects do not allow their members to have access to a hospital for treatment of all ailments, including prenatal checkups and childbirths, raising the risk of postnatal mortality and morbidity in young mothers (Balaj et al, 2021) and children between 0 and 5 years of age. This is against Article 24 of the CRC, because the young mothers are still children. The law enforcement agents should enforce the already existing pieces of legislation to promote the rights of children in Zimbabwe. Further, the lack of harmony among the pieces of legislation, specifically the Customary Law, the Constitution of Zimbabwe, and the Children's Act, is a recipe for disaster in upholding the rights of children. It leaves room for perpetrators to violate child rights since they can choose a piece of legislation that protects them if convicted. This has led to many cases of rape and sexual intercourse with minors being dismissed because the laws are not in harmony. A perpetrator may argue that they are protected by the customary law which allows people to marry at a lesser age, thus nullifying any claims of child rape as stated by the other pieces of legislation. There is a need, therefore, to align existing legislation to the new constitution, which is clear on the legal age of the majority and its relevance to only adults getting married after eighteen years of age and not minors, who should, at all costs, stay in school. Further, section 70 of the Criminal Law (Chapter 9:07) punishes people who engage in sexual affairs sex with children between the ages of twelve and sixteen, but only punishes those committing the crime outside marriage. This is an indication that marrying a minor and having sexual intercourse with her is not a crime at all, according to this law. Thus, the legal framework on the rights of children needs to be revised and harmonised in Zimbabwe.

The economic hardships in Zimbabwe, which remain unbearable, make children end up working on farms, mines, and in households as maids and gardeners. Child labour has increased and should be addressed so that children avoid working in mines or farms (ILO 2014) as they try to look for basic needs like food, shelter and clothing. For example, the Maintenance Act (Chapter 5:09), which was meant to promote the provision of basic needs for children born out of wedlock, is no longer effective to its maximum potential because many parents are out of formal employment. Some parents are letting their children work, which is against the Labour Act, Chapter 4 section 81(1) and 19:3b of the Constitution, Article 32 of the Convention and Article 15 of the Charter. This is caused by the fact that parents have failed to raise school fees for them, and the vicious cycle of poverty is never broken in such poor homes. Strong programs for the youth can help to empower children so that they do not fall prey to criminals who target children for marriage and sexual exploitation.

Some children continue to be victims of circumstances when they have to drop out of school to take care of their sick parents or their younger siblings, scenarios which can be handled by social welfare departments, churches, or Non-Governmental Organisations if enough research is done on the whereabouts of such children. Child rights programs can help to ensure that all children in difficult circumstances are identified and channelled into the correct system to get the necessary help. Situation analysis is critical so that the correct needs and challenges are identified and the correct stakeholders are communicated with for the sake of promoting the best interests of the child. According to the Convention on the Rights of the Child (1990), children have a right to be protected from child prostitution and child sexual exploitation. Many children in Epworth, located in the south-eastern part of Harare Province and other high-density suburbs, are picked up by adult exploiters who use them and pay only 25 cents (USD) and equivalent, which can only buy a small bundle of vegetables. This is a criminal offence, and the perpetrators, because they are adults, should be arrested, not the children. Rather than exploiting the child, the adult can be responsible enough to give the child their needs of the day and help them with information on how to get placed into an orphanage or any children's home. For this reason, penalties for adult perpetrators of child prostitution should be stiffer by three times stiffer than they are at the moment. However, in most cases, it's the children who are arrested, which makes one question the pragmatic implications of the laws being used, whether they are in the best interest of the child as stated by the four principles of the CRC. Some children may go into child prostitution out of their own accord, even if they have money, food, and school fees at home. These constitute a small percentage, though, and child situation analysis can help in establishing the causes of child abuse so that the best mitigation measures are put in place.

Another challenge is that national laws have not been fully harmonised with international and regional laws, thus exposing the children to missed opportunities in terms of enjoying their rights. For example, in Zimbabwe, the education system states that each child should pay school fees from primary to tertiary level, while Article 28 of the CRC maintains that there should be free and compulsory primary and secondary education for every child. This gap is therefore created by different levels of legal development in different countries, and the economic differences present a challenge to the universality of child rights. Children in first-world countries have a better chance of achieving primary and secondary education as compared to children in developing countries like Zimbabwe, where school fees are needed at every level, and the economic challenges reduce the opportunities for children in rural and urban areas. Child protection organisations (NGOs and the rest of the private sector) should therefore target the gaps which the Government lacks, complementing the efforts by the

Government. In addition, the cultural differences in the human rights discipline lead to differential access to resources and child rights globally. In Zimbabwe, in some cases, children are supposed to be trained to work at a tender age, which may be considered child labour in other countries. However, section 81 (1)(e) of the Constitution of Zimbabwe prohibits child labour, while section 19(3)(b) (i) and (ii) enshrined in the same Constitution states that children should not perform work which is inappropriate for their age nor hazardous to their wellbeing. This shows that if the law is followed closely, children will still be protected from child labour, but still be trained to do safe chores for training purposes.

Recommendation

Several recommendations can be noted from the preceding discussion. Firstly, laws promoting child rights and protection should be aligned with the new Constitution of Zimbabwe and the proposed Marriage Bill so that children's rights are uniform in all pieces of legislation. Secondly, there is a need for stiffer penalties should be enforced for rights violators. Thirdly, education, training, and awareness campaigns should be increased on human rights knowledge for the children, adults and parents, targeting church leaders, traditional leaders and other community leaders for safe spaces. Referral pathways should be clearly outlined and readily available (physical addresses and contact numbers in case of emergency) so that victims can easily find assistance. Moreover, cultural practices should promote the rights of the child as stated in the African Charter on the Rights and Welfare of the Child. Religious sects that do not respect the legal age of majority, the right to education, and the right to health for women and children should be prosecuted, since those rights are key to child survival and development for future generations. There is also a need to align cultural practices with the law and everyday life to close implementation gaps for the best interest of the child. Finally, there is a need for a multi-stakeholder approach in dealing with child rights issues. One organisation cannot handle all challenges alone; thus, the Government, Civil Society, Non-Governmental Organisations, church leaders, traditional leaders and all adults should join hands in educating the youth on their rights as well as resource mobilisation for youth empowerment programs.

Conclusion

Religion, culture, and economic hardships in Zimbabwe are fueling the violations of child rights. This continue to happen regardless of the national, regional and international legal instruments advocating for the rights of the child such as the African Charter on the Rights and Welfare of the Child (ACRWC), the Convention on the Rights of the Child (CRC), the Zimbabwean constitution, and many other Acts established in the country to uphold the rights of the child. Children's rights to education, health, survival, and development continue to be violated despite the existence of legislation promoting the rights of children. There is a mismatch amongst legislation promoting the child, leaving gaps that are being taken advantage of by child rights violators, showing that there is a need to harmonise the pieces of legislation and align them to the new constitution. The economic hardships in the country have led to children dropping out of school to work or to practice child prostitution; thus, efforts should be made at all costs to improve the economic environment so that parents can afford to pay for their children's needs. An enabling environment is needed so that even those male parents with children out of wedlock can pay for the maintenance of their children, but when everyone is out of employment, it becomes very difficult for single mothers to claim maintenance of their children.

References

Alderson, P. 2017, *Children's rights: Best practice*, Available at: https://www.researchgate.net/publication/320466791_Children's_rights_best_practice [Accessed 12 June 2023].

Amnesty International 2002, *The rights of the child in Argentina*, pp. 3–8. Available at: https://www.amnesty.org/en/wp-content/uploads/2021/06/amr130182002en.pdf [Accessed 5 May 2023].

Amoah, A. & Asamoah, M.K. 2022, 'Child survival: The role of a mother's education', *Heliyon*, Available at: https://doi.org/10.1016/j.heliyon.2022.e11403 [Accessed 22 April 2023].

Balaj, M., York, H.W., Sripada, K. & Brisnier, E. 2021, *Parental education and inequalities in child mortality: A global systematic review and analysis.* [No link provided].

Chigiti, J. 2012, *Kenya: Child labour is a human rights violation.* [No link provided].

Constitution Net 2013, *The Constitution of Zimbabwe*, Available at: https://constitutionnet.org/sites/default/files/copac_-_constitution_of_zimbabwe_2012.pdf [Accessed 18 July 2023].

Gradinarova, N. 2023, 'Children's rights and access to health care', *MEDIS – International Journal of Medical Sciences and Research*, vol. 2, no. 1, pp. 43–48. Available at: https://www.researchgate.net/publication/369363546_CHILDREN'S_RIGHTS_AND_ACCESS_TO_HEALTH_CARE [Accessed 11 June 2023].

Humanium Report 2019, *Realising child rights in Switzerland*, Available at: https://www.humanium.org/en/switzerland-2/ [Accessed 30 March 2023].

International Labour Organisation 2014, *Child labour in a nutshell: A resource for Pacific Island countries*, Available at: https://www.ilo.org/wcmsp5/groups/public/---asia/---ro-bangkok/---ilo-suva/documents/publication/wcms_304562.pdf [Accessed 6 May 2023].

International Labour Organisation 2021, *Child labour: Global estimates 2020, trends and the road forward*. [PDF document, no stable link] [Accessed 16 May 2023].

Leech, G. 2017, *Migrant children turned away from schools in Russia*, Available at: https://www.hrw.org/news/2017/02/09/migrant-children-turned-away-schools-russia [Accessed 27 April 2023].

Mahajan, R. 2016, *Laws on child marriages in India*, Available at: https://www.nationalgeographic.com/photography/article/child-brides-marriage-shravasti-india-culture [Accessed 21 March 2023].

Nygard, D. 2019, *Children's rights in Russia*, Available at: https://discretion.uib.no/ [Accessed 4 May 2023].

Ofosu Oti, G. 2017, *Promoting and protecting children in Ghana*, Available at: https://www.ghanaweb.com/GhanaHomePage/features/Promoting-and-protecting-child-rights-in-ghana-534530 [Accessed 9 May 2023].

Save the Children 2020, *Fundamentals of child rights in India*, Available at: https://www.savethechildren.in/child-protection/fundamentals-of-child-rights-in-india [Accessed 7 June 2023].

Selim, L. 2019, *What is birth registration and why does it matter?* UNICEF Publications, Available at: https://www.unicef.org/stories/what-birth-registration-and-why-does-it-matter [Accessed 25 April 2023].

Swissinfo 2021, *Child rights in Switzerland*, Available at: https://www.swissinfo.ch/eng/society/switzerland-among-best-countries-for-children-s-rights/46673946 [Accessed 18 March 2023].

Thum, J. 2021, *Realising child rights in Argentina*, Humanium Report, Available at: https://www.humanium.org/en/argentina/ [Accessed 9 May 2023].

UN 2012, *Child rights: CRC ratifications in chronological order*, UN Blogspot, Available at: https://unchildrights.blogspot.com/2011/01/chronological-order-ratifications-crc.html [Accessed 11 April 2023].

UNICEF 2017, *Inclusive education: Including children with disabilities in quality learning – What needs to be done?* Available at: https://www.unicef.org/eca/sites/unicef.org.eca/files/IE_summary_accessible_220917_brief.pdf [Accessed 13 April 2023].

UNICEF 2018, *Helping children with disabilities take their place in society*, Available at: https://www.unicef.org/eca/media/3646/file/in-focus-disability.pdf [Accessed 17 April 2023].

Chapter Seven
The Roles of Social Workers in Promoting Child Rights in Africa

Chika Rita Ikeorji

Introduction

The issue of child rights in Africa has deep historical roots that stem from colonial legacies, cultural norms, and economic disparities (Kaime, 2005). This is apparent in the imposition of foreign rule by European powers during the colonial era, where several traditional African values and practices were disregarded, leading to the erosion of indigenous child-rearing systems (Arowolo, 2010). Not only did the colonial administrations disrupt families and disregard the well-being of African children in pursuit of economic interests, but they also overlooked cultural norms and traditions. Children in Africa have been historically vulnerable to exploitation, abuse, and neglect. With approximately forty per cent of Africa's population being under the age of eighteen (Newell et al, 2004), it shows that ensuring the fulfilment of children's rights is crucial for sustainable development and social progress that the continent has sought over the decades. The recognition of child rights gained momentum with the adoption of the United Nations Convention on the Rights of the Child (UNCRC) in 1989, which articulated the fundamental rights that all children are entitled to, including the right to survival, development, protection, and participation (Assembly, 1989). The significance of child rights in Africa cannot be overstated because protecting children's rights not only guarantees their well-being but also fosters the creation of a just, equitable, and prosperous society in the long run. Despite the increasing awareness and international frameworks for child rights, African children continue to confront numerous challenges.

Ambrose (1995) asserts that numerous economic and social problems plague Africa, which oftentimes negate the effort made by its populace in struggling to survive and have a decent life. All categories of persons involved in these adversities include children who are supposed to be protected by both the system and the family. From the perspective of Rushubirwa and colleagues (2015), these adversities are multifaceted and interlinked, such that the negative effects of each factor on another make the situation more severe or intense. Amongst the most common social problems faced by children are poverty, child labour, and conflict. In Africa, widespread poverty remains a pressing issue that has forced many families to struggle to provide their children with necessities such as food, clean water, and shelter (Addae-Korankye, 2014). With this level of poverty in many families, there is limited access to other basic needs of the child, such as education and healthcare. There are several regions in Africa experiencing armed conflicts, leading to dire consequences for children (Williams, 2016) such that children in more than 50 countries are currently suffering from the effects of war, with Angola, Rwanda, Sierra Leona, Nigeria, and Liberia as mostly affected (Albertyn et al, 2003). In times of conflict, children become victims of violence, forced recruitment into armed groups, and displacement, disrupting their education and psychosocial well-being (Williams, 2016). According to Werner (2012), millions of children in Africa lack access to quality education due to economic hardships, which drive many children into exploitative labour practices. Eneji and Ikeorji (2018) posit that young people are often victims of conflict in some countries of Africa. Children are engaged in hazardous jobs, deprived of education, and robbed of their childhood, which hinders their development and future opportunities.

Amongst the front liners in propagating the goodwill of every African child are the social workers. Social workers are found in every aspect of society, in various settings (Berg-Weger, 2019), where they play a pivotal role in addressing the myriad challenges faced by individuals, including children. In Africa, social work is gaining recognition due to its mandate to resolve the social problems of people and enhance their social functioning (Rodriguez et al, 2017). There cannot be a stable society without social workers because they exist to fix the diverse social problems of people. It has been established that to get the desired positive social change depends on the knowledge and skills of a professional, which social workers possess and utilise during service delivery (Teater, 2019). In all settings, the core purpose of the social work profession is to enhance the well-being and quality of life of individuals, families, groups, and communities. With a dedication to promoting social justice, equality, and empowerment, social workers seek avenues to address the challenges and complexities of human life (Berg-Weger 2019). The primary focus is on helping vulnerable and marginalised populations, advocating for their rights, and supporting them in achieving their fullest potential. This shows the overarching importance of the social work profession in society and the need for social workers to be fully engrossed in care environments where they can render efficient services to individuals.

Overview of the Children's Rights Act in Africa

According to the United Nations Convention on the Rights of the Child (UNCRC), a child is defined as any individual under the age of eighteen years (UNICEF, 2013). The UNCRC considers anyone who has not yet reached their eighteenth birthday as a child, and it grants them specific rights and protections under the convention. The history of child rights legislation in Africa is a testament to the continent's commitment to protecting and promoting the well-being of its youngest citizens. There are specific timelines and details which may vary from country to country, but the overarching narrative reflects Africa's efforts to address the vulnerabilities and challenges faced by children (Sossou and Yogtiba, 2009). The recognition of child rights in Africa traces back to early initiatives during the colonial era and post-independence period (Kaime, 2005), where some African countries adopted legal provisions and policies to protect children from abuse, exploitation, and neglect (Williams, 2016).

However, these efforts were often limited in scope and lacked comprehensive protection for all children. This is partly because some cultural norms and practices in certain African societies inadvertently perpetuate child exploitation or hinder efforts to address it comprehensively (Pence, 2008). For example, early marriage, child labour, and traditional practices like child begging may be deeply ingrained in certain communities, making it challenging to fully eradicate such practices through policy alone. Also, many African countries face significant economic challenges, and their governments may have limited financial resources to allocate to social welfare programs (Albertyn et al, 2003). The constraints can lead to prioritising certain aspects of child protection over others, resulting in policies that may not address all dimensions of child exploitation comprehensively.

A significant turning point in the history of child rights in Africa was the adoption of the UNCRC by the United Nations General Assembly in 1989 and which came into force in 1990. The convention established a universal framework for children's rights, outlining a comprehensive set of protections and entitlements (Imoh and Ansell, 2014). The UNCRC consists of 54 articles which cover a wide range of rights and protections that are guaranteed to children to ensure their well-being, development, and safety. It recognised children as rights-holders, entitled to special care and protection. In the subsequent years, many African countries have ratified the UNCRC, signifying their commitment to safeguarding the rights of children within their borders. As developments progressed, the African Charter on the Rights and Welfare of the Child (ACRWC) was established, building on the principles of the UNCRC in 1990 but became operational in 1999 (African Union, 1999). The African Charter on the Rights and Welfare of the Child was adopted by the Organisation of African Unity (now the African Union) in 1990. The ACRWC provided a regional context to child rights, acknowledging the unique socio-cultural challenges faced by African children, but specifically, the ACRWC, as a regional human rights treaty, focused on the rights and welfare of children in Africa (African Union, 1999). It was created to complement and reinforce the provisions of the United Nations Convention on the Rights of the Child (UNCRC) with provisions that are tailored to the specific needs and challenges faced by children in Africa.

At the time of its promulgation, the ACRWC was to be the building block to salvage the pitiable plight of numerous African children. This is because it emphasised the importance of preserving children's identity, culture, and language while ensuring their overall development (Bakewell, 2013). Following the adoption of international and regional child rights frameworks, many African countries undertook the task of enacting or revising national legislation to align with these standards (African Union, 1999), which included incorporating provisions to protect children's rights to education, healthcare, protection from violence, and participation in decision-making processes. As opined by Ijeoma (2013), some countries also set a minimum age for marriage and employment to combat child marriage and child labour, thereby ensuring that the child is protected from all vices that hinder their full development. Though it is imperative to have strong legislation that safeguards the dignity of persons, implementation is equally crucial. In Africa, the implementation of policies has been a stumbling block to growth and sustainable development (Ajulor, 2018). In collaboration with civil society organisations and international agencies, governments have worked and continue to work toward translating child rights laws into effective policies and programs (Wessells, 2015). If these efforts yield positive results, they would improve access to education, healthcare, nutrition, and social services for children, with special emphasis placed on addressing the needs of vulnerable and marginalised children.

As the understanding of child rights evolved, the importance of child participation in decision-making processes gained recognition. African countries had to create spaces for children's voices to be heard, allowing them to actively participate in matters that directly affected their lives (Andersen et al, 2015). This gave rise to the emergence of child-led advocacy initiatives, empowering children to raise awareness about their rights and hold duty-bearers accountable for their fulfilment. In this light, children knew when they were not being treated fairly and could speak up for their rights. Despite the progress made, significant challenges remain in fully realising child rights in Africa (Musoke, 2011) as a result of persistent poverty, armed conflicts, and cultural norms that perpetuate harmful practices which threaten children's well-being. While governments and stakeholders continue to refine and strengthen child rights legislation, enhance child protection mechanisms, and invest in education and healthcare infrastructure, social workers will continue to play a key role in ensuring that the dignity of the African child is preserved.

Definition and Purpose of Social Work

Social work is an adaptable and ever-changing field that has a profound mission to assist and empower marginalised individuals and communities. Social work, as defined by the International Federation of Social Workers (2014), is a practice-based profession and an academic discipline that promotes social change and development, social cohesion, and the empowerment and liberation of people. Principles of social justice, human rights, collective responsibility, and respect for diversity are central to social work. Underpinned by theories of social work, social sciences, humanities, and indigenous knowledge, social work engages people and structures to address life challenges and enhance well-being. Across the globe, this definition has proven to assist practitioners as it underscores the importance of addressing both individual and systemic challenges to promote positive social change. This is a profession that seeks to enhance the social functioning and quality of life of individuals and communities. Social workers are trained professionals who apply social theories, knowledge, and skills to address social issues, support vulnerable populations, and advocate for social justice (Okafor, 2021). The scope of practice for social workers cuts across various domains, such as direct practice, community development, policy advocacy, research, and administration.

The main purpose of social work practice is to empower individuals and communities, especially those who face marginalisation and adversity, to achieve their fullest potential and access resources necessary for their well-being (Berg-Weger, 2019). This is achieved through eliminating social disparities, combating oppression, and promoting equity by advocating for the most vulnerable and underprivileged groups. Social workers are driven by principles of social justice, human rights, and inclusivity; this is what propels a sustainable society (Quzack et al, 2021), which aligns with the purpose of social work to build and promote a just and compassionate society. In most contexts, social workers seek to understand the causative factors of the social problems of people, believing that a problem can be solved if the root cause is known and addressed. Then they go further to help individuals ascertain how they can cope in situations where the immediate solution is not feasible, such that even in the incapability of people, they can lead a meaningful life. As stated by Okafor (2021), social workers combine theories, knowledge, and skills to ensure that individuals are helped to enjoy the basic amenities of life and also get relevant knowledge and information on how to resolve their social problems. In general, social workers do not leave their clients in the same situation they met them, but ensure to create positive and transformative lifestyle decisions that will make them responsible and productive.

In Africa, social work practice encompasses a diverse and vital field of professionals committed to addressing the complex social challenges faced by individuals, families, and communities across the continent to enhance the well-being of people and give them a better life and future (Cox, 2021). Practice settings for social workers include government agencies, non-governmental organisations (NGOs), schools, healthcare facilities, courts, and community-based organisations. Social work practice holds immense importance in Africa due to the critical role it plays in addressing a wide range of social issues and challenges such as providing crucial support and assistance to vulnerable populations, including orphaned children, refugees, internally displaced persons, people living with HIV/AIDS, and those affected by poverty, violence, or conflicts (Germain and Knight, 2020). The profession also empowers communities to identify their strengths and resources, fostering a sense of ownership and active participation in the development and implementation of solutions to their problems as well as challenging systemic inequalities, discrimination, and oppression, aiming to create a more equitable society. According to Wu and Karabanow (2020), social workers are important during crises and disasters as they provide psychosocial support, organise relief efforts, facilitate rehabilitation for affected individuals and communities, and provide mental health support.

Multidisciplinary Approach in Social Work

Social workers do not rely on their efforts alone to resolve the social problems of people; they collaborate with other professionals. This is what makes the social work profession a multidisciplinary one such that the practice and principles of the profession involve drawing knowledge, methods, and insights from various fields and disciplines (Ahmed, 2021) This shows that the professionals understand that addressing complex social issues, supporting individuals and communities requires a diverse range of perspectives and skills which they cannot provide alone because individuals could have diverse challenges aside from social challenges that are related to other aspects of their lives. The trust and confidence people have in the profession of social work over time stem from this realisation that the problems of people do not emanate from one source alone but build up from the diverse fragments of their social and economic environment

(Pink *et al*, 2022; Banks et al, 2021). During practice, social workers exhibit their multidisciplinary approach by combining knowledge from disciplines such as psychology, sociology, anthropology, economics, law, health sciences, and more (Berg-Weger, 2019). This collaboration with professionals from various fields helps to address the multifaceted needs of their clients, which in turn enhances the quality of care and support they provide. This diverse knowledge base of social work allows them to understand the multiple factors that contribute to social challenges and develop comprehensive solutions to assist people. They achieve this by holistically viewing individuals and communities and not considering only their immediate concerns, but also the broader context in which they live, which helps to identify underlying issues that may impact well-being and quality of life.

To ensure that solutions are effective and relevant to the unique circumstances of each individual, social workers build knowledge from different disciplines to create interventions and strategies that are tailored to the specific needs of individuals and communities (Ahmed, 2021; Basky, 2019; Berg-Weger, 2019). More so, using a multidisciplinary approach, social workers go beyond conducting comprehensive assessments and, with insights from different disciplines, make informed decisions that consider a wide range of potential impacts and outcomes. This approach gives the profession the flexibility to work with diverse clients and complex challenges which is imperative for effective service delivery and allows social workers to adapt their methods and interventions to various situations, populations, and settings (Wang *et al*, 2022). With all these, social workers ensure that their interventions are grounded in the best available knowledge, which is often obtained from research findings and incorporated into evidence-based practices in different settings.

Roles of Social Workers in Promoting the Children's Rights Act in Africa

Across the diverse and dynamic contexts in Africa, where the vital task of securing and ensuring children's rights remains a significant concern, the roles of social workers stand out as essential drivers of change. Encouraging child rights legislation in Africa represents a critical stride towards establishing a society that is just and fair for its youngest citizens. Social workers, armed with their extensive interdisciplinary knowledge, unwavering commitment, and dedication to equity, can be regarded as catalysts for transformation as they work towards safeguarding and promoting the rights of children across the African continent. There are several roles which social workers implement to promote the Children's Rights Act in Africa, thereby creating an environment where the interests, voices, and well-being of every child are given the utmost priority.

Advocacy

To ensure full legal protection and justice for children, social workers serve as advocates for children's rights, both on an individual and systemic level. An advocate is someone who actively supports, defends or promotes a particular cause, idea, or group of individuals to bring about positive change, raise awareness, and influence decisions and policies related to the cause they champion to create a positive impact by working towards the betterment of the cause or the well-being of the individuals they advocate for (Rogers et al, 2022). On an individual level, social workers work closely with children who may have experienced abuse, neglect, exploitation, or other rights violations. They act as a bridge between the child and the legal system, offering emotional support, guidance, and information about their rights, carving a niche for child-friendly juvenile justice systems that prioritise rehabilitation and reintegration over punitive measures. They work to ensure that children in conflict with the law are treated with dignity and respect through one-on-one interactions. Social workers help children understand the legal processes they might be involved in, empowering them to participate actively and make informed decisions (Germain and Knight, 2020). They make an effort to ensure that significant others who have a role to play in the children's case are available and accessible. Therefore, by fostering a supportive and trusting relationship, social workers create a safe space for children to express their concerns, fears, and needs, which contributes to a stronger legal case and better protection of their rights.

Social workers engage in advocacy efforts that go beyond individual cases, which is at the systemic level by leveraging their expertise and experiences while working with vulnerable children;

they can effectively advocate for legal reforms, amendments, and the development of child-friendly policies (Lynch and Liefaard, 2020). Most children in Africa do not understand their rights, and neither do their parents, especially those with little formal education. Also, some parents do not know the appropriate authorities to report cases of abuse and allow their children to struggle with their vulnerability. The advocacy efforts of the social worker can lead to more robust legal frameworks that prioritise the rights and best interests of children, as well as a platform that provides knowledge to parents on accessing the rights of their children. Furthermore, as advocates, social workers act as intermediaries between children, families, and the legal system. They provide vital support to families whose children have experienced abuse, neglect, exploitation, or other forms of rights violations (Cox, 2021). They do this by providing legal representation with legal authorities to ensure that the child's rights are upheld within the legal framework, as well as guiding families through the legal processes, ensuring that the Child Rights Act is effectively implemented to protect the child's best interests.

Advocacy in promoting the Children's Rights Act by social workers is also reflected in their task of pushing for provisions in the Children's Rights Act that protect children from all forms of abuse, including physical, emotional, and sexual abuse, neglect, and discriminatory practices (Rogers et al. 2022). It is not enough that the Act should contain the rights of the child, but also consider potential harms that children may face, which would prevent them from accessing those rights. Social workers ensure that mechanisms are in place for reporting, investigating, and addressing cases of abuse and neglect that would affect children in the future. They also advocate for children's right to education, such that policies provide a platform for every child to have access to quality schooling, regardless of their socio-economic background; promote education and vocational training opportunities as alternatives to child labour. In Africa, access to quality healthcare is a challenge, but social workers advocate for children's right to healthcare by promoting policies that ensure access to essential health services, including vaccinations, regular check-ups, and medical treatments. They work to reduce health disparities and improve overall child health outcomes (Pradhan et al, 2021). The advocacy role of social workers extends to measures to prevent child trafficking as well as to ensure that children are not subjected to exploitation, forced labour, or sexual abuse.

Education

Many African countries have remained underdeveloped and have made less progress, partly due to a lack of education. As social change agents, social workers are charged with the responsibility of educating society on the dangers of neglecting children and not helping them to access their basic rights as enshrined in the Act. According to Krappmann (2006), the first way to educate people about children's rights is to embed it as a human rights education so that both children, their teachers, and their parents understand it. This will help them to push for the full implementation and agitate when these rights are neglected. This requires taking education back to the root of learning, where children are taught in their early years to understand what they deserve and aspire to make it count in their lives. Also, recognising how culturally sensitive issues of children are, social workers ensure that educational settings for children in communities are interactive and culturally sensitive, such that educators in local areas hinge on teaching and promoting children's rights and empowering them to become advocates for children's well-being and protection.

As part of educating the larger populace, social workers train communities on child rights and how to eliminate harmful practices that may hinder quality education. Providing child-rights education is important to help communities harness resources within and outside the community that can aid in enhancing knowledge and promoting growth (Firmanto et al, 2020). It is only when people understand the importance of a thing that they continue to crave it. Also, through creating public awareness, social workers, through campaigns, workshops, and town hall meetings, sensitise communities and decision-makers about the importance of children's rights (Assembly, 1989). These campaigns aim to change societal attitudes and perceptions which have kept communities in the dark over the ages and foster a culture where child protection is prioritised and valued. This grassroots approach creates a groundswell of support for children's rights, encouraging individuals to demand legal protection and justice for children in their communities. Social workers often use their social media networks and platforms to educate communities about the provisions of the Children's Rights Act and the significance of its enforcement. It is important to note that social media handles have become viable channels for creating faster awareness that generates a prompt response (Siddiqui & Singh,

2016). Children have been rescued from kidnappers and retrieved from guardians who abuse and molest them in the guise of house help.

Empowerment

Social workers who work directly with children and their families often provide them with support and empowerment. This role helps them to strengthen families and create a protective environment for children's well-being (Andersen and Dolva, 2015). The concept of empowering children by creating safe spaces for them to voice their concerns and opinions and involving them in decision-making processes that affect their lives has proven to be an essential aspect of promoting their rights and overall well-being. As stated by Vis (2011), recognising children as active participants in their own lives, teaching children about their rights, personal boundaries, and how to seek help in case of rights violations is essential for their protection and development. When children are empowered through safe spaces, it acknowledges their need for expression and participation. Social workers must ensure that these spaces are truly inclusive, where children from diverse backgrounds, with different abilities, and varying communication styles feel comfortable sharing their thoughts. While involving children in decision-making is beneficial for their personal growth and development of decision-making skills, it is important to strike a balance. Social workers recognize that it is not all decisions that are suitable for children to be directly involved in, and some may require guidance from adults due to complexity or potential consequences, so they ensure that children participate meaningfully with considerate involvement such that their contributions are valued and integrated into the decision-making process (Andersen and Dolva, 2015). It is through empowering children that they recognise when those rights are being violated and are equipped with the tools to seek help when and where necessary.

Although the empowerment of children through safe spaces, participation, and education about their rights is a laudable approach, it requires careful consideration of age-appropriateness and cultural sensitivity. It is not enough to make children understand their rights, but more effort should be made to ensure they truly understand their rights and can apply this knowledge in real-life situations without interference. Understandably, the concepts of empowerment, rights, and boundaries can vary across cultures and societies (Kramsch, 2014). Social workers work to enhance cultural sensitivity with their empowerment initiatives by critically evaluating how they align with local values and traditions. Children and families are more likely to engage when the approach resonates with their cultural context. This enhances the effectiveness of empowerment initiatives for promoting children's rights. For example, the life of the community cannot be separated from their culture. A social worker would design programs that align with the norms of the community and engage with children and their families in their local environment, and ensure that workshops or programs respect specific cultural contexts. This is the only avenue they can utilise to eliminate language and cultural barriers to promote effective communication and empowerment initiatives that remain culturally sensitive and relevant.

Social workers empower children through education and skill building, which not only enhances their practical abilities but also boosts their self-esteem and prospects, and to attain their full potential (Scharf et al, 2017). There are viable learning experiences provided to equip children with the tools they can use to overcome challenges. While education and skill-building are essential, consideration should be given to the child's readiness and receptiveness. Some children might have experienced disrupted education or emotional trauma that affects their ability to engage in learning, which can have adverse effects on their well-being. Social workers often refine and enhance the way children are empowered and supported in realising their rights and potential. Empowerment opportunities for children provided by social workers go beyond education and skill-building, they also strive to ensure that children experience self-confidence and a sense of agency by establishing mentorship programs that connect children with positive adult role models where mentors offer guidance, support, and encouragement, helping children set goals and work towards them (Kearney and Levine, 2020). Also, social workers can involve children in community service and volunteering activities. This experience not only builds empathy and a sense of social responsibility but also boosts their self-worth by realising their ability to make a positive impact in their lives and within their community. This is an enabling opportunity for children to take on leadership roles in school or community projects, which paves the way for developing confidence, decision-making skills, and navigating challenging situations while maintaining their dignity and assertiveness.

Collaboration

Addressing the challenges of the African child through the promotion of the Children's Rights Act is a collective effort that requires social workers to collaborate with governmental and non-governmental organisations to develop and implement child protection policies, guidelines, and programs that align with the Children's Rights Act. To take a holistic plan in addressing children's needs, partnership with not just their parents but also families, teachers, and other significant others in their lives is required (Ishimaru, 2019). Collaboration in this context means the cooperation and interactive process that involves sharing ideas, resources, expertise, and responsibilities to collectively address challenges, solve problems, or create innovative solutions to achieve a common goal or objective. As collaborators, social workers are instrumental in establishing and strengthening child protection systems through training sessions for law enforcement agencies, educators, healthcare professionals, and community leaders to sensitise them to the rights of children and the significance of the Act.

Collaboration between social workers and governmental bodies can be a powerful catalyst for change in promoting the Children's Rights Act in Africa. This is an avenue for ensuring equitable partnerships and shared goals, which is important for sustainable development. Collaboration with the government includes maintaining open lines of communication to ensure that ongoing sessions enhance the capacity of all collaborators to address child rights issues effectively. As resource persons, social workers can use their expertise and best practices to maximise the impact of interventions and programs such that the government does not renege on its mandate on policies concerning children (UNICEF, 2020). Social workers can also collaborate with the government to ensure adequate monitoring and evaluation to produce comprehensive reports on the progress of children's policies, as well as monitoring and evaluation mechanisms to assess the outcomes of child rights initiatives. By this, they can track the implementation of child policies and decipher whether the impact of interventions is felt or identify areas for improvement

(WHO, 2020). Similarly, social workers, through their collaborative role with the government, can create a sense of accountability and encourage community involvement by developing awareness campaigns to inform the public about child rights initiatives, progress made, and areas that require attention (UNICEF, 2020). Oftentimes, new policies emerge based on these reports generated through monitoring and evaluation because they address shortcomings. Perhaps, if the government sees that the successes achieved through these collaborative efforts are publicly acknowledged and celebrated, it could motivate further commitment and dedication to child rights initiatives. Clarity on the needs of the child and how the government is involved can be achieved through this means.

Furthermore, social workers collaborate with relevant stakeholders, which include legal aid organisations, international organisations, child advocacy groups, human rights organisations, and community-based organisations, to mention but a few. The rationale behind this collaboration is to ensure that a holistic approach is employed in addressing the Children's Rights Act in Africa (Brodie 2018). Collaboration can also be extended to other stakeholders, including parents, teachers, and community leaders; this involvement will enhance decision-making processes such that their input will be valued and also give credit to strategies that are respectful and relevant. This introduces a critical lens as well as transparent communication and consistent actions, improving impacts for shared values (WHO, 2020). Effective collaboration of social workers with relevant stakeholders can help to provide training and workshops to enhance their understanding of child rights issues and their role in promoting them. As social workers continue to collaborate, they create a collective force that advocates for, protects, and enhances the rights of children, thereby creating a brighter future for generations to come.

Research and Data Collection

Due to the lack of implementation and maintenance of policies in most African countries, social workers have taken up the mandate to engage in research and collection of data on existing knowledge on children's rights, showcasing the loopholes and providing new data on recent and reoccurring issues with available policies

(Alston and Bowles, 2019). This is because when social workers analyse individual cases to gain a deeper understanding of complex situations, it provides valuable insights into systemic challenges and can inform targeted interventions. Social workers understand the broader context, identify gaps, and build on existing knowledge when they engage in reviewing existing literature and research on children's rights and other related topics. As social scientists, social workers engage in participatory observation within communities and settings where children are present (Jones, 2023). This direct observation can reveal nuances and insights not captured through other methods.

Most often, methods used by social work researchers to get valid information on children's issues include conducting interviews and focus group discussions with those concerned. This approach helps to uncover underlying motivations and emotions as well as fostering openness and honesty amongst participants (Adler et al, 2019). Social workers also anticipate the potential impacts of a policy before implementation. They are capable to mitigate unintended consequences and ensure that policies are aligned with long-term goals as intended. By this, they can make comparisons of policies with best practices and experiences from around the world, which enables the adoption of proven strategies and the avoidance of pitfalls. This confirms the global mandate of social workers in looking out for the best interests of their clients.

Evaluating why existing policies failed to work through research and data collection is an important yardstick in achieving full implementation of the Children's Rights in Africa. The idea is to stop the proliferation of policies and ensure that existing policies are working. More often than not, policies are established due to political interest, and they end with the political era of that particular government. This includes the Children's Rights Act, which is yet to be fully implemented despite how important it is in safeguarding the future of African children (Nnama-Okechukwu and Okoye, 2019). Engaging in research and collecting relevant data serves as the bedrock upon which effective policies are built. It empowers social workers and policymakers to make informed, evidence-based decisions that address societal challenges, allocate resources wisely (Owen et al, 2022), and create lasting positive impacts for meaningful change and improvements in the lives of individuals and communities.

Through research, gaps in current policies or areas where existing interventions might be falling short are revealed; having discovered these shortcomings, social workers as policymakers can develop targeted policies that address specific challenges of the child. More so, social workers use robust research evidence to garner public trust and support. This is due to basing their decisions on credible research findings that have been demonstrated through a commitment to rational decision-making and accountability. As opined by Kabeyi (2019), research facilitates the ongoing monitoring and evaluation of policies. This is an avenue used by social workers to assess whether the intended outcomes of policies are being achieved and make necessary adjustments based on real-time data and feedback from the research. This feedback helps in promoting policies that are comprehensive, well-rounded, and reflective of the diverse needs of children because it comes from the social workers' engagement with stakeholders, including affected communities, experts, and advocacy groups, who are involved in the policy development process.

Community Mobilization

In Africa, the child does not belong to the immediate family alone but also to the community; to ensure the promotion of the Children's Rights Act, social workers need to be involved in community mobilisation (Heywood, 2021). Since the child belongs to the community, it is expected that they would understand the needs of the child better than the larger society, just as a father would understand the child more than their teacher. Social workers as community mobilizers are often embedded within local communities, which gives them a nuanced understanding of cultural norms and practices. It is this knowledge that helps them tailor their approaches to promote the Children's Rights Act while respecting cultural values because social workers play a vital role as facilitators and agents of change (Teater, 2019). Integrated frequently into the very fabric of local communities, social workers are an invaluable advantage in shaping the community's dynamics. This shows how social workers can identify entry points for engagement that resonate with the community's cultural sensitivities and aspirations in solving issues bothering the African child. With this in mind, social workers build close ties and ongoing relationships with community members such that they can navigate the complexities of local contexts more effectively. This serves as a cornerstone for successful community mobilisation efforts.

While mobilising communities, social workers can identify both formal and informal networks within the community. They acknowledge existing power structures through influential figures, leaders, and potential advocates who can drive change from within (Dominelli, 2021). In essence, this localised knowledge not only informs the design of programs and initiatives but also contributes to sustainable outcomes by ensuring that efforts are contextually relevant and embraced by the community. As community mobilizers, social workers' deep cultural understanding forms the bedrock upon which they build relationships, foster empowerment, and they also act as catalysts of change. Again, because social workers have established relationships and reputations that make them effective advocates for children's rights through several media of discussions, they have earned trust within communities and can address the holistic needs of individuals and families (Banks, 2020). Social workers must address the various dimensions of children's rights, such as education, healthcare, and protection, by providing comprehensive support by using their relevant skills and knowledge in organising community meetings, workshops, and awareness campaigns. If the issue of the Children's Rights Act in Africa should incorporate a sense of ownership and collective responsibility, then mobilising community members in various discussions is key.

According to Ishimaru (2019), actively mobilising the community to develop strategies to implement local solutions that respect cultural norms and values is more likely to gain acceptance and allow social workers to address doubts that may arise. The central idea of community mobilisation is to emphasise the benefits of respecting children's rights and dispel any misconceptions from community members who are often custodians of children in the community. Most of the community leaders, religious figures, and elders are people who hold influence in the community and are in the right position to be involved in children's rights (HelpAge International, 2008). This is due to the significant impact they can make in changing certain attitudes and behaviours amongst community members. Mobilising community members also involves drawing resource maps after conducting a community needs assessment to determine the community's strengths, needs, and resources; the best approach to intervention, and creating a safe space for open discussions where community members can voice concerns and questions. Social workers can also use this avenue to relay the success they have recorded concerning children's rights and mobilise the community to leverage available resources that can enhance sustainable change and progress (Heywood, 2021). Mobilising the community concerning the Children's Rights Act aims to harness the strengths, skills, and assets of a community to create a sense of ownership and responsibility for the well-being of its children. This is also an important area of social work where they render services in community development; an avenue used to promote cultural sensitivity and community integration, such that they can bridge gaps between policy and practice that lead to effective implementation of children's rights in various communities across the globe.

Recommendations

Having examined the roles of social workers in protecting the rights of children in Africa, the following recommendations, if fully implemented, would help to ensure that children in Africa would enjoy all the benefits enshrined in the African Children's Act. Firstly, social workers need to be professionally equipped with skills and knowledge to help children because one cannot give what they do not have. There is a need for educational institutions to update and enhance social work curricula to cover the latest child rights issues, psychological support techniques, legal frameworks, and cultural sensitivities. There should be regular practical training opportunities, such as workshops, field placements, and internships, that can give social workers hands-on experience in dealing with real-world child rights situations. With access to continuous learning platforms, social workers will have the needed resources to handle multiple issues with children and enhanced case management.

Secondly, effective policy implementation comes from building knowledge and evaluation. Social workers should be abreast with current trends in events on children, since they are meant to fix the social problems of society. There is a need for continuous evaluation of existing policies and sharing new research findings, innovative approaches, and best practices on issues of children that have been resolved. This also creates an avenue for experienced social workers to guide and support newer professionals as mentors. Thirdly, government and social workers should be involved in decision-making on existing and new policies that promote the interests of the child. Engaging with lawmakers to influence the development of legislation that protects children and supports those working on their behalf is a way to ensure that budgets include adequate funding and provisions for children and social work programs. This provides opportunities for support and ensures consistent quality in interventions geared towards helping children. Finally, collective effort and collaboration with different government agencies, non-governmental organisations (NGOs), educational institutions, healthcare providers, and community leaders would create a platform where there will be a useful exchange of ideas, sharing of resources, and coordination of actions to address the challenges of the child in Africa. such a forum can also be used as a campaign to engage the general public, media, and policymakers on child rights issues. These campaigns can emphasise the importance of collective action and encourage individuals to participate in initiatives aimed at safeguarding children's rights.

Conclusion

This chapter emphasised the crucial role of social workers in safeguarding and promoting the rights of children in Africa. Despite the numerous challenges faced by children on the continent, such as poverty, armed conflict, child labour, and limited access to education and healthcare, social workers have continued to employ a multidisciplinary approach to address these issues effectively. Through their interventions, social workers play a pivotal role in creating a conducive environment for the holistic development and well-being of children. They tackle various challenges, including child abuse, exploitation, neglect, education, and healthcare, making a significant impact on children's lives. There is a need for social workers to sensitise communities and advocate for behavioural changes that eliminate harmful practices affecting children. The importance of comprehensive training programs, ongoing supervision, and supportive organisational structures to enhance social workers' knowledge and skills in protecting and advocating for child rights should be emphasised. There is a need for a collaborative effort to address the Children's Rights Act in Africa, recognising that children's rights are fundamental to their well-being and development. By continuously striving to enhance children's rights, society can work towards creating a safer and more nurturing environment for the younger generation.

References

Addae-Korankye, A. 2014, 'Causes of poverty in Africa: A review of literature', *American International Journal of Social Science*, vol. 3, no. 7, pp. 147–153.

Adler, K., Salanterä, S. & Zumstein-Shaha, M. 2019, 'Focus group interviews in child, youth, and parent research: An integrative literature review', *International Journal of Qualitative Methods*, vol. 18, pp. 1–15.

African Union 1999, *African Charter on the Rights and Welfare of Children*, Unpublished, Addis Ababa.

Ahmed, D. 2021, 'Importance of social workers in a multidisciplinary frontline environment during pandemics', *Issues in Social Science*, vol. 9, no. 1, pp. 1–14.

Ajulor, O.V. 2018, 'The challenges of policy implementation in Africa and Sustainable Development Goals', *PEOPLE: International Journal of Social Sciences*, vol. 3, no. 3, pp. 1497–1518.

Albertyn, R., Bickler, S.W., van As, A.B., Millar, A.J.W. & Rode, H. 2003, 'The effects of war on children in Africa', *Pediatric Surgery International*, vol. 19, pp. 227–232.

Alston, M. & Bowles, W. 2019, *Research for social workers: An introduction to methods*, Routledge, London.

Andersen, C.S. & Dolva, A.S. 2015, 'Children's perspective on their right to participate in decision-making according to the United Nations Convention on the Rights of the Child, article 12', *Physical & Occupational Therapy in Paediatrics*, vol. 35, no. 3, pp. 218–230.

Arowolo, D. 2010, 'The effects of Western civilisation and culture on Africa', *Afro Asian Journal of Social Sciences*, vol. 1, no. 1, pp. 1–13.

Assembly, U.G. 1989, *Convention on the Rights of the Child*, United Nations Treaty Series, vol. 1577, no. 3, pp. 1–23.

Bakewell, O. 2013, '"Keeping them in their place": The ambivalent relationship between development and migration in Africa', in *Globalisation and Migration*, Routledge, London, pp. 112–129.

Banks, S., Cai, T., De Jonge, E., Shears, J., Shum, M., Sobočan, A.M. et al. 2020, 'Practising ethically during COVID-19: Social work challenges and responses', *International Social Work*, vol. 63, no. 5, pp. 569–583.

Barsky, A.E. 2019, *Ethics and values in social work: An integrated approach for a comprehensive curriculum*, Oxford University Press, New York.

Berg-Weger, M. 2019, *Social work and social welfare: An invitation*, Routledge, New York.

Brodie, K. 2018, *The Holistic Care and Development of Children from Birth to Three: An Essential Guide for Students and Practitioners*, Routledge, London.

Cox, C. 2021, 'Older adults and Covid 19: Social justice, disparities, and social work practice', in *Gerontological Social Work and COVID-19*, Routledge, London, pp. 118–131.

Dominelli, L. 2021, 'A green social work perspective on social work during the time of COVID-19', *International Journal of Social Welfare*, vol. 30, no. 1, pp. 7–16.

Eneji, A.P. & Ikeorji, C.R. 2018, 'Youth political participation and electoral violence in 21st century Nigeria: Bridging the gap', *World Journal of Innovative Research*, vol. 4, no. 6, pp. 9–13.

Firmanto, A., Sumarsono, P. & Nur, F. 2020, 'A family-school partnership-based learning: An effort to organise early childhood education'.

Germain, C. & Knight, C. 2020, *The life model of social work practice: Advances in theory and practice*, Columbia University Press, New York.

HelpAge International 2008, *Older people in Africa: A forgotten generation*, Available at: https://www.helpage.org/silo/files/older-people-in-africa-a-forgotten-generation.pdf [Accessed 10 August 2023].

Heywood, M. 2021, 'The transformative power of civil society in South Africa: an activist's perspective on innovative forms of organising and rights-based practices', in *Challenging Inequality in South Africa*, Routledge, London, pp. 30–52.

International Federation of Social Workers. 2014, *Global definition of social work*, Available at: https://www.ifsw.org/what-is-social-work/global-definition-of-social-work/ [Accessed 30 June 2022].

Ijeoma, O.C., Uwakwe, J.O. & Paul, N. 2013, 'Education is an antidote against early marriage for the girl-child', *Journal of Educational and Social Research*, vol. 3, no. 5, pp. 73–79.

Imoh, A.T.D. & Ansell, N. (eds.) 2014, *Children's Lives in an Era of Children's Rights: The Progress of the Convention on the Rights of the Child in Africa*, Routledge, London.

Ishimaru, A.M. 2019, *Just Schools: Building equitable collaborations with families and communities*, Teachers College Press, New York.

Jones, H. (ed.) 2023, *Towards a New Social Work*, Taylor & Francis, London.

Kabeyi, M.J.B. 2019, 'Evolution of project management, monitoring, and evaluation, with historical events and projects that have shaped the development of project management as a profession', *International Journal of Science Research*, vol. 8, no. 12, pp. 63–79.

Kaime, T. 2005, 'The Convention on the Rights of the Child and the cultural legitimacy of children's rights in Africa: Some reflections', *African Human Rights Law Journal*, vol. 5, no. 2, pp. 221–238.

Kearney, M.S. & Levine, P.B. 2020, 'Role models, mentors, and media influences', *The Future of Children*, vol. 30, no. 1, pp. 83–106.

Kramsch, C. 2014, 'Language and culture', *AILA Review*, vol. 27, no. 1, pp. 30–55. *Work*, 63(6), 790-794.

Krappmann, L. 2006, 'The rights of the child as a challenge to human rights education', *Journal of Social Science Education*.

Lynch, N. & Liefaard, T. 2020, 'What is left in the "too hard basket"? Developments and challenges for the rights of children in conflict with the law', *The International Journal of Children's Rights*, vol. 28, no. 1, pp. 89–110.

Musoke, M. 2011, *Challenges to the realisation of children's Right to freedom of expression: A study carried out in Kabale District*, [Unpublished Thesis], Kampala International University.

Newell, M.L., Brahmbhatt, H. & Ghys, P.D. 2004, 'Child mortality and HIV infection in Africa: a review', *AIDS*, vol. 18, suppl. 2, pp. S27–S34.

Nnama-Okechukwu, C.U. & Okoye, U.O. 2019, 'Rethinking institutional care using a family-based alternative child care system for orphans and vulnerable children in Nigeria', *Journal of Social Work in Developing Societies*, vol. 1, no. 3.

Okafor, A. 2021, 'Role of the social worker in the outbreak of pandemics (A case of COVID-19)', *Cogent Psychology*, vol. 8, no. 1.

Owen, K.L., Watkins, R.C. & Hughes, J.C. 2022, 'From evidence-informed to evidence-based: An evidence-building framework for education', *Review of Education*, vol. 10, no. 1.

Pence, A.R. & Marfo, K. 2008, 'Early childhood development in Africa: Interrogating constraints of prevailing knowledge bases', *International Journal of Psychology*, vol. 43, no. 2, pp. 78–87.

Pink, S., Ferguson, H. & Kelly, L. 2022, 'Digital social work: Conceptualising a hybrid anticipatory practice', *Qualitative Social Work*, vol. 21, no. 2, pp. 413–430.

Pradhan, B., Bhattacharyya, S. & Pal, K. 2021, 'IoT-based applications in healthcare devices', *Journal of Healthcare Engineering*, vol. 2021, article ID 9986653, pp. 1–18.

Quzack, L.E., Picard, G., Metz, S.M. & Chiarelli-Helminiak, C.M. 2021, 'A social work education grounded in human rights', *Journal of Human Rights and Social Work*, vol. 6, pp. 32–40.

Rodriguez, M.Y., Ostrow, L. & Kemp, S.P. 2017, 'Scaling up social problems: Strategies for solving social work's grand challenges', *Research on Social Work Practice*, vol. 27, no. 2, pp. 139–149.

Rogers, A., Gullickson, A.M., King, J.A. & McKinley, E. 2022, 'Competitive champions versus cooperative advocates: Understanding advocates for evaluation', *Journal of MultiDisciplinary Evaluation*, vol. 18, no. 42, pp. 73–91.

Rushubirwa, L., Ndimande-Hlongwa, N. & Mkhize, N. 2015, 'Globalisation, migration, and local communities, one adverse upshot: A case review of xenophobia in eThekwini Municipality, Durban, KZN, South Africa', *Journal of Social Development in Africa*, vol. 30, no. 1, pp. 97–120.

Scharf, R.J. et al. 2017, 'Global disability: empowering children of all abilities', *Pediatric Clinics*, vol. 64, no. 4, pp. 769–784.

Siddiqui, S. & Singh, T. 2016, 'Social media has its impact both positive and negative impacts', *International Journal of Computer Applications Technology and Research*, vol. 5, no. 2, pp. 71–75.

Sossou, M.A. & Yogtiba, J.A. 2009, 'Abuse of children in West Africa: Implications for social work education and practice', *British Journal of Social Work*, vol. 39, no. 7, pp. 1218–1234.

Teater, B. 2019, *An Introduction to Applying Social Work Theories and Methods*, 3rd edn, McGraw-Hill Education (UK), London.

UNICEF 2013, *The Convention on the Rights of the Child: The children's version*, Available at: https://www.unicef.org/child-rights-convention/convention-text-childrens-version [Accessed 10 March 2023].

UNICEF 2020, *Global status report on preventing violence against children*. Available from: https://www.unicef.org/reports/global-status-report-preventing-violence-against-children-2020 [Accessed 20 June 2023].

Vis, S.A., Strandbu, A., Holtan, A. & Thomas, N. 2011, 'Participation and health–a research review of child participation in planning and decision-making', *Child & Family Social Work*, vol. 16, no. 3, pp. 325–335.

Wang, K. et al. 2022, 'Preference of older adults for flexibility in service and providers in community-based social care: a discrete choice experiment', *International Journal of Environmental Research and Public Health*, vol. 19, no. 2, article 686.

Werner, E. 2012, 'Children and war: Risk, resilience, and recovery', *Development and Psychopathology*, vol. 24, no. 2, pp. 553–558.

Wessells, M. 2015, 'Bottom-up approaches to strengthening child protection systems: Placing children, families, and communities at the centre', *Child Abuse & Neglect*, vol. 43, pp. 8–21.

Williams, P.D. 2016, *War and conflict in Africa*, John Wiley & Sons, Chichester.

World Health Organisation 2020, *Health policy and system support to optimise community health worker programmes for HIV, TB and malaria services: An evidence guide*.

Wu, H. & Karabanow, J. 2020, 'COVID-19 and beyond: Social work interventions for supporting homeless populations', *International Social Work*, vol. 63, no. 6, pp. 790-794.

Chapter Eight
Online Child Sexual Exploitation and Abuse in South Africa: A Review

Nokukhanya G Ndhlovu

Introduction

Child sexual abuse (CSA) is a global problem affecting millions of children every year. The United Nations Children's Fund (2020a) states that roughly 121 million children globally are forced to perform sexual acts in childhood; however, the exact number is much higher, as many cases go unreported. CSA remains pervasive globally with devastating consequences for girls and boys (UNICEF, 2020b; United Nations, 2020; World Health Organisation, 2017; Hillis et al. 2016; Horvath et al. 2014: 11). Globally, one out of five girls and one out of thirteen boys experience sexual exploitation or abuse before the age of eighteen. This is a prevalent challenge that affects children in almost all countries and cultures. CSA involves forcing or persuading children to take part in sexual conduct. These activities can involve physical contact, including sexual assault or abuse, or they can be non-contact, such as exposing children to sexual content or encouraging them to behave inappropriately. CSA can also involve grooming children, which is the process of building trust and gaining control over children in preparation for abuse. This can happen online or offline (UNICEF, 2020b; Independent Inquiry into Child Sexual Abuse, 2017:9). Child sexual abuse is a form of violence against boys and girls, and it has devastating impacts on both their physical and mental health.

Some harms that can be caused by sexual exploitation and abuse include depression, missing school, psychological trauma, self-harm, anxiety, drug and alcohol abuse, lower educational attainment and offending behaviour. Children who are sexually exploited or abused are also more likely to contract HIV and have problems in childbirth

(UNICEF, 2021a; UNICEF, 2020a). While CSA is a global challenge, it is particularly high in Africa (Selengia, Thuy and Mushi, 2020). However, despite its prevalence, it is often hidden, under-researched, and undocumented (Ndhlovu and Mfoafo-M'Carthy, 2022: 240). Other studies also show that due to the patriarchal nature of African society, Africa is still the continent with the most cases of child sexual abuse (Selengia *et al.* 2020; Badoe, 2017:33; Motsoeneng, 2015). This chapter contributes to the growing body of knowledge on online child sexual exploitation and abuse by providing a more nuanced understanding of the link between digital platforms and child sexual abuse in Africa. The chapter specifically examines the dynamics and the severity of the issue in South Africa. The research questions are: What are the different forms of online child sexual exploitation and abuse that children experience? What are the dynamics of online child sexual exploitation and abuse in Africa and South Africa?

Understanding OCSEA: Definition and Manifestations

Online child sexual exploitation and abuse (OCSEA) is a broad term encompassing various forms of child exploitation facilitated or enabled by digital or communication technologies. This can occur through any internet-based platform, including social media, email, and text messaging. The Australian Centre to Counter Child Exploitation (2021) defines OCSEA as the misuse of technology or the internet to directly or indirectly contribute to child sexual exploitation and abuse. This includes activities like producing, sharing, or distributing child sexual abuse material or other exploitative content. The Interagency Working Group (2016) further expands on OCSEA, highlighting the abuse and exploitation of children facilitated by the misuse of information and communication technologies. End Child Prostitution and Trafficking International (ECPAT), International Criminal Police Organisation (INTERPOL) and UNICEF (2022:15) collectively emphasise that OCSEA can manifest entirely online or through a combination of online and offline interactions between offenders and children. Therefore, OCSEA encompasses a spectrum of harmful activities where technology plays a key role in sexually abusing and exploiting children.

Online-facilitated child sexual abuse (OCSA), as termed by ECPAT International (2016), encompasses any form of child sexual abuse involving the use of the internet or other electronic communication technologies to coerce or entice children into participating in sexual abuse activities. UNICEF (2021a) highlights the interchangeability of this term with technology-facilitated child sexual abuse and exploitation, encompassing exploitation and abuse made possible or facilitated by technology like the internet or wireless communication devices. For example, CSA takes on an online dimension when acts are photographed, filmed, or recorded and subsequently uploaded to the internet, either for personal consumption or sharing with others. Each viewing or sharing of such recorded material constitutes a new violation of the child's rights (UNICEF, 2021a). The United Nations (2022) further defines OCSEA as the use of information and communication technologies (ICTs) to sexually abuse children.

While OCSEA crimes can occur within a specific country, effective prevention, investigation, and prosecution necessitate national and international collaboration across disciplines to identify, locate, and protect victims (Quayle, 2021:279). OCSEA crimes include making, preparing, viewing, distributing, or possessing child sexual abuse material, as well as soliciting children for sexual purposes, whether or not it leads to or is intended to lead to a physical assault (Quayle, 2021:279). Online child sexual abuse is a major concern for parents, practitioners, and policymakers. The threat of online predators who may pose as children in chat rooms to lure children into abusive situations is widespread. This type of abuse is often reported in the media, but other forms of online-facilitated abuse may be more common. These forms of abuse reflect the growing interconnectedness of the online and offline worlds (May-Chahal and Kelly, 2020:5). These forms of online child sexual abuse include online grooming, Child sexual abuse/exploitation material and live streaming of child sexual abuse.

The first form of online child sexual abuse, grooming, involves an adult building an online relationship with a child to sexually exploit or abuse them. Research indicates that this behaviour is predominantly perpetrated by men, but women can also be involved (United Nations Office on Drugs and Crime, 2020; Interagency Working Group, 2016). Nyasuguta (2020) defines this as online grooming for child sexual exploitation, which refers to using online platforms to build a relationship with a child with the ultimate goal of engaging them in online or offline sexual abuse or exploitation.

This can involve manipulating the child into participating in sexual acts or creating or sharing sexually explicit content involving them. By contrast, child sexual abuse material (CSAM), also known as child pornography, as the second form of online child sexual abuse, refers to materials that depict acts of child sexual abuse or focus on the child's genitalia. CSAM can be used in a broader sense to refer to any material that depicts children in a sexualised way, regardless of age, including both boys and girls. The severity of the sexual abuse can range from children posing sexually to gross assault (Nyasuguta, 2020). The United Nations Office on Drugs and Crime (2020) defines it as the depiction of a child, through any means, in real or simulated explicit sexual acts or the depiction of a child's sexual parts for mainly sexual purposes. As the final form of online child sexual abuse, live streaming of child sexual abuse is the broadcasting of child sexual abuse in real time to viewers in remote locations. This happens over the internet, which often means that the violence is being transmitted across national borders. However, it is important to note that some countries have also reported cases of domestic live streaming of child sexual abuse. Live streaming of child sexual abuse can be found on online chat rooms, social media platforms, and communication apps that allow video chat (Drejer et. 2023; United Nations Office on Drugs and Crime, 2020).

Despite the lack of a universally accepted definition, it is evident that the widespread sexual abuse and exploitation of children online is a pressing and defining issue of our time. Not only is it a threat to the health, safety, and well-being of girls and boys, but OCSEA is also a major obstacle to achieving gender equality and sustainable development goals.

Ubuntu Theory

Ubuntu is a philosophy that originated in Africa. Rooted in the concept of shared humanity, Ubuntu fosters a holistic perspective that recognises the inherent interconnectedness of individuals and communities. Ubuntu is best understood as a social ideology that highlights the interconnectedness of human beings and their shared values of care, collectivism, harmony, friendliness, respect, and responsiveness (Bhuda and Marumo, 2022). Ubuntu is a Bantu word that means 'humanity towards others', a philosophy that is built on the importance of community (Mugumbate and Chereni, 2019:28). Building on the traditional emphasis on present social connections, Van Breda (2019) proposes a broader understanding of Ubuntu that encompasses respectful interactions with diverse communities, responsibility towards past and future generations, and a deep commitment to the well-being of the Earth. *Umuntu ngumuntu ngabantu* means that we are who we are through others and reflects the notion of Ubuntu, which emphasises the importance of compassion, justice and respect for others, including children.

Ubuntu is a philosophy that has been used by many African communities for centuries to guide, educate and preserve positive human interactions and relations (Bhuda and Marumo, 2022). The notion of Ubuntu is important in examining the high levels of child sexual abuse in a continent that values Ubuntu. Ubuntu is used to examine the disconnect between the ideals of Ubuntu and the lived experiences of children who suffer abuse. It interrogates and exposes the hypocrisy of a society that readily invokes Ubuntu while dehumanising children through sexual abuse and tolerating the dehumanisation and maltreatment of its most vulnerable members. By grounding its analysis in the core principles of Ubuntu – respect, compassion, and shared humanity – it is important to challenge the normalisation of OCSEA since these same principles of Ubuntu must extend to the protection and well-being of children. Ubuntu's true essence lies not in mere pronouncements but in extending its protective embrace to all individuals, particularly those who are dependent and vulnerable. This entails ensuring the well-being and safety of children, including protecting them from the devastating consequences of sexual abuse.

The Dynamics and the Scale of OCSEA

The internet has revolutionised societies worldwide, and children are particularly impacted. They now have unlimited access to mobile devices and computers, and many of them start using these technologies from a young age. As a result, the internet has become an integral part of their lives (United Nations, 2022). Many children spend a lot of time online. Research suggests that one child uses the internet for the first time every half-second. This trend is not surprising, given the increasing availability and affordability of internet-connected devices. The internet offers a wealth of opportunities for children. They can learn new things, explore their interests, and connect with friends and family from all over the world. When used safely and responsibly, the internet is a powerful learning and personal development tool (UNICEF, 2022a). The widespread adoption of digital technology has reportedly had a profound impact on children and young people's lives worldwide. As the Committee on the Rights of the Child has noted, digital technologies have the potential to realise a variety of children's rights, for example, the right to education, the right to play, and the right to protection (UNICEF, 2021b). These opportunities are not without their risks. The most alarming threat is OCSEA because offenders can now more easily contact possible victims, distribute sexual images, and encourage other perpetrators to commit crimes due to the proliferation of technology. Children can be harmed through the creation, sharing, and viewing of CSA content – perpetrators can also groom them for sexual abuse and exploitation. They may try to meet children face to face or coerce them into producing sexual material (UNICEF, 2022b).

Global legal instruments like the 1989 Convention on the Rights of the Child (CRC) and the Optional Protocol to the CRC on the sale of children, child prostitution, and child pornography of 2000 underscore the critical role of nations in protecting children from harmful practices. These legal frameworks establish children's rights and hold governments accountable for safeguarding them. Similarly, Ubuntu emphasises the interconnectedness of humanity, urging adults to treat children with compassion, respect, and concern for their well-being. Both legal and cultural perspectives, therefore, converge in demanding a world where children are valued, protected, and empowered. However, with the rise of the internet and computer-mediated communication, children find themselves exposed to online abuse and exploitation. The rise of the digital world has coincided with the emergence of numerous online behaviours deemed deviant, some existing within supportive subcultures. While many of these practices may not pose significant public safety threats, others, like child sexual abuse and the creation or distribution of related material, inflict immense harm on victims. Researchers increasingly focus on the internet's role in facilitating CSA, exploring online paedophile networks and predatory tactics used to target children (Holt, Blevins and Burkert, 2010:4). The ubiquity of online interaction has become so widespread that it's likely interwoven into nearly every instance of child sexual exploitation and abuse. Technological advancements and increased internet access have empowered perpetrators to exploit and abuse children in unprecedented ways, shrouded in a veil of secrecy and anonymity (UNICEF, 2021b).

COVID-19 increased CSA, particularly online. Children and adolescents faced increased emotional vulnerabilities, economic hardship, and unsupervised time online. In addition, child protection services were disrupted in many countries, leaving vulnerable children without access to adequate protection (UNICEF, 2021a). Consequently, the COVID-19 pandemic led to increased screen time for children, especially younger children. This is because schools were closed, and children were spending more time at home (UNICEF, 2021b). In 2020, UNICEF (2020) predicted that the COVID-19 pandemic had heightened the risk of OCSEA. Due to stay-at-home measures, children were forced to spend more time at home away from family and friends, which meant an increase in the likelihood that children would meet online predators. This exposed them to sexual exploitation by predators who used grooming techniques to gain the trust of their victims. With more adults isolated at home, there was also an increased demand for online child sexual abuse material, which meant that more children would be sexually abused and exploited for commercial purposes. Stay-at-home orders also forced families to remain in close quarters. This also likely escalated child sexual abuse, both offline and online.

Despite the emphasis on human dignity and the importance of treating others with respect in the Ubuntu philosophy, many children are subjected to dishonourable and dehumanising treatment (Ndhlovu and Mfoafo-M'Carthy, 2022:243) – and the digital age has aggravated their situation. The growing presence of online platforms has exposed countless children to various forms of harmful content, making them vulnerable to OCSEA. This blatant disregard for children's safety and respect deeply undermines the fundamental values of human dignity and interconnectedness. The rise of social media and internet access has further amplified this risk by creating new avenues for perpetrators to target and exploit vulnerable individuals. This calls for urgent action to protect children in the digital age and foster a safer online environment. To this end, Kloess etal. (2014) argue that the widespread online availability of child sexual abuse content and the ease with which perpetrators can target vulnerable children online raise serious concerns. The internet has become a breeding ground for online child sexual exploitation activities, providing offenders with interactive platforms to fulfil their deviant desires, engage in CSA acts, and form communities that normalise and validate child sexual abuse (Ali, Haykal and Youssef, 2023:405; Kloess et al., 2014).

The true scale of the online child sexual abuse threat remains ambiguous, but concerning trends emerge from global data indicating a rise in reported cases to national hotlines and clearinghouses in recent years (UNICEF, 2021). A 2021 study by WeProtect Global Alliance revealed that INHOPE's platform for collecting and classifying child sexual abuse material witnessed the exchange of a staggering 1,038,268 individual media files. In 2021, a dark website with more than 400,000 recorded users that was dedicated to the sexual abuse of children was shut down by Europol. There are over 3 million accounts on the dark web's 10 most harmful online CSA sites. The National Centre for Missing and Exploited Children grapples with a staggering influx of OCSEA reports, exceeding 60,000 daily on the CyberTipline. Each report is entrusted to one of only 30 analysts, exposing a critical gap in resources. The ever-growing tide of OCSEA cases threatens to overwhelm global efforts to combat this heinous crime.

Constrained by inadequate funding, OCSEA programs struggle to keep pace with the escalating crisis, leaving countless children vulnerable to online exploitation. Previous Global Threat Assessments have shown that online exploitation and abuse are on the rise. The alarming growth of OCSEA outpaces worldwide response efforts, leaving the horrific crime chronically underfunded and inadequately addressed. The problem is getting worse, as new trends (such as online grooming, livestreaming for payment, among others) are emerging that are making it more difficult to identify and stop cases of exploitation (WeProtect Global Alliance, 2021). A study by the National Institute for Health and Care Excellence (NICE, 2017) found that children facing OCSEA often stay silent. Key findings point to a higher prevalence among girls, while predisposing factors include childhood exposure to physical/emotional abuse, parental conflict, and excessive internet use. Notably, vulnerability rises when these factors intersect, particularly for children with disabilities or low self-esteem (NICE, 2017).

Exploring OCSEA in South Africa

The 1990 African Charter on the Rights and Welfare of the Child calls on the continent of Africa to protect the rights and welfare of African children (African Union, 1990:8). To raise awareness among representatives from all 55 African Union member states about the dangers of OCSEA, a rising cybercrime and to mobilise political as well national obligation to combat the heinous act – the African Union held its first continental consultation on combating OCSEA on March 6, 2019, at the African Union Conference Centre in Addis Ababa, Ethiopia. The consultation was held under the theme of 'protecting children from abuse in the digital world.' The African Union (2019) highlighted the growth of internet usage in Africa by more than 20% since 2010. This increase has led to a higher risk of OCSEA. However, there is inadequate awareness and comprehension of OCSEA among many African policymakers and governments. Some don't perceive OCSEA as a priority and cannot address it effectively (African Union, 2019). The African Union (2019) further noted that the rapid growth of internet usage in Africa, combined with inadequate awareness and regulation of the danger, could result in an explosive increase in OCSEA in the years to come, which is a serious concern, as seen in other parts of the world (African Union, 2019).

Traditionally, research on the prevalence of OCSEA has focused on high-income countries. While the issue of OCSEA receives significant attention in high-income countries, its prevalence in low- and middle-income nations remains under-researched. Analysing reported cases can offer valuable insights, albeit with limitations. For instance, the National Centre for Missing and Exploited Children (NCMEC) saw a 28% surge in suspected OCSEA reports in 2020, reaching 21.7 million. However, such data may not fully represent the situation in resource-constrained countries, where reporting mechanisms and awareness often lag. These figures represent a significant increase in the number of industry referrals of OCSEA, which increased by 700% between 2013 and 2017. It is important to note that these numbers are only a reflection of reported child sexual abuse and exploitation content, and the true degree of the problem is likely much higher (ECPAT, INTERPOL and UNICEF, 2022a; UNICEF, 2021a). While there was no comprehensive data on the increase of OCSEA in developing nations during the COVID pandemic, existing data from Cambodia and Ghana suggest a significant increase in some forms.

In Cambodia, reports of OCSEA material to a hotline increased by 20% in the first half of 2020. In Ghana, reports to the CyberTipline increased by 63% in 2020 between January and September compared to January and September 2019 (UNICEF, 2021b).

South Africa is a country that upholds the principles of Ubuntu, but its children are raped and sexually abused at an alarming rate. The staggering prevalence of child sexual abuse stands in stark contrast to the ideals of Ubuntu – principles of respect, compassion, and shared humanity that the South African society readily embraces. While Ubuntu emphasises respect and nurturing of all, the rampant exploitation of children reveals a glaring disconnect between rhetoric and reality. The epidemic of child sexual abuse exposes a critical failing within society, where the vulnerable children are subjected to unspeakable cruelty despite claims of Ubuntu. Consequently, South Africa has been named the "rape capital of the world" due to the prevalence of sexual violence in the country (Govender, 2023:1).

According to statistics, CSA is pervasive and has been on the rise in recent years. Studies continue to indicate that the sexual violence of both girls and boys is extensive and is linked with severe health challenges (Artz et al. 2018:791; Ward et al. 2018: 461; Vermeulen and Greeff, 2015:557). Despite South Africa's laws and policies on CSA, the problem has become so severe that current interventions are not enough to help families (Vermeulen and Greeff, 2015:557). Exacerbating an already dire situation is the 'emergence' of online child sexual abuse and exploitation, a relatively new phenomenon that poses a significant danger to child safety.

In South Africa, OCSEA is increasingly facilitated through digital technologies, despite the nation's strong emphasis on Ubuntu values that prioritise child protection and human dignity. This gap between principles and practice raises important questions on the efficacy of current safeguards and the need for stronger measures to ensure child safety in the digital era. The ubiquity of digital technology is fuelling a concerning rise in reported OCSEA cases. There is a direct correlation between technological advancements and increased CSA incidents. This includes offenders leveraging technology to facilitate online CSA in diverse forms (UNICEF, 2021a). Kloess et al. (2019) note that there are two common online CSA offenders, namely creators and consumers – creators are those individuals who create, share, and sell content that depicts the sexual abuse and exploitation of children. This content can include images, videos, and text that depict violence against children, while consumers are the individuals who purchase or view child sexual abuse content. They may also seek out vulnerable children online to abuse them (Kloess et al, 2019).

Although there is currently limited empirical data on the pervasiveness of OCSEA, research seems to suggest that South African children are at risk of exposure. The pandemic and the related lockdown measures led to increased emotional vulnerability and stress, which may have contributed to an increase in child abuse. Poverty and job losses caused by the pandemic, especially in low- and middle-income countries, could have also made it more difficult for parents to cope, which could have led to child abuse (UNICEF, 2020). In light of the above, Sekudu (2019) argues that the erosion of Ubuntu values is evident in South Africa, and this has resulted in the dehumanisation of children through sexual abuse. The dehumanisation of children through online CSA directly contradicts the fundamental Ubuntu tenet of valuing shared humanity, exposing a deep moral hypocrisy within our society.

In South Africa, the South African Kids Online (SA Kids Online) Study by UNICEF found that over 95% of the country's children have regular internet access, but their online conduct can put them at risk of online sexual violence, exploitation as well and abuse. The SA Kids Online is a nationally representative survey of 2,643 children (ages 9-17) and 1,393 parents and guardians about their online behaviours, wellness, and well-being. Conducted in about 176 towns and cities across the country's nine provinces, the survey included a representative sample of the population by age and gender. According to the study, children use the internet primarily for educational purposes, such as learning new things or doing schoolwork. They also use it to watch videos. However, limited awareness of online risks and access to the internet without parental permission can put vulnerable children in danger (UNICEF, 2022a). The study revealed that:

> 70% of children surveyed used the internet without their parents' permission, 25% of the children confirmed that they had added people they had never met in person to their friends or contacts list, [and] 18% of the children had sent a photo or video of themselves to someone they had never met in person. Of the children who had seen sexual images, 67% were exposed to them on an online device.

Numerous children exploited online kept their experiences hidden, potentially leading to long-term mental health consequences. Only 41% of the surveyed children had received any online safety instruction (UNICEF, 2022a). This emphasises the negative impact and highlights the low level of awareness. A significant portion of online child sexual abuse and exploitation incidents in South Africa occur on Facebook and WhatsApp. According to available data, 65% of reported OCSEA cases took place on Facebook or Facebook Messenger, making it the most prevalent platform for this harmful activity. WhatsApp followed closely, accounting for 27% of incidents. The remaining platforms, including TikTok, Instagram, Twitter, and YouTube, saw significantly lower rates of OCSEA, with each platform contributing between 1% and 4% of reported cases (McCain, 2022).

A study involving 1,639 South African children aged nine-seventeen who use the internet revealed significant concerns among their caregivers regarding online interactions with strangers. A staggering 79% of caregivers deemed this highly risky for children. Interestingly, while 53% of the children themselves echoed this sentiment, thirteen per cent saw no risk at all in such interactions. Despite these concerns, the data indicated that children do engage with unfamiliar individuals online. For example, about fifty-two per cent of children shared that they had added people to their social media whom they had never met in person in the past year; thirty-three per cent said that they had a face-to-face meeting with an online contact; most children who conducted themselves in this manner reported positive experiences and that they did not feel harmed. Eight per cent reported sharing nude images or videos of themselves online in the past year because they were in love, or because they were flirting. More sixteen–1seventeen-year-old children engaged in dangerous online activities compared to the younger children in the sample (ECPAT, INTERPOL and UNICEF, 2022).

The study further investigated children's experiences of OCSEA and found the following: 9% said they have been asked to share sexual pictures or videos in exchange for either gifts or money, and seven per cent reported that their sexual images were shared without their consent. Additionally, seven per cent were blackmailed, coerced or threatened to engage in sexual conduct, while nine per cent were asked to meet for sexual activities. This type of online sexual extortion is not overtly criminalised in South Africa, which is a major gap within the country's response. Additionally, a survey of forty-nine frontline social support workers conducted by Disrupting Harm found that men were much more regularly identified as offenders than women in OCSEA cases. The statistics from this survey may also be underreported due to the stigma surrounding sexual abuse and because children may be reluctant to divulge the abuse (ECPAT, INTERPOL and UNICEF, 2022).

As a part of the African Union, the South African government is committed to tackling child sexual abuse, including OCSEA. The country has signed and ratified many international agreements that protect children. South Africa also has a comprehensive legal and regulatory framework in place to protect children. In South Africa, the primary laws governing OCSEA are the Criminal Law (Sexual Offences and Related Matters) Amendment Act (Republic of South Africa 2021) as well as the Children's Act (Republic of South Africa 2005). However, UNICEF (2022b) contends that despite its comprehensive legislation regarding OCSEA, implementation remains a challenge in South Africa (UNICEF, 2022b), which further exposes children to the risk of online sexual abuse and exploitation.

Conclusion

This chapter explored the issue of online child sexual exploitation and abuse globally, with a focus on South Africa. It discussed the different forms of online child sexual exploitation and abuse that children experience and also examined the dynamics of OCSEA in Africa and South Africa. The study found that the scope of OCSEA is vast and concerning, despite the lack of a universally accepted definition. This form of abuse can take various forms, leveraging any internet-based communication platform like social media, email, or text messaging. Quantifying the true extent of OCSEA crimes remains a challenge. However, mounting evidence suggests a worrying upward trend in these crimes.

Using the concept of Ubuntu, the paper questioned the conduct of adults who have dehumanised children and normalised child sexual abuse. This study explored the dissonance between claims of Ubuntu and the ongoing reality of online child sexual abuse perpetrated by mostly men. It identified a double standard within society, where the principles of Ubuntu – emphasising communal responsibility and respect for human dignity – are readily invoked, yet children experiencing abuse are dehumanised and denied their fundamental rights. By highlighting Ubuntu's core tenet of treating others with compassion and recognising their innate humanity, the study emphasises the urgent need to prioritise the safety and dignity of children by dismantling harmful societal norms.

To combat online abuse, the chapter suggests reorienting societal attitudes towards shared respect and protection. Schools can equip children with digital literacy and responsible online conduct. Social workers and community structures can offer trusted spaces for reporting. Parents can foster open, non-judgmental conversations about online safety and potential dangers. Ultimately, children themselves need education on navigating online risks, responsible online behaviour, and avenues for seeking help if they encounter harmful content or actions. In light of the limited scholarly attention paid to OCSEA in Africa, the paper advocates for continued research efforts to fill this critical gap. Recognising the insufficient reporting and response mechanisms for OCSEA in Africa, the paper recommends strengthening these systems to effectively address this issue. Lastly, to uphold the spirit of Ubuntu, the study advocates for a reorientation of male socialisation, moving beyond simply respecting and valuing other men to encompass broader respect and protective instincts towards women and children.

References

African Union 1990, *African Charter on the Rights and Welfare of the Child*, Addis Ababa, Ethiopia. [Accessed 18 June 2023].

African Union 2019, *African Union Continental Consultation on Combatting Online Child Sexual Exploitation*, Available at: https://au.int/en/pressreleases/20190306/african-union-continental-consultation-combatting-online-child-sexual [Accessed 12 April 2023].

Ali, S., Haykal, H.A. & Youssef, E. 2023, 'Child sexual abuse and the Internet—A systematic review', *Hu Arenas*, vol. 6, pp. 404–421, Available at: https://doi.org/10.1007/s42087-021-00228-9 [Accessed 12 April 2023].

Artz, L., Ward, C.L., Leoschut, L., Kassanjee, R. & Burton, P. 2018, 'Guest editorial: The prevalence of child sexual abuse in South Africa: The Optimus Study South Africa', *South African Medical Journal*, vol. 108, no. 10, pp. 791–792.

Australian Centre to Counter Child Exploitation 2021, *Terminology and definitions of online child sexual exploitation*, Available at: https://www.accce.gov.au/sites/default/files/2021-06/Factsheet%20-%20Definitions%20of%20Online%20Child%20Sexual%20Exploitation.pdf [Accessed 16 June 2023].

Badoe, E. 2017, 'A critical review of child abuse and its management in Africa', *African Journal of Emergency Medicine*, vol. 7 (Supplement), pp. 32–35, Available at: https://doi.org/10.1016/j.afjem.2017.09.002 [Accessed 11 May 2023].

Bhuda, M.T. & Marumo, P. 2022, 'Ubuntu philosophy and African indigenous knowledge systems: Insights from decolonisation and indigenisation of research', *Gender & Behaviour*, vol. 20, no. 1, a31, Available at: https://hdl.handle.net/10520/ejc-genbeh_v20_n1_a31 [Accessed 30 May 2023].

Drejer, C., Riegler, M.A., Halvorsen, P., Johnson, M.S. & Baugerud, G.A. 2023, 'Livestreaming technology and online child sexual exploitation and abuse: A scoping review', *Trauma, Violence, & Abuse*, vol. 25, no. 1, pp. 260–274, Available at: https://doi.org/10.1177/15248380221147564 [Accessed 11 May 2023].

ECPAT, INTERPOL & UNICEF 2022, *Disrupting harm in South Africa: Evidence on online child sexual exploitation and abuse*, Global Partnership to End Violence Against Children, Available at: https://www.unicef.org/southafrica/media/7076/file/ZAF-disrupting-harm-South-Africa-2022.pdf [Accessed 18 June 2023].

ECPAT International 2016, *Terminology Guidelines for the Protection of Children from Sexual Exploitation and Sexual Abuse*, ECPAT, Luxembourg.

Govender, I. 2023, 'Gender-based violence – An increasing epidemic in South Africa', *South African Family Practice*, vol. 65, no. 1, a5729, Available at: https://doi.org/10.4102/safp.v65i1.5729 [Accessed 18 June 2023].

Hillis, S., Mercy, J., Amobi, A. & Kress, H. 2016, 'Global prevalence of past-year violence against children: A systematic review and minimum estimates', *Pediatrics*, vol. 137, e20154079, Available at: https://doi.org/10.1542/peds.2015-4079 [Accessed 10 May 2023].

Holt, T.J., Blevins, K.R. & Burkert, N. 2010, 'Considering the pedophile subculture online', *Sexual Abuse*, vol. 22, no. 1, pp. 3–24, Available at: https://doi.org/10.1177/1079063209344979 [Accessed 30 May 2023].

Horvath, M.A.H., Davidson, J.C., Grove-Hills, J., Gekoski, A. & Choak, C. 2014, *"It's a lonely journey": A rapid evidence assessment on intrafamilial child sexual abuse*, Office of the Children's Commissioner, London.

Independent Inquiry into Child Sexual Abuse 2017, *Victim and survivor voices from The Truth Project*, Available at: https://www.iicsa.org.uk/key-documents/3304/view/victim-survivor-voices-from-truth-project.pdf [Accessed 15 July 2023].

Interagency Working Group 2016, Terminology Guidelines for the Protection of Children from Sexual Exploitation and Sexual Abuse, *ECPAT International and ECPAT*, Luxembourg.

Kloess, J.A., Beech, A.R. & Harkins, L. 2014, 'Online child sexual exploitation: Prevalence, process, and offender characteristics', *Trauma, Violence, and Abuse*, vol. 15, no. 2, pp. 126–139.

Kloess, J.A., Hamilton-Giachritsis, C.E. & Beech, A.R. 2019, 'Offence processes of online sexual grooming and abuse of children via internet communication platforms', *Sexual Abuse*, vol. 31, no. 1, pp. 73–96, Available at: https://doi.org/10.1177/1079063217720927 [Accessed 28 April 2023].

May-Chahal, C. & Kelly, E. 2020, *Online child victimisation*, Bristol University Press, Bristol.

McCain, N. 2022, *Children are most likely to be sexually abused on Facebook and WhatsApp*, Available at: https://www.news24.com/news24/southafrica/news/children-most-likely-to-be-sexually-abused-on-facebook-whatsapp-report-finds-20221107 [Accessed 26 June 2023].

Motsoeneng, B. 2015, *Rape within families remains under-reported*, Available at: https://www.news24.com/health24/news/public-health/rape-within-families-remains-under-reported-20150821-2 [Accessed 16 April 2023].

Mugumbate, J. & Chereni, A. 2019, 'Using African Ubuntu theory in social work with children in Zimbabwe', *African Journal of Social Work*, vol. 9, no. 1, pp. 27–34.

National Institute for Health and Care Excellence 2017, *Child Abuse and Neglect: recognising, assessing and responding to abuse and neglect of children and young people*, Available at: https://www.nice.org.uk/guidance/gid-scwave0708/documents/draftguideline [Accessed 26 May 2023].

Ndhlovu, G.N. & Mfoafo-M'Carthy, M. 2022, 'Exploring the culture of silence on child sexual abuse within the family in Zimbabwe: A review of the literature', *African Journal of Social Work*, vol. 12, no. 5, pp. 239–248.

Nyasuguta, F. 2020, *Six types of sexual abuse that children face online*, Available at: https://www.the-star.co.ke/news/big-read/2020-07-16-six-types-of-sexual-abuse-that-children-face-online/ [Accessed 30 June 2023].

Quayle, E. 2021, 'Online Child Sexual Exploitation and Abuse', in Brown, J.M. & Horvath, M.A.H. (eds), *The Cambridge Handbook of Forensic Psychology*, Cambridge University Press, Cambridge, pp. 279–295.

Republic of South Africa 2005, *Children's Act*, Government Printers, Pretoria.

Republic of South Africa 2021, *Criminal Law (Sexual Offences and Related Matters) Amendment Act, 2021*, Government Printers, Pretoria.

Sekudu, T. 2019, 'Ubuntu and xenophobia: The challenges of reconciling two competing moralities in South Africa', *Journal of Human Rights*, vol. 18, no. 3, pp. 307–326.

Selengia, V., Nguyen Thi Thuy, H. & Mushi, D. 2020, 'Prevalence and patterns of CSA in selected countries of Asia and Africa: A review of literature', *Open Journal of Social Sciences*, vol. 8, no. 9, p. 157, Available at: https://doi.org/10.13189/oss.2020.8.9.157 [Accessed 14 June 2023].

United Nations 2020, *No country is free from child sexual abuse, exploitation, UN's top rights forum hears*, Available at: https://news.un.org/en/story/2020/03/1058501 [Accessed 16 June 2023].

United Nations 2022, *Countering online child sexual exploitation*, Available at: https://www.unodc.org/westandcentralafrica/en/westandcentralafrica/stories/2022/countering-online-child-sexual-exploitation.html [Accessed 17 June 2023].

United Nations Children's Fund 2020a, *Action to end child sexual abuse and exploitation: A review of evidence*, UNICEF, New York.

United Nations Children's Fund 2021a, *Ending online child sexual exploitation and abuse: Lessons learned and promising practices in low- and middle-income countries*, Available at: https://www.unicef.org/media/113731/file/Ending%20Online%20Sexual%20Exploitation%20and%20Abuse.pdf [Accessed 27 June 2023].

United Nations Children's Fund 2021b, *Addressing technology-facilitated child sexual exploitation and abuse in the face of COVID-19*, Available at: https://www.unicef.org/media/113751/file/Addressing%20Technology-Facilitated%20Child%20Sexual%20Exploitation%20and%20Abuse%20in%20the%20Face%20of%20COVID%2019.pdf [Accessed 16 June 2023].

United Nations Children's Fund 2022a, *UNICEF: One third of children in South Africa at risk of online violence, exploitation and abuse*, Available at: https://www.unicef.org/southafrica/press-releases/one-third-children-south-africa-risk-online-violence-exploitation-and-abuse [Accessed 19 June 2023].

United Nations Children's Fund 2022b, *UNICEF: Protecting children online*, Available at: https://www.unicef.org/protection/violence-against-children-online [Accessed 19 June 2023].

United Nations Office on Drugs and Crime 2020, *Online child sexual exploitation and abuse*, Available at: https://www.unodc.org/e4j/zh/

cybercrime/module-12/key-issues/online-child-sexual-exploitation-and-abuse.html [Accessed 19 June 2023].

UNICEF 2020b, *Sexual violence against children*, Available at: https://www.unicef.org/protection/sexual-violence-against-children [Accessed 19 June 2023].

Van Breda, A.D. 2019, 'Developing the notion of Ubuntu as an African theory for social work practice', *Social Work*, vol. 55, no. 4, pp. 439–450.

Vermeulen, V. & Greeff, A.P. 2015, 'Family resilience resources in coping with child sexual abuse in South Africa', *Journal of Child Sexual Abuse*, vol. 24, no. 5, pp. 555–571.

Ward, C.L., Artz, L., Leoschut, L., Kassanjee, R. & Burton, P. 2018, 'Sexual violence against children in South Africa: A nationally representative cross-sectional study of prevalence and correlates', *Lancet Global Health*, vol. 6, no. 4, pp. e460–e468, Available at: https://doi.org/10.1016/S2214-109X(18)30060-3 [Accessed 10 April 2023].

WeProtect Global Alliance 2021, *Global threat assessment 2021: Working together to end the sexual abuse of children online*, Available at: https://www.weprotect.org/wp-content/plugins/pdfjs-viewer-shortcode/pdfjs/web/viewer.php?file=https://www.weprotect.org/wp-content/uploads/Global-Threat-Assessment-2021.pdf&attachment_id=143651&dButton=true&pButton=true&oButton=false&sButton=true#zoom=0&pagemode=none&_wpnonce=1daac639cd [Accessed 10 June 2023].

World Health Organisation 2017, *Child sexual abuse global estimates*, Available at: https://www.who.int/ [Accessed 19 June 2023].

PART 3

Lived Realities and Emerging Child Rights Challenges

Chapter Nine
Child Marriage as a Major Challenge in Rural Communities: A Case Study of Binga District, Zimbabwe

Willard Muntanga and Taruvinga Muzingili

Introduction

The issue of child marriage continues to affect the lives of girls in Africa. Several factors contribute to the issue of child marriages in Zimbabwe, including peer pressure, lack of parental support, poverty, drug substance abuse and cultural practices. This chapter identifies the causes and effects of child marriages on girls' education, as well as coming up with community-driven measures to minimise child marriages in Zimbabwe and beyond. The fact that socio-cultural customs negatively affect girls' performance in rural primary formal education justifies the need to examine the issue of child marriages and their effects on girls' social capital development.

This chapter is based on the research findings in Binga, a district in Zimbabwe with a total population of 159,982, about 72,393 males and 87,589 females (ZIMSTAT, 2022:126). Most inhabitants in the district are Tonga people who were relocated from the Zambezi valley around the 1950s by the government of the federation to pave the way for the construction of the Kariba dam. Prior to the relocation processes, young people engaged in various activities, which included fishing, herding goats, hunting and farming. A significant proportion of BaTonga households and families in Binga depend on subsistence rural agriculture and informal fishing in the Zambezi River as their main sources of livelihood. Households within the district are considered extremely vulnerable, and the majority of families struggle for survival.

The Basilwizi Trust, SAFAIDS and Actionaid Policy Brief Report (2023:3) indicates that there is limited network coverage, with some areas in the district completely out of network range, thereby compromising communication for development and citizens' access to public services. The high prevalence of poverty in Binga may also be attributed to poor supportive economic activities, which fail to link or address their basic needs of the time. As a result of this, it is drastically lacking in essential public services such as health, education, communication and agricultural development. BaTonga people are often overlooked were priorities are concerned.

The overarching problem concerns the rampant child marriages, school dropouts, and underperformance of school children at school under the influence of tradition and culture in the Zambezi valley communities in Binga rural district. It is crucial to understand child marriages in rural areas and recommend appropriate and effective social work responses that benefit rural communities. The outbreak of child marriages in schools by students in secondary schools in Binga has given school teachers and parents a predicament in running the routine activities and administration of schools. Various reasons have led students to become victims of child marriages in the Zambezi valley communities. The problem of child marriages by children in schools will further magnify and increase the propensity of school dropout among students, and may be difficult to curtail if not addressed at the early stages. In Zimbabwe, efforts aimed at addressing child marriages have not been fully explored to draw key lessons on child marriages in the rural communities. This owes to perceptions predicated on culture and tradition regarding child marriages by adolescent children in schools. The policies and laws of Zimbabwe prohibit child marriages by learners who are still of school-going age. This was because children fail to complete school intentionally or unintentionally.

Understanding the Challenge in Rural Communities

Child marriages have been a problem affecting rural communities, though such cases go unreported. Muntanga and Muzingili (2019:671) discuss the cumulative impact of early marriages in rural areas, which has left a girl child in obscurity. This demonstrates that child marriages in the rural areas have been under the carpet and often go unreported due to the norms and values within traditional societies. In many traditional settings, poor woman uses early marriage of daughters as a strategy for reducing their economic vulnerability, shifting the economic burden related to a daughter's care to the husband's family

(Muntanga and Muzingili, 2019:671). The infiltration of fishing camps by girls in Binga has its genesis in unstable economic fortunes in the communities, for example, in 2012 nationally child headed households were the largest with an average household size of 7.6 people (Zimbabwe National statistics, 2012:7). There are cases where girl children were awarded scholarships or bursaries though they still lacked other school materials (Muzingili *et al*, 2018:5). Locally, Binga rural district has several children engaging into marriages at a tender age though such cases are often not documented. The problem of child marriages is centred on several factors, including lack of enforcement of marriage laws, poverty, cultural beliefs and the lack of role models (Kalimbuka, 2020:1). In many African societies, child marriages serve to cement family, clan and tribal connections. For example, *Trokosi* is a traditional practice in rural Ghana, Benin and Togo that involves sending a young virgin girl to a shrine as atonement for a crime committed by a family member. Child marriages in the rural areas, such as Binga, require an inter-disciplinary approach to unveil hidden information on child marriages in rural communities.

The participants in Zambezi valley community schools were selected methodically to participate in the research based on registers at the schools. Data was collected from secondary and primary students in Binga rural district who have been participating in sexual reproductive health and rights trainings. The group of students who were involved in school health activities such as health clubs, environmental cleaning and other profitable activities were recruited using school registers, which were collected from the school head. Most participants were beneficiaries of locally based organisations such as Basilwizi Trust and were trained on comprehensive sexual reproductive health and rights trainings (SRHR). These participants knew SRHR issues, health club formation and community health. Over and above, most of the participants had more than 3 years of learning in these schools, and this ensured data collection, which was a true reflection of what is happening in these schools and the communities.

Understanding of Child Marriages

Child marriage is a common problem which has disrupted Zambezi valley communities and throughout Africa. One respondent defined child marriages as:

> *Kukwatana kwa bana baniini mulombe amusimbi bali ansi aminyaka ili kkumi amusanu atutatu kabachi zyotololwa abazyali babo (The marriage between two children (a boy and a girl) who are below the age of 18 and still under the control of their parents).*

Another respondent defined it as:

> *A marriage between a man and a girl child who has not reached the age of consent for marriage and will be going for primary education. In most cases, it occurs to girls who are orphans who are forced by the situation at home, as there will be no one to look after the family members.*

The definitions describe what child marriages entail in the context of Zambezi valley communities in Binga rural district. The Convention on the Rights of the Child (1989) defines a child as anyone under the age of 18 years (Bunting, 2005:19). Plan International (2016:1) defines child marriages as any marriage where at least one of the parties is under 18 years of age. Child marriage can be considered a form of forced marriage given that one or both parties have not expressed their full, free and informed consent. These definitions are in line with the current legal framework in Zimbabwe, which legislates against marriage before the age of 18 for both boys and girls.

Causes of Child Marriages

Lack of Parental Support and Poverty

Child marriages in rural areas such as Binga are partly a result of parents who are unable to financially support their daughters to continue with their education. A girl child from Kalungwizi Secondary School lamented that:

> *Bazyali baangu me baka ndilekelezya, tako tibakali kuduulila pe ma bbuku a mpesulo zyaku belesya kuchikolo kuti ndijane maanu akuti ndizwidilile mukupona (My parents neglected me; they never bought books and pens for me at school for me to complete my education in my life).*

Another girl from Sinakatenge village of Binda district echoed that:

> Our parents do not provide advice to us as girls to guide us in the sense of right and wrong, but instead they send us to fetch water from the river for domestic use. They don't have time to discuss with us about life for the net benefits of our future as a girl child.

The lack of support on the part of parents remains a genuine concern insofar as girls' education is concerned. Parents in rural areas fail to pay fees for their children to attend school, and they end up dropping a girl school. This is often linked to poverty, which remains one of the major driving factors for child marriages in rule areas such as Binga. One girl child from Sizemba Primary School said:

> Iswe tubana bachisimbi buchete mbubo butupa kuti tufwambane kukwatwa katuchili bana bachikolo. Alubo kufwaba nkuko kupa kuti tuleke kuya kuchikolo akambo kakuti ngatwabula zisamo zyakusama mpawo kukwatwa ngachaba chintu biyo chakuti tukajane kuyusa akulondolwa kumakwatwe. As a girl child, poverty drives us to get into child marriages while we are still going to school. Poverty also leads to school dropouts for girls as we fail to get clothes (school uniforms), and entering into marriages becomes the last solution.

A School head teacher from Binga district attested that:

> Most of the parents are failing to pay fees for a girl child at my school. I don't know why. Some parents say that we don't have money or livestock, so we can sell and get money to pay the fees for their children.

The sentiments indicate that poverty is one of the major factors contributing to child marriages in rule areas such as Binga in Africa. In some cases, parents are not employed, and they depend on peasant farming, which is not sustainable for them, and hence, they fail to take their children to school. As a result, girls get into child marriage, trying to move away from the poverty in their families. Some families in rural areas also marry off their daughters to reduce their economic burden or earn an income. Child marriages are sometimes high during times of drought, as this leads to food deficiency. Thus, child marriages remain on the rise in rural areas such as Binga since the drought crisis intensifies the situation, threatening food security.

Peer Pressure

Child marriages are sometimes caused by peer pressure (*jungwe*) in the rural areas, such as Binga. One school teacher from Sinamwenda Primary defined peer pressure as an influence by children of the same age or group to do or accept certain behaviour, which negatively affects them. Adolescents influence others as well as being influenced by them (Brown et al, 2009:78). A village head noted that:

> *Bana bachikolo bachisimbi bali kufwambana kujana mala na kumita akambo ka jungwe, babu chijanina zyabasankwa chindi kachitana sika pe kuti bakwatwe biya achiindi cheelede* (Girls are being impregnated at a tender age, and they rush for boys when they are not yet matured in mind and physically).

Another learner attested that 'a girl child, in our community, is being forced to get into a relationship with a married man in the community and drop out of school at the end'. The sentiments indicate that girls get into child marriage due to peer pressure. One major reason for them to be involved in sexual affairs with married men is the need for money or food, as these lure and attract girls. Dhull (2017:256) defines peer pressure as an influence from friends or classmates to do something that is not normally done, such as stress or strain one feels from friends and schoolmates to act, behave, think and look a certain way. However, the Girls Empowerment Movement (2017:01) maintains that many adolescent girls are hindered from fulfilling their potential and developing into productive members of society. Peer pressure can be dangerous when girls grab and accept wrong things, which have a negative impact on their lives. This is different from positive peer pressure, which should be celebrated by everyone in the community.

Drug and Substance Abuse

Drug substance abuse is among the top causes of child marriages in rural areas such as Binga. One parent from Malube Primary School noted that:

> *Bana bachisimbi balansi aminyaka ilikkumi atubili mazuba ano babunywa tunjengu abalombe muchindi chakkisimusi, babuchesya mumabbawa kaba fwepa tombwe wamazuba ano. Kumamanino, bana bachisimbi ngabazikumita mala abasankwa mbubatazi pe mpawo banjila mumapenzi* (Girl children who are below the age of 12 years drink alcohol with small boys during Christmas days, and they go out for the whole night in a beer hall, smoking marijuana. At the end, they get impregnated by men, and they fail to identify them.

Another villager in Malube said that.

> Girls in our community have been addicted to alcohol, and they are no longer concentrating much on their schoolwork. Drug and substance abuse has become one thing which has changed the minds of girls, and they are no longer listening to advice from their parents.

The sentiments indicate that drug and substance abuse contribute to child marriages in Binga rural district, Zimbabwe. Parents often complain about the behaviours of a girl child, as they now compete with boys on drugs. Many teenage girls use drugs to escape problems like bullying, not getting along with others, growing apart from family members and friends. The use of illicit drugs continues to increase in rural African communities, especially among young boys and girls. Of major concern is the fact that children are targeted as the new market for drugs (Odhiambo, 2021:454). Consequently, drug and substance abuse remain an important factor which drives girls into child marriages.

Cultural Practices

Child marriages in rural areas are also conducted in religious and/or cultural settings. This increases the cases of child marriages in rural areas. One village head attested that:

> Some of the cultural practices and traditions of BaTonga people in Binga are no longer being followed or are being ignored by children because of the advent of Christianity. Thus, girls are no longer undergoing certain trainings which make and prove to them that they are mature enough they stand for marriage.

> *Practices such as Nkolola (initiation or training which is undergone by a girl child before she is married) have been long ignored and avoided by BaTonga people, which thus why child marriages are looming.*

One religious leader defined cultural practices as:

> *The norms and values which are followed by the community members uphold a sense of unity and purpose in the society. These cultural practices and traditions determine the forms and types of marriages which take place in the traditional society.*

Cultural practices have a bearing on society's ability to facilitate and minimise child marriages. In the traditional society of Binga, child marriages occur because of cultural practices such as wife inheritance and prophetic pronouncement of choosing a young girl. Some spiritual leaders might ascribe that it is God who spoke to them in spirit to select her. The common religious sects which instigate child marriages, such as *Johane Masowe* and *Madzibaba,* have several cases of child marriages. Mobile prophets in Binga marry young girls who are still going to school. They secretly tell youthful girls that they want to drive away bad omens on their bodies so that they get married without any problems.

Net Effects of Child Marriages

Child marriages are one of the heart-rending forms of abuse faced by young girls in Binga rural district, Zimbabwe. A girl child faces problems which range from personal to socio-economic, with ripple effects on the social capital development. The net effects of child marriages include socio-economic, educational and health consequences.

Socio-economic Consequence

In the traditional society, girls suffer from reduced self-identity and opportunities for receiving basic life survival skills, which could be a means for a better life. Young girls who are married remain in subservient and acquiescent roles in the family where they are married, performing domestic overload wifely duties beyond their capacity. Chant (2010:357) maintains that many young women succumb to arranged marriages. Some girls return to live with parents and guardians and are perceived to be a financial burden to the same parents who allowed or pressured them to marry early in the first place. As the Tonga adage goes, '*Mwana uleegwa kuku joka*", *mwana ulilila nyeele ya bbonobono mumuleke imunyanine mumaboko*' (A child is advised after a bad thing has happened to them). This shows that in some cases, these children get into marriages more willingly, and often against the advice of their parents. Child marriages rob girls of their childhood, virginity and threaten their well-being, and it is one of the most hidden forms of violence against women and girls in society.

One of the major reasons why pregnant teenagers or teenage mothers fail to continue with their schooling is a lack of parental support. The majority of girls expressed that their parents were no longer interested in looking after them after getting pregnant. The understanding is that the alleged fathers or relatives of the alleged fathers should take responsibility. Pregnant and mothering teenagers acknowledged that there were shifts in the responsibilities as parenting their children brought new burdens. One of the key informants noted that:

> *Married children do not finish and complete their academic education due to the demanding basic needs of the family at home. The child will be demanding soap, clothes, and nutritious food, and she will not be able to balance the two (Education and basic needs of the child).*

In concurrence, one girl expressed that:

> *My parents told me that they will not support me or the child. Even if I go or demand something from the father of the child, I will get it, as he comes from a poor family. His relatives are also poor. I can only get support here, but my parents leave me to look after the baby. They even refused to allow me to find someone to stay with the child if I went back to school.*

After experiencing an overwhelming situation, one of the girls noted that:

> *As a pregnant girl child, I thought of committing suicide after being segregated and isolated by family members, by taking poison. I was chased away from home. I ended up staying with my sister at her marital home.*

The sentiments show that girls often feel that their parents and relatives do not give them enough support to go back to school after they become pregnant. The situation is worsened by poverty from the alleged father's family. Mothering is associated with new responsibilities, which affect young mothers' re-entry into schools.

Health Consequences

The health risks attributed to teenage pregnancy and childbirth as a result of child marriage are copious, and these contribute to maternal and child mortality. In Binga rural district, child marriages pose many dangers to young girls' reproductive health and psychological well-being. Though there are limited cases of obstetric fistula reported in rural areas in Zimbabwe, birth complications and miscarriages are common. The practice of girls having sexual relations with many boys and men has exposed them to sexually related diseases; some succumb to HIV/AIDS. One girl noted that 'during pregnancy check-up by the nurses at the clinic, most girls test positive with HIV/AIDS'. A Nurse at Tyunga clinic attested that:

> *Complications during childbirth and delivery are most common in girls under the age of 18, significantly raising the risk of death, premature delivery, infant mortality and low birth weight. In 2022, we recorded 50 young females under the age of 18 who registered for ANC (Antenatal care) bookings.*

This is an indication that child marriages have many consequences which affect the health and life of girls. In terms of health, girls who give birth at a tender age fail to maintain hygiene as they are divorced by their husbands, and they have access to basic needs such as clothes and soap to wash nappies for the newborn baby. Thus, they become susceptible to diseases like cholera, which affects the health of individuals in the society. Married women who were as children are also consistently less likely to give birth in healthcare facilities or with assistance from skilled providers (Fan and Koski, 2022:01).

Educational Consequences

Child marriage is a serious deterrent to girls' education in rural schools in Africa. It blocks young girls' educational and other life opportunities and negatively affects their personal and social development; it diminishes girls' opportunity to acquire survival skills, which enables them to escape poverty-related conditions. One respondent from Binga noted that:

> *Iswe tubana bachisimbi tujana buyumuyumu maningi kuti tweendelele Anembo achikolo na ndamitisigwa amulombe, ngatwayowa kusekwa abamwi besu* (As a girl child, we find it difficult to go to school and our friends laugh at us).

Apart from the parents' ridicule, pregnant teenagers are also shunned by teachers at schools in rural areas. Due to the negativity associated with teenage pregnancies, some learners associate with friends outside their schools. In some cases, girls who associate with friends who are pregnant or mothering while schooling are also ridiculed. One of the girls noted that "as pregnant girl children at school, we feel embarrassed and isolated as our friends shun and avoid interacting with us; they isolate us and leave us in the cage of loneliness". To show the extremity of the situation, another girl added that:

> I tried to wear a jersey to cover my pregnancy so that teachers and other students could not see that I am pregnant. Some learners, especially boys, scold pregnant or mothering teenagers. We became their daily topics, and we always felt embarrassed.

The above sentiments show that girls are often in a dilemma in as far as child marriages are concerned in rural areas; their future is blocked and soiled as they shun continuing with their education. Parents also claim that when a child finds out that she is pregnant and it is not planned, they often experiences high levels of stress, and some experience depression, confusion, fear and stress. Parents also experience shame, embarrassment and humiliation from the community when their daughters are pregnant. In such instances, girls prefer to be out of school. However, Kurevakwesu and colleagues (2023:03) found out that parents often feel that the money spent on sending their daughter to school is wasted if she becomes pregnant.

Challenges in the Legal Sphere and Marriage Laws

Child marriage is constitutionally not permissible. However, the country is suffering from legal plurality; there are so many laws and policies around child protection and child marriages, though these laws have no real impact in addressing issues related to child marriages in the traditional communities, such as Binga. There are several challenges in addressing child marriages, including poor implementation of already existing laws, corruption and bribery and lack of awareness about marriage laws.

Poor Implementation of Existing Marriage Laws and Corruption

Although the legal framework on marriage is clear in Zimbabwe, it is generally not known by people in rural areas. In most cases, there is poor implementation of the laws at grass grassroots level as there are no resources put aside to support trained officers to reach rural areas to talk about marriage laws and child marriages in the traditional society. One child protection committee member asserted that:

> *The committees for child protection were established, but they are not trained and capacitated on the rights of children. We were only told to form a committee by a ward councillor without receiving any form of training for us to be able to execute our roles and duties.*

Lack of enforcement of marriage laws by the government is an indication of failure to implement the laws. Scholars such as Mutale (2015:35) and Muzingili (2014:38) argue that the rural areas of Zimbabwe lack proper child protection structures to ensure that every child is protected. The implementation failure of marriage laws is attributed to the malfunction of committees which look after children in the rural communities, as well as the unprofessional legal officers.

Corruption is another factor which is making the perpetrators win cases of child marriages in the rural communities. This is because when cases of child abuse are reported to the police, the perpetrators end up not being imprisoned. One elderly man noted that:

> *So many married men have impregnated girls who are under the age of 18, and not even one was imprisoned or charged a fine by the court. They are reported to the police, and some of the cases do not even reach the court.*

Another woman maintained that:

> Some of the village heads are given goats and chickens to address issues of child marriages at the village level, and the cases are not even reported to the police. Even the school heads do not take up the issues as they are bribed by the parents who want their girl child to be married.

The issues are common in rural communities such as Binga Rural District. Child marriage issues are not often reported, and if reported to the police, most cases are not taken the court. This shows that corruption and bribery take place and contribute to the plight of child abuse.

Marriage laws are not known to community members

The civil marriage laws require marriage registration with the court, a requirement that marriages be of individuals who have reached eighteen years of age. Such laws are not known in most rural areas, such as Binga. One village head affirmed that:

> I don't know what civil marriage is all about. What I know is the unregistered marriage which we do here, where I just agree with my partner and parents as long, I give them 3 beasts as lobola, it will be enough. These marriage laws are not even known to us as village heads, and it's alien to us.

Another respondent attested that:

> Our daughters are being married at a tender age because we don't know marriage laws practised in our country, the magistrate court is very far from us, so that we can enquire and be apprised of the requirements. Those in the office of the magistrate do not come to the ground to share with us information on marriage laws.

The laws of marriage are often unknown in rural areas, which explains why child marriages are on the rise. Due to economic constraints, responsible officers do not do their job of imparting knowledge to the communities so that they can have an appreciation of the legal laws related to marriages.

Measures to Minimise Child Marriages

There are several measures which can be implemented to address the challenge of child marriages in rural communities. From a socio-cultural perspective, there is a need for cultural awareness on the issues of child marriages in rural communities and even in urban areas. It is also important for robust engagements with religious and local structures, such as village heads and chiefs, so that they are aware of the age of marriage in line with legal frameworks. Moreover, cultural practices such as *Kunjilila mun'anda* (wife inheritance) and *Kutangila musimbi* (promissory marriage), which promote child marriages in the traditional society, should be abandoned. Churches should create platforms for youths to share their experiences, debating on the issues of child marriages and their effects. In the traditional society, religious and traditional leaders play a pivotal role in ending child marriages in their communities, especially through awareness campaigns on the negative effects of child marriages in rural communities.

From a poverty eradication perspective, it is important to empower girls on life-based skills education (LBSE) such as sewing, carpentry, leather work and welding so that they can stand on their own if she does not get formal employment. This includes educating a girl child who is being taken to school so that she can progress up to the tertiary level. This will delay a girl child delay to getting into marriage, and because of that, child marriages in the society would have been minimised. There is also a need to create employment for community members so that they are able to take their children to school, and they will be able to provide basic needs for their children, hence the tendency of exposing a girl child to child marriages will be limited. Moreover, harmonised cash and voucher assistance (CVA) might be useful in rural areas so that communities can receive goods or services for use at the household level. This will ensure that children get food to eat and also get money for payment of school fees at school. Finally, provision of social support to orphans (both girls and boys) can be helpful so that children are not exposed to sexual and other forms of abuse by other people outside the family.

Finally, from legal and political perspectives, there is a need to strengthen the legal framework and ensure swift measures are put in place to guarantee implementation. The Southern African Development Community model law requires countries to set the minimum age of marriage at 18, register all marriages and take effective action to eradicate child marriages. This is in line with the Zimbabwean Constitution. Thus, for any person who wants to marry or get married must be 18 years or above, verification of the age must be done by means of birth certificates, identification cards or other official documents that may reveal the identity and possible age of the child. There is also a need for training of the law enforcement officers, traditional leaders and religious authorities on the dangers and effects of child marriages, human and child rights, as well as reporting matters related to child marriages. Moreover, perpetrators should be given penalties in the form of a fine or imprisonment for disobeying marriage laws. It is also important to establish community committees or structures which look after child protection issues, including child marriages. Finally, Marriage laws (customary marriage and civil marriage) must be observed and followed by community members in the traditional contexts.

Conclusion

Child marriages in rural areas have harmful effects on the lives of girl children more than boys. Major causes of child marriages include poverty, drug substance abuse, lack of parental support, peer pressure and cultural practices. Discussion around legal frameworks on child marriage and suggested measures to minimise child marriages in Binga rural district. Some traditional societies have norms and values that harm the girl child, and they need to be checked and verified on their impact on how they affect and injure the girl child's social capital development in society. Girls are often denied access to education and other opportunities which are crucial to their lives. Above all, civil laws and the Constitution of Zimbabwe should be in tandem so that perpetrators of child marriages should be held accountable. The recommendations emphasise the need for an interdisciplinary and holistic approach to end child marriage in Zimbabwe and beyond.

References

Basilwizi Trust, SAFAIDS & ActionAid 2023, *Strengthening access to friendly sexual and reproductive health services in resource-constrained settings: Experience and lessons from Binga, Zimbabwe, June–July report 2023*.

Bunting, A. 2005, 'Stages of development: Marriage of girls and teens as an international human rights issue', *Social and Legal Studies*, vol. 14, no. 1, pp. 17–38.

Chant, S. & Evans, A. 2010, 'Looking for the one(s): Young love and urban poverty in the Gambia', *Environment & Urbanisation*, vol. 22, no. 2, pp. 353–369.

Dhull, P. & Beniwal, D.R. 2017, 'Dealing with peer pressure', *Online International Interdisciplinary Research Journal*, vol. 7, Special Issue, Nov.

Girl Empowerment Movement 2017, *Helping girls and young women to shape South Africa's future*, UNICEF for Every Child, South Africa, May.

Fan, S. & Koski, A. 2022, 'The health consequences of child marriages: A systematic review of the evidence', *BMC Public Health*, vol. 22, 309.

Kalimbuka, C.B. 2020, *The very traditions that support child marriages in Malawi can be used to end them*, World Bank Blog, Youth Transforming Africa. Available at: https://blogs.worldbank.org [Accessed 14 July 2023].

Muntanga, W. & Muzingili, T. 2019, 'The obscurity of early marriages in Binga rural district, Zimbabwe: Implications of the girl child', *Journal of Advances in Social Sciences and Humanities (JASH)*, vol. 5, no. 3, pp. 670–673.

Mutale, Q. 2015, 'Challenges facing school children in rural areas of Zimbabwe: A case of Tyunga and Luunga wards of Binga District', *Research on Humanities and Social Sciences*, vol. 5, no. 9, pp. 32–38.

Muzingili, T. 2014, *Factors affecting school completion rate by the girl child in remote areas: Case of Binga district, Ward 1*, Dissertation, University of Zimbabwe, Zimbabwe.

Muzingili, T., Muchinako, G.A. & Mutale, Q. 2018, 'Child protection concerns: Situations of girls in fishing camps in Binga, Zimbabwe'.

Plan International 2016, *Ending child marriages in Zimbabwe: Gaps and opportunities in the legal and regulatory framework*, Policy Brief 2016.

Kurevakwesu, W., Mthethwa, E., Chirangwanda, K. & Mabeza, T. 2023, 'Parental perceptions towards reintegration of pregnant girls and teenage mothers into the education system in Zimbabwe'.

Odhiambo, D.O. 2021, 'Effects of drugs and substances on academic performance in secondary schools in Nakuru County, Kenya', *International Journal of Science and Research*, vol. 10, no. 8.

Brown, B.B. & Larson, J. 2009, 'Peer relationships in adolescence', in R.M. Lerner & L. Steinberg (eds), *Handbook of Adolescent Psychology*, Wiley, New Jersey.

ZimStats 2012, *Zimbabwe population census: Women and men profile summary report 2012*, Government of Zimbabwe, Harare.

ZimStats 2022, *2022 population and housing census: Preliminary report on population figures, Zimbabwe*, Government of Zimbabwe.

Chapter Ten
Child Marriages in Zimbabwe: Interrogating Culture, girls' rights, and HIV and AIDS in Hurungwe District, Mashonaland West Province

Francis Maushe, Wilberforce Kurevakwesu, Noel Garikai Muridzo, Etiya Edith Chigondo, and Albert T Mashambanhaka

Introduction

Child marriages are one of the daunting problems the African continent is experiencing. Children's future is heavily threatened by the increase in child marriage cases in most Zimbabwean provinces, resulting in calls for establishing measures to protect them from abusive cultures. This chapter explores the cultural practices that promote child marriages in the Hurungwe District of Mashonaland West Province in Zimbabwe. The chapter also discusses the consequences of child marriages to children and their families regarding their welfare, and the intervention measures needed to reduce child marriages.

Background: Child Marriages in Zimbabwe

The existence of child marriages, particularly in the African continent, is alarming because it threatens the well-being and future of girls across the globe. UNICEF (2022) defines child marriages as any formal or informal marriage arrangement or union between a child who is under eighteen years of age with an adult or another child. There are combined efforts to fight against child marriages and improve child protection measures across the globe. Various frameworks inform this legislation, such as the United Nations Sustainable Development Goals (SDGs), to eradicate human rights violations practices by 2030. Child marriages mainly affect girls compared to boys.

The bid to fight child marriages is influenced by the devastating effects of the practice, in which young girls' health and lives are heavily threatened. UNICEF (2022) states that girls involved in child marriages experience domestic violence, HIV/AIDS and STIs, adverse economic and health outcomes, education deprivation, pregnancy-related complications, and childbirth complications. Child marriages in Northern Nigeria are high, with several implications for children's lives (Iyabode, 2011:2). Girls Not Brides (2019) observes that child marriage is a severe global problem across countries, cultures, religions, and ethnicities. About 12 million girls marry before the age of 18 annually, while one in five girls globally marries before eighteen years (Child Not Brides, 2019). Approximately forty per cent of girls marry before reaching eighteen years in Sub-Saharan Africa. Africa has about fifteen to twenty countries with the highest rates of child marriages (Gumbonzvanda and Bihlmaier, 2019). For instance, about seventy-seven per cent of girls in Niger, and above 60% in Chad marry before eighteen. There is a need to increase efforts to combat child marriages to prevent the increase in child marriages, expected to double by 2050.

In Zimbabwe, one in three girls marry before reaching age eighteen, and problems associated with early marriages, particularly pregnancy and birth-related complications, have increased (ZIMSTATS, 2019). For example, a fourteen-year-old girl was reported by the police to have died while giving birth at an Apostolic Sect site in Manicaland Province in Zimbabwe. Zimbabwe National Statistics Agency (2019) states that about 33.7% of girls in Zimbabwe are married before age eighteen, compared to two per cent of boys who marry before 18. ZIMSTATS (2019) has also noted that rural girls are more likely to marry early than urban girls, influencing calls for action. ZIMSTATS statistics on child marriages in Zimbabwean provinces are presented below.

Province	Girls married before the age of 18
Mashonaland Central	52.1%
Mashonaland East	45.1%
Masvingo	43.4%
Mashonaland West	42.2%
Manicaland	38.1%
Midlands	29.4%
Matebeleland North	23%
Harare	20.3%
Matabeleland South	10.9%
Rural	21.3%
Urban	43.7%

As shown in the table, Mashonaland West has a 42.2% rate of child marriages. Another survey by the Multiple Indicator Cluster Survey (MICS) established that about 50.9% of child marriages in Zimbabwe emanate from families who affiliate with traditional religions, particularly the Apostolic sect. Having presented statistics on child marriages, it is crucial to establish the factors contributing to them. The significant factors that contribute to child marriages, as argued by Gumbonzvanda (2014:2), include poverty and lack of education, gaps in laws and enforcement of laws, and customary practices and beliefs. Several laws have been set around the globe and locally to contain the problem of child marriages and improve child protection measures. The legal responses and initiatives to child marriages include the Campaign for Accelerated Reduction of Maternal Mortality (CARMMA), Maputo Protocol, National Convention on the Rights of the Child, Children's Act (Chapter 5:06), the 2013 Zimbabwe Constitution, the Criminal Law (Codification and Reform), and the Marriage Act.

Child Marriages in the Kanyati area in Hurungwe, Zimbabwe

Cultural Practices that Promote Child Marriages in Hurungwe

Child marriages are prevalent in places such as Hurungwe. A female respondent noted that:

> Many girls here are dropping out of school and getting married at very tender ages. Few girls finish school in our area. The majority start to engage in early sexual activities with older men, resulting in unwanted pregnancies, early marriages, and even exposure to HIV/AIDS and other STIs" (Interviewed Woman).

The sentiment shows that early marriages are high. This is partly due to the historical exploitation and marginalisation of women in poor communities remain high and detrimental to the health and wellbeing of girls and women. The social and cultural practices promoting child marriages include cultural initiation ceremonies (*Chinamwali*), sexual cleansing rituals, spiritual beliefs and instructions in apostolic churches, and community pressure. A female professional respondent maintained that:

> *The cultural practices of initiating girls through the practice, in which girls are taught how to please men (husband), yet this process is done when the girls are as young as twelve years old. It is said that girls are taught how to please a man in bed, yet she is still children. Girls are mostly influenced to engage early in sexual activities to experience what they have been taught during the initiation process. In some scenarios, meaning is brought to the initiation shrines to sleep with the girls.*

Another female respondent expressed similar sentiments by saying, 'My friend was married by a much older husband after church leaders approved the union, now she is the fourth wife. They live in absolute poverty.' This is in line with what another woman said: "I feel that *tsika yekuti vasikana havaiti zvechikoro vanoroorwa ndoirikukonzera kuti vasikana varoorwe vari vanana* (Children are getting married earlier because parents do not value educating girls)". Similarly, a professional participant also indicated that:

> *Children become brides based on the notion that parents use them as a source of getting money or relieving themselves from poverty if the girls are married to richer men. This has largely exposed children to several problems that mainly affect their sexual health.*

Thus, the noted cultural practices are vital for the understanding of the prevalence of child marriages in rural areas such as Kanyati village in Hurungwe. In the same vein, most children do not have the opportunity to express their choices because cultural practices undermine them. As already pointed out, the central cultural practices that promote child marriages in Hurungwe include cultural initiation practices *(Chinamwali)*, sexual cleansing rituals, community pressure, and spiritual beliefs and practices in Apostolic churches. This is in line with Kalimbuka's (2020:3) investigation that revealed that cultural beliefs in rural communities promote the proliferation of early marriages. Similarly, rural Gambia also experiences high rates of child marriages perpetuated by ethnicity (Lowe, 2019:4). The issue of poverty and community pressure to ease poverty by marrying off girls early was also found in Tanzania. Families take marrying off girls as a pathway to a better life. A study by Stark (2017) established that early marriages in urban Tanzania are perpetuated by poverty and the traditional practices of marrying off girls to gain resources.

Impact of Child Marriages on Child and Family Welfare

Several effects of child marriages affect the lives of girls and their families. One of the young women said:

> Since I got married, ndakapindana nenhamo dzakawanda sekusiya chikoro ndiri form 1 ndiine 15 years, kutambudzika pakuzvara, kurohwa nemurume, nekushaya zvekudya zvinokwana (I have been through a lot of problems since I got married, in which I dropped out of school, experienced birth-related complications, violence from the husband, and other stressful situations)

Similar sentiments were expressed by a child bride:

> Chakanyanyondirwadza ndechekuti pandakatizira murume wangu akazoroora vamwe vakadzi vaviri mushure mangu. Pari zvino ndogara ndichichema ndichiona vezera rangu vakaenda mberi nechikoro vavanemabasa akanaka. Vabereki vangu vose vakashaika chero ndikarwara hapana wekuudza ndinogara ndichierera musodzi. Barika rinorwadza nezera rangu tinogara tichirwa, kugara mumaricho nekuda kwenzara (My life is full of misery because my husband married two other women after marrying me. A polygamous life is harrowing, and I always cry seeing my peers who are now thriving because they are furthering their education. All my parents died, and I didn't have anyone to turn to. I always got depressed, and we survived on piecemeal jobs to make ends meet."

Similarly, an official highlighted that 'It is unfortunate that child brides in Kanyati are victims of domestic violence, poverty, and high exposure to STIs such as HIV/AIDS. May reports lodged about domestic violence involve victims of child marriages.' Since the onset of COVID-19, the rate of child marriages highly increased significantly. The alarming rates of birth-related complications are often reported to local health centres, and the burden of mother-to-child transmission is often high in these young brides. Child brides suffer traumatising experiences that harm their well-being. In the same vein, young women are being exploited at the expense of getting married. The range of problems they face is embedded in the name of patriarchal beliefs that one should marry her husband. Regarding the contribution of child marriages to the spread of HIV/AIDS and STIs, one of the professionals explained that:

> *Most stakeholders are hard hit by the high prevalence of HIV/ AIDS cases in adolescents. Child brides are being exposed to HIV/AIDS and other STIs due to a lack of knowledge on sexual health and limited safe sex negotiating power. The rate has increased because of limited accessibility of health centres in rural areas and the COVID-19 restrictions.*

The sentiments portray the need to help young women who are indebted to a range of social problems that they cannot escape on their own. Their lives are troubled and captured by cultural practices that continually exacerbate their oppression and suffering. Thus, the consequences of child marriages include dropping out of school, poverty, intimate partner violence, birth-related complications, high exposure to HIV/AIDS and other STIs, as well as stress and depression. Nour (2006:5) explored the health consequences of child marriage in Africa and found that sexually transmitted diseases, cervical cancer, and deaths during childbirth are other significant problems of child marriage. However, child deaths were not reported in Kanyati, though they occurred in Zimbabwe, for example, the recent story of Memory Machaya in Zimbabwe, in which a fourteen-year-old girl was said to have died while giving birth at a Marange shrine in Manicaland. Machaya's story reflects the dangers of child marriages and the need for effective responses to protect the girl child from these life-threatening practices. Therefore, this chapter has established the significant consequences of early marriages on the well-being of girls and women.

Intervention Measures to Reduce Child Marriages

Several measures can be employed to reduce child marriages. These include increasing information dissemination to young girls and rural households, ensuring the enforcement of child marriage laws and indicting perpetrators, economic empowerment of young women, and engaging stakeholders who work on child protection and girls' rights. One professional said:

> *Young girls should be empowered to stay in school to mature and understand sexual health issues and refrain from early sexual relationships, particularly with older men, to avoid being exposed to early pregnancies, abuse, and HIV/AIDS.*

One young bride argued:

> As a victim of child marriages, I feel that I have been accorded a chance. I would have worked hard on my schooling, other than getting involved in childbearing and being a housewife. All my intelligence is now down the drain.

The expressed opinions show that child marriages are detrimental to the welfare of children and their families, and addressing the problem would need the use of laws to prevent further girls' exposure to child marriages, among other suggested interventions. Notably, the maximisation of child protection initiatives will bring sanity to the gender discourse in which the historical marginalisation of women is at its peak. Thus, the suggestions given would support the trajectory of ending child marriages in line with the SDGs. As noted, interventions in a bid to address child marriages include enforcement of laws to persecute perpetrators of child marriages, economic empowerment of young girls and women as well as the community, information dissemination about sexual health to rural girls and households, as well as engaging child rights and protection organisations. Kalamar, Lee-Rife and Hindin (2016:1), in response to the overarching detrimental effects of child marriages, assessed what could be interventions to address child marriages and concluded, from several literature sources, including Gray literature, that law enforcement, empowerment of marginalized rural communities, and increasing school funding opportunities could reduce the menace. Mehra (2018:7) also suggests using youth information centres as the sources of sexual and reproductive health information for young girls and boys and their households to drastically reduce exposure to early sexual relationships.

Conclusion

The problem of child marriages in Hurungwe in relation to rights, culture, and HIV/AIDS remains a major stumbling block to the success of girls in their lives. This chapter unearthed the devastating experiences that the girl child is exposed to and the overarching experiences related to HIV/AIDS, violation of rights and other cultural vices. Child marriages are highly prevalent in Mashonaland Central Province, posing greater negative consequences for this historically exploited and socially discriminated gender. Huge gaps exist regarding addressing the problem of child marriages and law enforcement to persecute the perpetrators and empower the community, especially young girls, which is key to overcoming this problem.

Thus, grassroots leaders such as village heads, chiefs, and educational leaders should be trained to work as watchdogs to identify potential victims of child marriages. This will promote the reduction of the number of those who perpetrate the increase in child abuse cases. Secondly, the Social Services Department should mobilise funds to promote educational and economic empowerment to ensure that young girls and women are informed about the dangers of girls' early engagement in sexual relationships. Healthcare human service professionals in rural areas should endeavour to empower young girls to access sexual health and related issues. This will strengthen the move to prevent the high increase of girls who marry early and encounter unwanted pregnancies.

References

Girls Not Brides 2019, *Where does it happen?*, Available at: https://www.girlsnotbrides.org/about-child-marriage/where-child-marriage-happens/ [Accessed 1 December 2021].

Gumbonzvanda, N. & Bihlmaier, M. 2019, 'The invisible wall to the Beijing space', *Rural 21*, vol. 53, no. 4.

Human Rights Watch 2015, *Ending child marriage in Africa*, Available at: https://www.hrw.org/news/2015/12/09/ending-child-marriage-africa [Accessed 1 December 2021].

Iyabode, R. 2011, 'Child bride and child sex: Combating child marriages in Nigeria', *Nnamdi Azikiwe University Journal of International Law and Jurisprudence*, no. 2, Available at: https://www.ajol.info/index.php/naujilj/article/view/82389 [Accessed 12 December 2021].

Kalamar, A.M., Lee-Rife, S. & Hindin, M. 2016, 'Interventions to prevent child marriage among young people in low and middle-income countries: A systematic review of the published and grey literature', *Journal of Adolescent Health*, vol. 59, no. 3, Available at: https://www.jahonline.org/article/S1054-139X(16)30161-6/fulltext [Accessed 2 December 2021].

Kalimbuka, B.C. 2020, *The very traditions that support child marriages in Malawi can be used to end them*, Available at: https://blogs.worldbank.org/youth-transforming-africa/very-traditions-support-child-marriages-malawi-can-be-used-end-them [Accessed 6 December 2021].

Khan, S. & Hancioglu, A. 2019, 'Multiple indicator cluster surveys: Delivering robust data on children and women across the globe', *Studies in Family Planning*, vol. 50, no. 3, pp. 279–286.

Lowe, M. 2019, 'Social and cultural factors perpetuating early marriage in rural Gambia: An exploratory mixed-methods study', *F1000Research*, vol. 8, Available at: https://www.ncbi.nlm.nih.gov/pmc/articles/PMC6974925/ [Accessed 4 December 2021].

Mehra, D., Sarkar, A. & Mehra, S. 2018, 'Effectiveness of a community-based intervention to delay early marriage, early pregnancy, and improve school retention among adolescents in India', *BMC Public Health*, vol. 18, no. 732, Available at: https://bmcpublichealth.biomedcentral.com/articles/10.1186/s12889-018-5586-3 [Accessed 8 December 2021].

Nour, N.M. 2006, 'Health consequences of child marriage in Africa', *Emerging Infectious Diseases*, vol. 12, no. 11, pp. 1644–1649, Available at: https://www.ncbi.nlm.nih.gov/pmc/articles/PMC3372345/ [Accessed 7 December 2021].

Stark, L. 2017, 'Early marriage and cultural constructions of adulthood in two slums in Dar es Salaam', *Culture, Health & Sexuality: An International Journal for Research, Intervention and Care*, vol. 20, no. 8, Available at: https://www.tandfonline.com/doi/full/10.1080/13691058.2017.1390162 [Accessed 10 December 2021].

UNICEF 2022, *Child protection: Child marriage*, Available at: https://www.unicef.org/protection/child-marriage [Accessed 12 December 2021].

Chapter Eleven
Access to Services for Children in Zimbabwean Streets: A Case of Harare Central Business District

Natalie Simbini, Takudzwa Chikombe and Witness Chikoko

Introduction

The street children phenomenon continues unabated globally, and Africa is no exception. In Africa, particularly in Zimbabwe, the problem has burgeoned over the last two decades, threatening the growth and development of children and exposing the inadequacies of interventions. To curb this anomaly, several governments in Africa, including Zimbabwe, ratified the provisions of the United Nations Convention on the Rights of the Child and the African Charter on the Rights and Welfare of the Child. In Zimbabwe, the National Orphan Care Policy of 1999, the National Action Plan for Orphaned and Vulnerable Children of 2004, the Children's Act (Chapter 5.06) and the Basic Education Assistance Module (BEAM) are some of the major strategies meant to protect and safeguard vulnerable children.

Despite the availability of these international and local legal instruments, programs, statutory measures, among other customised interventions, street children find themselves at the bottom of the social division of welfare in Zimbabwe. Whilst some of the manifestations of the phenomenon are contextual, there are many commonalities around the globe. At the core of this problem is a global consensus on the complex nature of street children. Street children live outside normal society structures, are nomadic, constantly mobile and a transient population (Manjengwa et al, 2016:55). These moving targets are difficult to assess, hence complex to define. In 1985, the Inter-NGO Programme for Street Children and Street Youth defined street children as "those for whom the street has become more than their family has become their home, a situation in which there is no protection, supervision or direction from responsible adults".

Some agencies maintain that the term 'street children' is inappropriate because it creates an artificial category and diverts attention from the interconnected dimensions of child vulnerability (Volpi, 2002). In Harare, the capital city of Zimbabwe, many children are finding sanctuary in the streets, and this reality is spread across other urban and peri-urban areas. Given the insufficiency of statistics on street children, this chapter analyses the issue of street children and their access to services, taking into account the prevailing socio-economic and political changes.

Understanding the Challenge of Streets Children

Whether children *of* the streets or children *on* the streets, the realisation of their rights is a rigorous process due to the manifold dimensions of the problem. By definition, children of the street live alone in streets, without proper and secure shelter, have lost contact with their parents and due to this are missing out on the parental protection, love and care; they are the most crucial group as they do not have any protection from the vagaries of nature and society. By contrast, children of the streets are seen as "children such as orphans, runaways, refugees, and displaced persons who do not have any contact with their families" (UNICEF, 1986; Srivastava, 2013:502).

In Asia and Pacific, street children have limited access to services like healthcare, education, food and shelter among other basic needs due to lack of identification cards and any other forms of identification including birth registration (West, 2003:18). The lack of access to services can be further attributed to the social marginalization, customary beliefs, lack of respect for street children and poverty. Due to a lack of access to education, children spend most of their time eking a living in the street and scavenging for food. At the same time, diseases such as HIV/AIDS, scabies, epilepsy and broken limbs, among other chronic illnesses such as tuberculosis, malaria, jaundice and typhoid, are a common phenomenon. This can be attributed to a lack of access to diagnosis and treatment services, and no access to water and proper sanitation (West, 2003:18). Street children have been further marginalised worldwide, and the realisation of their rights is imperative in all corners of the world so that they gain access to basic services and other forms of public goods.

In some parts of Europe, the problem of street children can be attributed to refugees and/or immigrants. It manifests in many forms of poverty, not limited to homelessness, child poverty and disability poverty (Volpi, 2002). Lack of shelter, lack of assistive devices for persons with disability living and working in the streets, lack of disposable income and child labour spell out the need to improve interventions and also the lives of children in the streets. Street children require equal care and protection as other children; hence, failure to meet their needs leads them to seek *substitute* families and chronically live on the street (Ochola, 2000:14). However, these families mostly provide shelter and protection from other families in the streets. Exploitation and abuse remain a reality. Hunter (2017) notes that street children are creative and adaptive, a sign of resilience after conducting studies in Ghana, Zimbabwe and the Democratic Republic of Congo.

Children and youth growing up on the streets live in conditions of chronic poverty and social exclusion (Hunter et al, 2017). Children use negative coping mechanisms to escape violence and marginalisation, such as drug abuse, crime, and prostitution. Evidence from Asia, the Pacific and Southern Africa especially South Africa shows that if the problem of street children persists, in the long run negative consequences such as high crime rate, disobedient and violence citizens, drug cartels and human trafficking will significantly increase (West, 2003:6). The observation is relevant to about Zimbabwe as evidenced by moral decadence in the name of prostitution, unsafe sexual behaviours, drug abuse and substance use, physical and mental abuse, and violence (Chikoko *et al*, 2019:83; 2021). Exploitation, stigma, and discrimination complement the list of unending challenges faced by children living and working on the streets. As a response, local authorities should provide avenues for the vulnerable group to access education, health, food, shelter and other essential services.

There are various interlocking variables ranging from institutional, personal, structural, to relational factors that act as obstacles for street children to access services. Zimbabwe, just like several other developing nations, experience many problems, including policy inconsistency, corruption, scarcity of resources, economic instability, and erosion of culture. A UNICEF study in 2000 estimated that at least 12,000 children lived and worked on the street in Zimbabwe and

150 million globally. However, there is a lack of current statistics on street children in Zimbabwe, but the assumption is that the number has reached alarming levels (Mhizha et al, 2016:40). Noteworthy among these problems is the macro-economic instability induced by the inflationary measures of the 1991 Economic Structural Adjustment Programme. In addition, the negative effects of the HIV/AIDs and COVID-19 pandemic, respectively, add to the dire situation of poverty in Zimbabwe. Also noteworthy are the effects of natural disasters such as cyclones and droughts, which affect the country. The total of these adversities creates a situation where children have to scavenge for food, as they may have lost their parents or guardians. The ubiquity of poverty caused by the aforementioned adversities also drives children to work in the street, thus forgoing education due to absenteeism at school.

At the same time, high urbanisation rates corroborate the increase of street children in urban and peri-urban areas in Zimbabwe and beyond. Pull and push factors are idiosyncratic to individuals, among them are runaways from abuse and exploitation by a parent or guardian, rural to urban migration in search of jobs due to poverty, refugees and internally displaced people. Over the last two decades, a significant increase in woman and child-headed households has been recorded, making the household set-up a source of the problem (Manjengwa *et al*, 2016:54). Further, the Operation Murambatsvina of 2000 in Zimbabwe cities was propelled by a statutory decision. The operation left many people homeless and hopeless after local authorities embarked on the destruction of illegal settlements and slums. Families were stranded and vulnerable, which forced them to move to peri-urban areas, and some to live and work on the streets. In the absence of adequate social safety nets, free healthcare and education, children turned to the street to eke a living for themselves and their families.

The Government of Zimbabwe, to this end, put in place various measures in the continuum of care in respect of children, including street children. Locally crafted policies and programs include the National Orphan Care Policy of 1999, the National Plan of Action for Orphans and Vulnerable Children 2004 (currently under review) and the 2017 National Case Management System for the Welfare and Protection of Children in Zimbabwe. These mechanisms reflect international best practices, and their implementation is guided by the confinements of the Children Act (Chapter 5.06). The Department of Social Development (DSD) under the Ministry of Public Service, Labour, and Social Welfare (MoPSLSW) was mandated by the law to be the custodian of a child in need of care. The Department presides over the implementation of child welfare targeted measures in collaboration with other Government Ministries and Departments, among them the Ministry of Health and Child Care, the National Aids Council, the Ministry of Primary and Secondary Education, the Ministry of Justice, and Home Affairs. Other statutory players intervene at certain levels, assisting preventive and remedial measures, including private sector players, Non-Governmental Organisations, Civil Society, and other voluntary organisations that play an imperative role in the protection of children in Zimbabwe. However, there is limited scope of coverage of social services due to fiscal constraints in Zimbabwe.

The aforementioned players, in collaboration with the community, attempt to ensure a safe and healthy environment for the development of children in their respective contexts. The Government of Zimbabwe strives to provide education, health, nutrition, registry, and legal services, among other imperatives. A study by Mwapaura (2022:3; World Bank, 2014) notes that the fluctuating social, economic, and political environment erodes the sustainability of Government interventions, rendering them inadequate. They further highlight that corruption, fiscal or budgetary limitations, policy inconsistencies, brain drain, lack of operational research, incapacity of DSD and the COVID-19 pandemic are among a myriad of obstacles in the provision of Children Protection Services in Zimbabwe. The resultant effect of this quagmire manifests in many forms of child abuse, neglect, and violence. Measures put in place point to the need to curb both direct and indirect causes of *streetism*. However, the implementation remains limited and fragmented (Mwapaura *et al*, 2022:3). On top of that, many street children have limited access to government services and programs as they chronically live and work on the streets. They are involved in car washing, selling of goods, waste picking for resale and other menial jobs (Ncube, 2015). Chikoko et al. (2019:38) corroborate this by purporting that street boys and girls are involved in perilous sexual behaviours like threesomes or oral sex for money, and they engage under the influence of drugs and substances in cities such as Harare. Taking cognizant of HIV/AIDS and other sexually transmitted diseases, there is a need for the provision of such services relevant to this end. The same can be written about drugs and substance abuse. The need for rehabilitation services targeted at this population is imperative. The aggregate of issues raised by this paper calls for more responsive mechanisms to foster child rights guided by the principles of non-discrimination, survival, and development of the child. Moreover, the socio-economic and political changes adversely affecting the general populace have negative externalities, which are more devastating on vulnerable groups.

Human Rights Approach

The chapter traversed the street children phenomenon using a human rights lens. According to the human rights perspective, everyone is born equal with rights and legal entitlements, street children included. Mwapaura and colleagues (2022:4) utilised the human rights perspective in their study on the challenges faced in the delivery of child protection services in Zimbabwe. They argue that the main thrust of the human rights perspective is the acknowledgement that unequal power relations and social exclusion prohibit people from their human rights and keep them in poverty. The human rights approach's relevance is imbued with the need to promote the rights and entitlements of marginalised groups, in this case, street children. As rights holders, street children must realise basic rights such as education, health, survival, and development, amongst others. On the other hand, the government is mandated with the provision and promotion of these rights and entitlements. The approach thus promotes critical understanding of the dynamics of power and their significant effect on children's welfare. In the context of the human rights approach, limited access to services or basic needs among street children in cities such as Harare unequivocally demonstrates a human rights abuse.

For street children to realise equal rights and legal entitlements, the human rights-based approach principles should be employed. Sida (2021) suggests that the perspective is anchored on participation, links to human rights, accountability, non-discrimination, and transparency. The approach promotes the participation of children in the formulation of programs and policies, and decision-making on issues related to their welfare. Participation breeds ownership of actions or decisions and gives a voice to the voiceless. The approach highlights the exploitation and violation faced by street children in Harare and the need to tailor-make remedies using their lived experiences.

According to Mwapaura (2022:4) also considers ways in which provisions from international legal instruments are utilised to advance child protection goals. The principle of accountability promotes the effectiveness of policy implementation. It acknowledges that children as rights-holders are legally entitled to question decisions and courses of action taken by their government. The government, in return, should put in place mechanisms and operating procedures that promote authority questioning and auditing mechanisms or obligations targeted at street children. The approach gives the power to hold the agency responsible for the lack of basic needs, such as shelter and food, for vulnerable children in Harare.

Non-discrimination is another principle of the human rights approach. The principle promotes access to children's related services regardless of the child's background. It encourages relevant stakeholders to 'leave no child behind'. To add on, empowerment refers to a social contract between the government and children towards the realisation of a child welfare state. The equilibrium point of this contract is reached when the government extends a platform for children to express themselves. On the other hand, transparency refers to the availability and accessibility of evidence-based information on street children-centred interventions, including statistics, research and policy instruments, among other relevant documents that contain authentic and credible information. The human rights approach promotes the use of empirical data to shed light on the adversities being faced by street children in Harare CBD, including their exploitation and violation, to inform policy.

The Government of Zimbabwe is a signatory to the UNCRC (1989), and the provisions of this international instrument trickle down to child protection policies and programs. According to Save the Children (2009), child protection systems must be anchored on human rights, and through this understanding, the vulnerability of street children takes a holistic approach and exposes the obstacles being faced in accessing mainstream services. Street children in cities such as Harare do not have access to basic needs such as education, health and food among a spectrum of rights.

Access to Services for Children in Street Situations

Children in street situations consist of runaways of abuse, delinquency, poverty, and peer pressure, and children on the move migrating across districts (UNICEF, 2001:1) or country borders using irregular migration corridors. Children on the move in street situations learn the language of the land to blend in and survive. Apart from those who traverse the streets, there are children born on the streets, usually adolescents, or products of generations of street families. Amongst them are those who solely work on the streets as a form of child labour. Children of caregivers with disabilities are forced onto the streets to support the family, whilst children *with* disabilities are used to solicit donations from well-wishers. For survival, children sell wares and consumables and provide informal services using proceeds for sustenance and mobility (Manjengwa, 2016:61), with some children attaining seasonal independent living in low-cost housing, particularly during cold and rainy seasons.

Young people and children on the streets have para-societies living in 'bases' amongst adopted informal 'families' (Hunter *et al*, 2017:2). The base is a pseudo-home fulfilling children's shelter, protection, and social needs. Once acculturated, the group provides protection, resources, and access to services such as shelter, nutrition, medical assistance, and other support through referral. Leaders emerge from natural selection, typically older members experienced on the streets, giving them social authority. Street leaders typically become street educators. Most bases are typically located close to open water sources; however, these tend to be unsafe. Children who live and work full time on the streets are typically primary school dropouts. Non-formal education (NFE) is offered by non-profit organisations coupled with access to safe and clean water, sanitation, and hygiene (WASH) facilities, and nutrition as a supplementary package. However, these facilities are not alternative care institutions, and children access them periodically, lowering retention in NFE programs.

Children in street situations suffer from lice, diarrheal diseases and infections related to poor hygiene and nutrition, and are susceptible to colds and flus due to exposure to the elements (UNICEF, 2001:17) without access to routine treatment. When pregnant, girls on the street access pre- and post-natal care from government hospitals where family planning is integrated into maternal care. However, these services are not consistently accessed, especially when there are no outward pregnancy complications. Law enforcement and the DSD periodically round up children on the street for cleanup programs and protection (Mhizha, 2016:48). Children are placed in residential and foster care, and training centres, the latter designated for children with behavioural issues. The process while in care involves profiling, care planning, family tracing and reunification. Rehabilitation is unstructured, determined by the resident superintendent. Additionally, there are high incidences of absconding with children relapsing onto the streets.

Children are vulnerable to risks whilst working and living on the streets, the most obvious being the risk of abuse and exploitation from other children and the public (Mhizha, 2016:50). Noted forms of abuse were physical, sexual, psychological, and financial. Whilst both boys and girls are exposed, girls have layered vulnerability, being subjected to sexual assault for money by other children and exposed to violence from their kin whilst they sleep at night. Protection is mostly sought from social networks in the streets rather than from law enforcement or the DSD; thus, cases go unreported, and child protection and justice services are not discharged. Socio-economic challenges have led to the erosion of the family as a primary safety net for children, leading to decreased household resilience and promotion of child labour as previously stated. Children work in all-weather conditions, and girls typically become involved in sex work, posing health and protection risks (UNICEF, 2001:24).

Children in street situations are also at risk of drugs and substance use as a means of escapism (Manjengwa, 2016:62). Drugs are self-manufactured or purchased for cheap on the streets, the most popular being glue and, more recently, illicit substances such as methamphetamine. Rehabilitation facilities are mostly privately run, high-cost and inaccessible to children in street situations. However, government-run institutions are available for drug and substance use rehabilitation, albeit with limited infrastructure and under-resourced. Training institutions are earmarked to provide rehabilitation support to children; however, they lack an evidence-based rehabilitation strategy/module, capacity building on illicit drugs and adequate equipment and infrastructure to provide aftercare for recovering children. Educational risks for children enrolled in school and working on the streets are a result of the number of hours spent after school meant for study, resulting in poor educational outcomes (Goodman, 2016:52). In addition, the gap widens for second chance education to those with prolonged periods out of school.

Children conflict with authorities whilst on the streets through raids, cleanup programs, or criminal activity (Schmidt, 2003:846). They risk arrest and detention along with adults due to a lack of identification, exposing them to violence, sexual exploitation, and abuse. This is further exacerbated by lack of coordination between law enforcement and the DSD inhibiting children from accessing Pre-Trial Diversion (PTD), a programme launched by the Ministry of Justice with support from UNICEF to provide children in conflict with the law with a child friendly criminal justice system which caters for their special needs by by-passing the adult court system, prioritizing rehabilitation for young offenders and protection them from violence.

During the COVID-19 pandemic, street interventions were reactionary. Whilst personal protective equipment was provided, children could not access previously accessible child-friendly service delivery sites such as drop-in centres closed during the national lockdown, although alternative care services were accessible through the DSD. Child protection surveillance was decreased, and informal trade was disrupted, prohibiting children's means of income. Children on the street were detained by law enforcement for noncompliance with isolation guidelines and delayed access to PTD due to a lack of civil registration (Better Care Network, The Alliance for Child Protection in Humanitarian Action, UNICEF, 2020). The case management of children in street situations has taken the perspective of the best interest of the child, overlooking child participation (NAP for OVC III, 2020), resulting in a one-size-fits-all approach involving profiling, family tracing and reunification without the exploration of independent living. In addition, Zimbabwe has experienced an exodus of professionals migrating to Europe, Australia, and North America, incapacitating the DSD to provide quality services for vulnerable children (Mwapaura et al, 2022:5).

Zimbabwe has made progress in developing legislative and policy frameworks to fulfil its obligations to safeguard children's rights as per ratification of the ACRWC. This includes child-centred plans in the National Development Strategy I (NDSI) and the NAP for OVC.

Within these strategies are social protection programs including the Food Deficit Mitigation Strategy (FDMS), Harmonised Social Cash Transfer (HSCT) and the Basic Education Assistance Module (BEAM), the latter envisioned to become free basic education for all. Zimbabwe has included a pillar on Child Labour in the NAP for OVC III's successor, deliberately programmed around children in street situations (NAP for OVC III Review Report, 2023) and validated the National Alternative Care Policy (2022) for children in need of care pending approval by cabinet. Further, the establishment of the NCMS involving multi-sectoral actors is a step towards supporting vulnerable groups, including children in street situations.

Moreover, Zimbabwe has established child parliamentarians to amplify the voice of children. Coordination structures such as the Working Party of Officials, committees and technical working groups in child protection, victim-friendly services, PTD and Risk Reduction all aim to provide specialised services for children (NAP for OVC III Review Report, 2023). Noting the emerging problem of illicit substances on the street, a task force with technical working groups focusing on prevention, prosecution and rehabilitation of children and youth has been established. An analysis of the social protection budget by UNICEF in 2021 showed an upward trend in spending by the government, although the MoPSLSW remains under-resourced.

These are notable gains at the national level in the pursuit of safeguarding and supporting service provision for children in street situations. However, there are micro and macro threats to these gains. Evidence shows that developed countries contribute more funding towards social protection and welfare as their economies grow. However, Zimbabwe is developing and faces inflation, exchange rate instability and limited economic growth. Moreover, shocks such as cyclones, floods, droughts, and disease outbreaks have further affected the country's economy. Geo-political instability has resulted in dwindling external funding as donors redirect funds towards in-country social protection programs, and support Western crises such as the Ukraine saga, amongst others. The child protection sector purse has shrunk significantly, inhibiting the capacity to support children.

A Human Rights Lens on Street Children's Access to Services

Children in street situations are exposed to layered vulnerabilities, including child labour, sexual exploitation, and abuse. Their circumstances impede them from accessing basic services such as health, education, protection, justice, and civil registration, amongst others, robbing them of their rights to survival and development, name and nationality, protection from abuse and child labour, amongst other protections and rights. Children in street situations do not enjoy the protection of the family and parental care as a primary safety net. Thus, the state and development actors need to support children in street situations to ensure access to services and establish sustainable solutions. It is important to outline notable challenges in service provision that prohibit children from enjoying their rights and their nature, leading to informed recommendations.

Education, Health, Family Planning and SRHR

The human rights approach pushes for the acknowledgement of power relations and their impact on exclusion. Findings outlined that education is inaccessible for children living on the streets, mostly made up of school dropouts and children who have never been to school. Factors vary, but the most common are families' inability to enrol and retain children in school. Further, children on the street are left behind as education programs are not designed to bridge the gap for children with prolonged periods and who have never been to school. Marginalised rural schools are under-resourced to establish NFE programs, which would otherwise prevent streetism and support reunified families. The Zimbabwean government has a vision to provide free basic education for all; however, this has not been operationalised due to a lack of funding. The current BEAM manages to support children in vulnerable circumstances; however, the program benefits children in the community as community-based committees influence beneficiary selection. This is systematic exclusion, and the governments and development actors should address these discriminatory practices and ensure that all marginalised groups are included in education interventions as is their right.

Furthermore, there is an unjust distribution of resources in the health sector, as systems strengthening has been focused on communities, leaving street societies behind. The health sector has established Community Health Workers (CHWs), foot soldiers of the MoHCC who conduct community health education, mobilisation, information dissemination, and case management. Additionally, health education is largely integrated into service provision for efficacy, excluding children in street situations who do not access routine health services. Whilst children on the streets report awareness of health care services, their information is largely from untrained, informal street educators. These inequalities are glaring, and measures must be taken to afford children in street situations the same liberties as children in the community when accessing healthcare. Illicit drugs and substance use are a problem on the streets. There are limited to no rehabilitation facilities readily accessible to children in street situations, nor do front-line workers have the know-how and equipment to provide adequate rehabilitation. Facilities are mostly privately owned, thus expensive, and children are discriminated against based on affordability. Drug and substance use are a gateway to delinquency, sexual exploitation, and abuse, and the ACRWC implores governments to protect children from substance use. Children in street situations are entitled to access to rehabilitation, care, and support for these reasons.

Mental Health, Psychosocial Support and Child protection and/or Welfare

Children are entitled to the best attainable mental health. Community volunteers and front-line workers in health, education and child protection sectors have been trained in mental health and psychosocial support (MHPSS), psychological first aid, and basic counselling. However, these interventions have largely been focused on children in the community and in alternative care. Focus group discussions showed that children heavily rely on friendships for emotional support. They report a sense of isolation alleviated by peer support. Whilst these are coping mechanisms and means to achieve social networks and bonds outside of the family, this support is given from an untrained perspective. From a human rights perspective, MHPSS must be equitably practised, including marginalised groups in most need of care, such as children in street situations, given the complex challenges and risks faced affecting their mental health. Moreover, mental health instability contributes to behavioural issues such as substance use, delinquency and exploitation and abuse of others, thus should be prioritised. Additionally, MHPSS promotes independent living, further positioning children to reach their full potential.

The NCMS facilitates effective identification, referral, service provision and follow-up support of child protection and welfare cases. Through this system, children in street situations have received alternative care services. Whilst children are involved in care planning as per the Alternative Care Policy, children do not have the liberty to adequately claim their rights, that is, exploration of technical and vocational education training (TVET) and independent living, for example, as possible care plan alternatives. The end goal is almost always family tracing and reunification. This is a violation of the human rights approach, as children must be empowered to express themselves for meaningful participation and sustainable solutions. Community Childcare Workers (CCWs) are community-based cadres who identify, refer and support service delivery for children in the NCMS. However, as previously noted, children have their societal structures on the streets and street educators are not recognised in the NCMS. This programmatic gap marginalises children in street situations in the NCMS and leads to systematic exclusion.

A mindset shift is critical to redress these discriminatory outlooks that lead to unjust biases in development interventions. Access to justice for children in street situations is inconsistent. The DSD and specialised justice CSOs have the mandate to monitor corrections and detention centres to identify children, albeit these activities are subject to the availability of funding. Children fall through the cracks if not identified, exposing them to violence in detention with adults. This violates children's rights with regard to accessing the. Representation from probation officers and lawyers also positions children to claim their rights in accordance with established international law and guidance on child rights.

Social Protection and Civil Registration

The government funds social protection programs to alleviate the effects of poverty on the most vulnerable households. A key tenet of the human rights approach is the need to interrogate inequalities that lie at the core of development problems and social exclusion.

Children in street situations have not typically benefited from social protection programs, as household selection and verification processes are community-based. Orphans and Vulnerable Children registers maintained at the village level are used as primary data sources for identifying and verifying vulnerable households, resulting in exclusion errors for children living on the streets, as they do not appear on vulnerability registers, especially when they have lived in the streets for prolonged periods. In addition, these programs are underfunded and do not include all marginalised groups. Further, urban areas where children living on the streets are not typically selected for social protection programs. This is an area which requires recourse as it unjustly excludes the most vulnerable of children, unable to represent themselves and have their voices heard to benefit from poverty reduction programs.

The ACRWC states that children have a right to an identity and countries must eliminate barriers to civil registration and discriminatory citizenship provisions that promote statelessness. Most children on the street do not have a form of identification and express the desire for civil registration for legitimacy and to break barriers to employment. Civil registration also positions children to participate in socio-political discourse. Children must be provided the opportunity to hold the Government accountable and interrogate the Registrar's mechanisms and standard operating procedures, identifying barriers to access to civil registration for children in street situations for redress of discriminatory procedures and practices. This includes administrative fees and bottlenecks for foreign nationals.

Disability and Child Participation

Children with disabilities (CWD) have a right to special measures of protection, independent living, and social inclusion. There is a glaring gap when it comes to CWD on the streets as they do not have access to aides, rehabilitation, care and MHPSS related to their condition. The government has a Disability Fund coordinated by a permanent Disability Desk within the DSD. However, disability is capital-intensive as it requires specialised infrastructure, diagnostic and rehabilitation equipment and personnel. Based on this, the Disability Fund has been stretched. There are no known development partners who focus on supporting CWD on the streets. This is an underrepresented, marginalised group with limited power to influence decisions, and so limited resources are funnelled towards the development of CWD, particularly those on the streets.

The United Nations states that nations must position children as rights-holders, to claim their rights by empowering them to express themselves and hold government and development actors accountable, corresponding to established international law and guidelines which governments have ratified. To this end, various child participation platforms have been established, including child-led child protection committees (CLCPCs), child advisory boards (CABs) and junior parliamentarians. These committees and boards are typically established in wards, building up to the national level, usually selecting the best and brightest with explicit talent. Children in street situations are marginalised and underrepresented in these groups as they are not in communities and schools where child advocacy is focused. Resultantly, their issues remain unheard, and they continue to be excluded from programming, policy, and national strategies for vulnerable children. Another aspect in which children are excluded from participation is in research, as most research methodologies for national studies and surveys sample households, completely missing children in street situations. This brings into question the validity of statistics and contributes to the chronic lack of information around children on the streets, resulting in inequitable distribution of resources. Recourse must be taken from these discriminatory research methodologies, as all children have a right to be heard and not left behind.

Recommendations

Several recommendations for the government, multi-lateral agencies, international nonprofit organisations, civil society, community, and faith-based organisations should emphasized. Whilst Zimbabwe has been cited as an example, themes resonated in studies of children in street situations across Africa in Kenya, Uganda, Ghana, the Democratic Republic of Congo, South Africa, and Ethiopia. Therefore, recommendations may apply to country contexts outside of Zimbabwe. Firstly, there is need to increase financing for DSD. Countries with less fiscal capacity spend less on social welfare, likely due to their limited ability to raise revenue through taxation. A benchmark for spending on social welfare has not been determined for best practice, and budget processes and budgeting capacities may be a factor that relates to low funding on social welfare. The government needs to capacitate Social Development personnel to budget according to caseloads, continuum of care, social welfare and protection program needs, human resources, and infrastructural development, in addition to the ability to lobby for proposed budgets.

Additionally, the government should have a benchmark of commitment to funding towards social development as MoPSE commits 10% of the fiscus towards ECD financing as per the Tashkent Agreement. Funding of social protection and welfare programs will improve the DSD's ability to provide a continuum of care for children in street situations, and outreach and community-based service provision programs across sectors should be resourced to absorb children in street situations. Further, preventative, and early intervention youth development, economic strengthening and family preservation programs should be considered as funding priorities, as well as drug and substance use rehabilitation infrastructural development, equipment, and personnel to promote family integration and independent living. The Disability Fund must be equitably resourced based on its cross-sectoral nature, allowing the DSD to coordinate services for CWD. Zimbabwe has experienced a massive brain drain of social workers, contributing to a gaping deficit in the social work workforce due to a lack of incentivisation. Thus, financing around human resources is critical to retain social workers and attract an additional workforce to reduce caseload ratios and provide quality services to children.

Second, case management of children in street situations should be strengthened. Whilst the DSD employs licensed social workers, capacity building is required on care work for children in street situations, given their unique complexities. Social workers must be knowledgeable about their needs, developmental experiences, and case management apart from other children in need of care. Social workers must promote child participation in care planning for children in street situations exploring adaptable alternatives that combine the perspectives of professionals and the child's own needs assessment which include exploration of Technical and Vocational Education and Training (TVET) combined with literacy, numeracy and life skills where reintegration into formal schooling is not feasible nor desirable to the child. All children in street situations must have individualised assessments, care, and development tracking plans. An Alternative Care Panel may be established to discuss complex cases with experts. Children in street situations already have a para-society mirroring that of community living. It is beneficial for the DSD to integrate these structures into the NCMS, thereby improving data around children on the streets, service uptake, information dissemination, child participation, and engagement. Caregivers in residential care facilities and foster care homes should be capacitated to cope with handling challenging behaviour when caring for children in street situations.

Third, there should clear integration strategies for children in street situations in development and social protection programs. The DSD must consider mechanisms for the inclusion of children in street situations in OVC registers. This will facilitate inclusion when identifying beneficiaries of social protection programs. Basic services should be popularised amongst children in street situations, and mechanisms developed to ensure that they have access to them. Sectoral social services such as health, HIV, Sexual Gender-Based Violence, SRHR, family planning, substance use, civil registration, justice, education and NFE must include children in street situations amongst their marginalised target groups and not only community, school, and facility-based interventions. Social protection programs must also be disability inclusive, deliberately targeting households led by caregivers with disabilities as a mechanism to prevent child labour and family separation.

Fourth, the development of national strategies for children in street situations, drawing lessons from Uganda and South Africa, highlights the importance of context-specific, rights-based approaches to addressing the complex needs of these vulnerable children. Durable solutions are a critical tool to address the problem of child trafficking. Uganda and South Africa are countries that have developed national strategies for the children in street situations involving the provision of TVET and apprenticeships, promoting technology-based innovations in education and training to develop employable skills and entrepreneurial capabilities, building on their existing enterprising nature. Due to inaccessible startup capital, children must be supported with startup packages. Interventions should be gender and disability inclusive. This may be achieved through vertical expansion of BEAM, extending from formal education, and Public-Private Partnerships. The government may support drop-in centres and places of safety as platforms for children to access services without compromising the children's independence, as evidence has shown that children in street situations need long-term contact before family reunification.

Family disintegration has been a key push factor for child streetism. Household economic strengthening (HES) coupled with social protection programs for families at risk of separation are critical family preservation tools. The DSD should fully operationalise its strategies to address child labour and implement parenting education and support programs. Specialised support is also critical for children with mental health challenges and disabilities, substance users, young mothers and children involved in sex work, as these are factors that contribute to relapse. Further, the DSD must develop and implement an evidence-based national Rehabilitation Strategy to ensure the provision of quality rehabilitation services for children in street situations.

Further, there is a need to enhance coordination around children in street situations. Coordination of the various moving parts of the national strategy to support children in street situations is critical and may be achieved through a Technical Working Group, National Child Protection Committee or Working Party of Officials. The coordinating body must include stakeholders from Health, Education, Justice, Home Affairs, Social Development, Labour, local government, civil society and multilateral agencies, and the private sector. Representatives of children should also have a direct link to this group to ensure that their issues are adequately and correctly represented.

The importance of establishing child participation for children in street situations in policy and legislation should not be overlooked. Representation in policy and legislation facilitates systemic change for children in street situations. The formation of representative groups comprised of children in street situations is encouraged to create forums for children to articulate their problems and craft their solutions. These should find fair and transparent representation in existing CLCPCs, CABs and junior parliamentary groups to ensure representation of their issues at the national level. Adult-led groups such as the National Protection Committee and Parliamentarians must request child-led policy briefs and actively participate in engagements with child-led groups to influence their decision-making.

Children in street situations should also be integrated into emergency preparedness, response, and recovery. Due to the COVID-19 pandemic and climatic crises in recent years, Zimbabwe has developed mechanisms to manage disasters coordinated by the Civil Protection Unit. Children in street situations must be integrated into Child Protection in Emergencies (CPiE). Drop-in centres should be classified as essential service providers in emergencies for continuity of alternative care, health, WASH, protection, education, and nutrition information and services. Law enforcement must not detain children in street situations for noncompliance with emergency mitigation measures and instead coordinate with the DSD to provide access to alternative care and referral to support services. Disaster Risk Reduction Plans should include the rescue, provision of emergency support, resettlement and rehabilitation of children in street situations.

The inclusion of development plans for children in street situations in the city council development plans is equally important. Children are typically attracted to urban cities for street living due to the perceived opportunities. Although the DSD is the custodian of children, the City Council has a role to play in the maintenance of public WASH facilities as an essential service for access to clean WASH facilities for the public, including children in street situations. The Urban Council Act makes provisions for 'regulation and licensing of hawkers and street vendors and persons who employ or engage hawkers or street vendors as agents'. Thus, the City Council has the mandate to support the regularisation of businesses run by adolescents working on the streets and the provision of designated, accessible marketplaces.

In the process, the private sector is an important partner in achieving social development goals. Social Cooperative Responsibility (SCR) resources must be channelled towards supporting marginalised groups. The largest number of children in street situations is in capital cities, where most companies are headquartered, posing an opportunity. Whilst financial contributions are necessary, companies may be positioned for in-kind support, creating space for youth apprenticeships and on-the-job training, market linkages, value chain analyses, information, communication and technology, amongst other expertise, as an incentive to contribute in an economic climate where capital contributions may not be feasible.

Finally, monitoring and evaluation of children in street situations should be strengthened. Monitoring and evaluation around children in street situations has been weak, evidenced by a lack of definitive qualitative and quantitative street data accessible to stakeholders. By tapping into the resource of street structures, the DSD has a potential entry point to improve data flow. Status analysis studies should be resourced to provide disaggregated data by geography, vulnerability groups, educational levels, duration on the streets and so on for evidence-based decision making, investment and advocacy. Moreover, the inclusion of children in street situations in research such as national statistics, operational research, assessments, and evaluations is critical for adequate planning. On a global scale, Ward (2007) developed a comprehensive set of prevention, early intervention, protection, and reintegration indicators for children living and working in the street. The MoPSLSW and development actors must include these indicators within their results framework, enabling reporting on a global level on the status of children in street situations. Further, countries must use this evidence to report on the status of children, including those in street situations, to the ACRWC Committee to track milestones in improving the status of children contributing to related Sustainable Development Goals.

Conclusion

Children in street situations across the continent have commonalities when it comes to themes regarding access to services. This marginalised group is largely denied their rights of access to basic services, care and support, and there is evidence of the unjust distribution of power, inequitable allocation of development resources and disempowerment of children in street situations to claim their rights. Children are systematically excluded from development programs, research, and policy dialogue, begging the need for development actors to adopt inclusive mechanisms that leave no one behind. Further, para-societies on the streets are generally unrecognised as mechanisms for change. The COVID-19 pandemic, disease outbreaks and climatic hazards such as Cyclone Idai, whilst leading to emergency preparedness, response, and recovery planning, have largely failed to provide sustainable solutions for children living on the streets. Although complex, comprehensive strategies for children in street situations are critical if the issue of homelessness amongst children is to be resolved.

References

Better Care Network, The Alliance for Child Protection in Humanitarian Action & UNICEF 2020, *Protection of Children During the COVID 19 pandemic*, Available at: https://www.unicef.org/sites/default/files/2020-05/COVID-19-Alternative-Care-Technical-Note.pdf [Accessed 10 June 2023].

Chikoko, W., Muzvidziwa, V.N., Ruparanganda, W. & Chikoko, E. 2019, 'Early sexual debut and substance abuse among street children of Harare Central Business District, Zimbabwe', *African Journal of Social Work*, vol. 9, no. 1, pp. 79-87.

Chikoko, W., Zvokuomba, K., Mwapaura, K. & Nyabeze, K. 2021, '"Three some" and substance abuse among street children of the Harare Central Business District, Zimbabwe', *Journal of Development Administration*, vol. 6, no. 2, pp. 52-60.

Shephard, D.D. 2014, Nonformal education for improving educational outcomes for street children and street youth in developing countries: A systematic review, *International Journal of Social Welfare*, vol. 23, no. 4, pp. 349-361.

Mbokazi, D.D. 2022, The role of public administration in serving children living in and off the streets of Durban, *African Journal of Public Affairs*, vol. 13, no. 6, pp. 1-15.

Mulugeta, E. 2005, 'Working on the Streets to Cope with Childhood Poverty: Problems and Resilience of Working Children in Addis Ababa', *Journal of Ethiopian Studies*, vol. 38, no. 1/2, pp. 151–173.

Sitienei, E.C. & Pillay, J. 2018, 'Life Experiences of Children Living on Streets in Kenya: From the Pot into the Fire', *Journal of Child & Adolescent Trauma*, vol. 12, no. 2, pp. 201–209.

Ogan, E.P. 2021, 'Dynamics of Street Children in Africa'. Available at: https://www.researchgate.net/publication/348539465_DYNAMICS_OF_STREET_CHILDREN_IN_AFRICA [2 May 2023]

African Committee of Experts on the Rights and Welfare of the Child 2021, *Report of the Thirty Eighth Ordinary Session Videoconference (3-4 Feb.)*, Addis Ababa.

Hunter, J., van Blerk, L. & Shand, W. 2018a, 'Building Assets on the Streets: Street Children and Youth in Three African Cities', University of Dundee.

Hunter, J., van Blerk, L. & Shand, W. 2018b, 'Friendship on the Streets: Street Children and Youth in Three African Cities', University of Dundee. Available at: https://www.streetchildren.org/resources/growing-up-on-the-streets-briefing-paper-13-friendship-on-the-streets-street-children-and-youth-in-three-african-cities/ [2 March 2023]

Hunter, J., van Blerk, L. & Shand, W. 2017, 'Play on the Streets: Street Children and Youth in Three African Cities', University of Dundee. Available at: https://www.researchgate.net/publication/320870305_Briefing_Paper_10_Play_on_the_Streets_Street_Children_and_Youth_in_Three_African_Cities_August_2017 [2 June 2023]

Hunter, J. & van Blerk, L. 2017, 'Resilience on the Streets: Street Children and Youth in Three African Cities', University of Dundee. Available at: https://www.streetchildren.org/wp-content/uploads/2018/01/Briefing-Paper-11-Resilience-on-the-Streets-Street-Children-and-Youth-in-Three-African-Cities.pdf [2 May 2023]

Government of Uganda, Ministry of Gender, Labour and Social Development 2020, *National Child Policy*, [National policy]. Available at: https://www.mglsd.go.ug/wp-content/uploads/2023/04/National-Child-Policy-2020.pdf [2 July 2023]

Government of Zimbabwe 2001a, *Children's Act (Chapter 5:06)*, Government Printers.

Government of Zimbabwe 2013, *Constitution of Zimbabwe Amendment No. 20*, Government Printers.

Government of Zimbabwe 2001b, *The Social Workers Act (Chapter 27:21)*, Government Printers.

Manjengwa, J., Matema, C., Tirivanhu, D. & Tizora, R. 2016, 'Deprivation among children living and working on the streets of Harare', *Development Southern Africa*, vol. 33, no. 1, pp. 53–66.

Krah, E., Hunter, J., van Blerk, L. & Shand, W. 2016, 'Spirituality on the Streets: Findings from Participatory Research with Street Children and Youth in Three African Cities', University of Dundee. Available at: https://www.streetchildren.org/resources/growing-up-on-the-streets-briefing-paper-9-spirituality-on-the-streets-findings-from-participatory-research-with-street-children-and-youth-in-three-african-cities/ [2 June 2023]

Mwapaura, K., Chikoko, W., Nyabeze, K., Kabonga, I. & Zvokuomba, K. 2022, 'Provision of child protection services in Zimbabwe: Review of the human rights perspective', *Cogent Social Sciences*, vol. 8, no. 1.

Mwapaura, K., Magavude, T., Munyanyi, S., Rufurwokuda, A. & Chisosa, T. 2022, 'The adversities in the lives of street children with disabilities during the COVID-19 pandemic: The case of Masvingo, Zimbabwe', *Journal of Social Issues in Non Communicable Conditions & Disability*, vol. 1, no. 1, pp. 1–10.

Myburgh, C., Moolla, A. & Poggenpoel, M. 2015, 'The lived experiences of children living on the streets of Hillbrow', *Curationis*, vol. 38, no. 1, pp. 1520.

Ochola, L. & Dzikus, A. 2000, 'Street children and gangs in African cities: Guidelines for local authorities', *Urban Management Programme Working Paper Series*, no. 18. Available at: https://unhabitat.org/street-children-and-gangs-in-african-cities-guidelines-to-local-authorities [2 May 2023].

Republic of South Africa, Department of Social Development 2010, *Strategy and Guidelines for Children Living and Working in the Streets*, Pretoria: Department of Social Development. Available at: https://www.gov.za/sites/default/files/gcis_document/201409/strategyandguidelineschildrenlivingworkinginthestreets50.pdf [2 May 2023].

Kakuru, R., Byaruhanga Rukooko, A. & Tusabe, G. 2018, 'Social protection mechanisms for children living on the streets: Perspectives from Uganda', *Journal of Social Distress and the Homeless*, vol. 27, no. 1, pp. 44-53.

Mhizha, S., Tandire, J., Muromo, T. & Matika, M. 2016, 'Ecological self-image and behaviours for children living on the streets of Harare', *Development Southern Africa*, vol. 33, no. 1, pp. 39–52.

Goodman, M.L., Martinez, K., Keiser, P.H., Gitari, S. & Seidel, S.E. 2016, 'Why do Kenyan children live on the streets? Evidence from cross sections of semi-rural maternal caregivers', *Child Abuse & Neglect*, vol. 51, pp. 257-266.

Russell, W. & Stenning, A. 2020, 'Beyond active travel: children, play and community on streets during and after the coronavirus lockdown', *Cities & Health*, vol. 4, no. sup1, pp. S186-S195.

West, A. 2003, 'At the margins: Street children in the Asia-Pacific region', *Asia Development Bank Working Paper*.

ZimStat 2018, *Poverty, Income, Consumption and Expenditure Survey 2017 Report*, [Research report]. Available at: https://catalog.ihsn.org/catalog/9250/download/92944 [2 March 2023]

Save the Children 2006, *Child rights programming: How to apply rights based approaches to programming*, Available at: https://resourcecentre.savethechildren.net/document/child-rights-programming-how-apply-rights-based-approaches-programming/ [Accessed 12 April 2023].

Sida 2021, 'Human rights based approach', Available at: https://www.sida.se/en/for-partners/methods-materials/humanrights-based-approach [Accessed 10 August 2023].

UNICEF 2001, *A Situation Analysis of Orphans and Other Vulnerable Children and Adolescents in Zimbabwe*, Harare: UNICEF, [Brief]. Available at: https://sid-inico.usal.es/idocs/F8/FDO7002/orphans.pdf [Accessed 10 August 2023].

UNICEF 2021, *Social Protection Budget Brief, Zimbabwe*, [Brief]. Available at: https://www.unicef.org/zimbabwe/media/7486/file/Zimbabwe-Social-Protection-Budget-Brief-2021.pdf [Accessed 10 August 2023].

United Nations 2020, *Policy Brief: The Impact of COVID-19 on Children*, [Brief]. Available at: https://unsdg.un.org/resources/policy-brief-impact-covid-19-children [Accessed 10 August 2023].

Volpi, E. 2002, *Street Children: Promising Practices and Approaches*, The World Bank Working Paper, Washington, DC.

Chapter Twelve
Child Sexual Abuse in Zimbabwe: A Case of Street Children of the Harare Central Business District

Witness Chikoko

Introduction

Child sexual abuse is a persistent global problem. Although there is no consensus on the definition of child sexual abuse, Muridzo (2014:49) defines child sexual abuse as "an act perpetrated by an adult or a more knowledgeable child on a child, for the perpetrator's sexual gratification, to which the child is unable to give consent due to unequal power in the relationship." Child sexual abuse involves sexual gratification that ranges from fondling the child's sexual or private parts to attempted or actual penetration. Child sexual abuse also includes sexual behaviours such as child pornography, voyeurism and exposure among others. Incest involving children is another form of child sexual abuse (Ndhlovu and Mfoafo-M'Carthy, 2022). Trafficking of children for sexual exploitation is also considered a form of child abuse, violence and exploitation (Jera, 2019). Child sexual abuse is on the increase in Latin America, Africa, Asia Pacific, among others (Chitereka, 2010; Muridzo, 2017). In a study in Zimbabwe, Rumble and colleagues (2015) observed that one-third of girls and one in every ten boys are victims or survivors of child sexual abuse before they reach the age of 18 years. Child sexual abuse is also more pronounced among vulnerable children.

Street children are more vulnerable to child sexual abuse (Atkinson-Shepherd, 2016; Kaiser and Sinanan, 2020; Chikoko, 2014; 2017; Sewpaul et al, 2012; Mhizha, 2010; Ruparanganda, 2008; Wakatama, 2007). The vulnerability of girls on the streets to sexual abuse is a result of many factors. In India, girls on the streets have multilayered vulnerability to sexual abuse as they are females on the streets with very few forms of protection, and also, they are socialised to be sexually subservient to males (Bhattacharya and Nair, 2014). An estimate of twenty-five per cent of street boys of Harare have been victims or survivors of violence and sexual abuse (Manjengwa et al, 2016).

In Bangladesh, both street boys and girls are vulnerable to sexual abuse, violence and exploitation, with the problem being more pronounced among street girls (Kaiser and Sinanan, 2020). Most street girls in Bangladesh are survivors or victims of sexual abuse perpetrated by their peers, homeless men, law enforcement agents, male staff members of public utilities, among others (Kaiser and Sinanan, 2020). Given the scant literature on the nature and magnitude of child sexual abuse among street children of the Harare Central Business District, Zimbabwe, this chapter problematises the nature and magnitude of child sexual abuse, violence and exploitation among the street children.

The Empowerment Theory

The word empowerment has been defined by Adams (2003:8), as 'how individuals, groups, and communities become able to take control of their circumstances to achieve their own goals, thereby being able to work towards helping themselves and others to maximise the quality of their lives'. In social work, the empowerment theory has also been defined by Adams, (2003:8) as, 'concerned with how people may gain collective control over their lives to achieve their interests as a group and a method by which social workers seek to enhance the power of people who lack it'. Empowerment is very important as social workers have ethical responsibilities to respect and promote clients' right to self-determination, pursuit of life purpose and goals (Turner and Maschi, 2015). Empowerment is a rationalistic approach in the sense that it is linked with humanistic theory, humanistic and existential theory and practice (Adams, 2003). It emphasises self-knowledge, accepting that people can control their own lives by rational and cognitive means (Adams, 2003). In addition, social workers have an ethical responsibility to increase choices and opportunities for community, collective and political empowerment, especially among vulnerable individuals and groups (Turner and Maschi, 2015).

The empowerment theory is also explained in the context that the environment can be changed directly in favour of the service user (Adams, 2003). For example, the social environment in the name of structures and institutions on the streets has not been flexible enough to prevent and protect street children from child sexual abuse, violence and exploitation. The empowerment theory includes a wide range of principles such as social justice, human rights, equality, inclusivity, and understanding of oppression among others (Turner and Maschi, 2015).

Utilising the empowerment theory, sexual abuse, violence, and exploitation among the street children in Zimbabwe demonstrate the vulnerabilities of these children. The empowerment theory supposes that victims of sexual abuse are less empowered. Therefore, the street children are not empowered to control their own lives by rational and cognitive means. It illustrates that, as a result of the sexual behaviours of the street children, they are part of the vulnerable members of the Zimbabwean society and beyond. Sexual abuse, violence and exploitation among the street children are at variance with the key principles of the empowerment theory, such as human rights, social justice, equality, among others.

Understanding the Child Sexual Abuse Plight in Zimbabwe

Forms of child sexual abuse in Zimbabwe include unprotected sex, sodomy, pornography, oral sex, early sexual debut, commercial sex, intergenerational sex, multiple sexual relationships, and masturbation, among others.

Unprotected Sex and Masturbation

Unprotected sex is one of the common sexual behaviours among the street children of the Harare Central Business District (Chikoko, 2017; Mhizha, 2010; Ruparanganda, 2008; Wakatama, 2007). Some of the major reasons account for unprotected sex among these children include misuse of substances, limited access to contraceptives such as condoms, and negative attitudes towards condom use. Some street children practised unprotected sex as this is regarded as more enjoyable compared to the one in a condom. The adolescent street girls who practice commercial sex work also engage in unprotected sex, known as *nyoro* in Shoma (Chikoko, 2014). The girls prefer *nyoro* (unprotected sex) as it attracts more rewards. *Nyoro* (unprotected sex) has been associated with better rewards or prices for the adolescent street girls who engage in commercial sex work.

In another study, Mhizha (2010) observed that street children of the Harare Central Business District engaged in unprotected sex as a result of negative attitudes towards condom use. The street children would rather sell condoms that they would have been given at the Drop-in Centre to raise money for beer, food, among others. After selling the condoms, they subsequently engage in unprotected sex (Mhizha, 2010; Wakatama, 2007). Most street children engage in *nyoro* (unprotected sex) as a result of limited access to contraceptives. The adolescent street children face stigma and discrimination when accessing reproductive health services at local clinics, as they are considered people of no fixed abode (Ruparanganda 2008). The intricate relationship between unprotected sex and substance abuse among the street children. Some of the street children who engage in unprotected sex abuse psycho active substances to cope with the traumatic experiences associated with unprotected sex (Chikoko, 2017).

Most street children engage in masturbation, which is referred to as *gwetengwe* (Mhizha and Muromo, 2013; Ruparanganda, 2008). One against five is also another name for masturbation among the adolescent street children (Chikoko, 2017; 2019). The street children engage in competition on who ejaculates faster than the other. Some of the street children are filmed while masturbating. The street children would be filmed when engaging in a competition of masturbation. After doing the filming of masturbation, they are paid some money by the pedophiles. There is an intricate relationship between substance abuse and masturbation among the street children.

Multiple Sexual Relationships and Intergenerational sex

The adolescent street girls of the Harare Central Business District who engage in multiple sexual relationships refer to themselves as *poto dzemaratsa*, which means something that is shared generously and frequently (Mhizha, 2010). Such adolescent girls also had several sexual partners on the streets. Multiple sexual relationships are not only confined to adolescent street girls but also to their male counterparts. The adolescent street boys also engaged in various episodes of multiple sexual relationships. Some of their sexual partners were both from the mainstream society and those staying, living and working on the streets. Chikoko (2017) has noted a close relationship between substance abuse and multiple sexual relationships among adolescent street children.

The adolescent street children engage in sex with sugar mummies or daddies (Mella, 2012; Ruparanganda, 2008; Wakatama, 2007; Mhizha, 2010). Ruparanganda (2008) observed that some of the adolescent street girls had relationships with sugar daddies in exchange for expensive gifts, money, among others. As a result of intergenerational sex, some of the adolescent street children can sustain their lives. Rather, intergenerational sex is part of their livelihood strategies (Ruparanganda, 2008). There is a close relationship between intergenerational sex and substance abuse among adolescent street children. Some adolescent street children misuse psycho active substances to manage traumatic experiences associated with intergenerational sex (Chikoko, 2017). Some of the psycho active substances include *chitongo* (a highly intoxicating substance), *chamba* (cannabis) and *bhurongo* (Cough syrup), among others. Conversely, some adolescent street children engage in substance abuse, such as aphrodisiacs, to manage the demanding nature associated with intergenerational sex among others (Chikoko, 2017). Some of the aphrodisiac substances include *vuka vuka, muchemedza mbuya, muvhomora kwaedza*, seven hours, among others.

Commercial Sex

Commercial sex work is one of the common sexual abuses among adolescent street children of Harare Central Business District (Bourdillon, 1991, 1993 and 1995; Mhizha, 2010; Wakatama, 2007; Ruparanganda, 2008; Rurevo and Bourdillon, 2003). *Huruwork* is a term that refers to commercial sex work among adolescent street girls. The adolescent street girls who engage in commercial sex work identify themselves as *majoki* or *mahure*, which means prostitutes (Mhizha, 2010). There are multiple and varied reasons why adolescent street girls engage in commercial or transactional sex. Some of them include lack of employment opportunities, poverty, failed child marriages, peer pressure, autonomy or freedom through sex work, obstacles to education, among others (Chikoko *et al*, 2019).

The adolescent street children who engage in commercial or transactional sex work use traditional medicines to enhance their work (Chikoko, 2019). Some of the traditional medicines used include *guchu, Makoko emabanana, mudzora, mushonga wejeko, mudhonza nzeve, muputa, mudiwa diwa, mushonga weluck, mugeza chiereko, mudzinga mhepo,* among others (Chikoko et al, 2019). However, some of such traditional medicines have negative side effects on these adolescent girls. For example, *mudzora* has been associated with several negative effects, including exposure to cervical cancer, dry sex leading to contracting sexually transmitted diseases, including HIV and AIDS (Chikoko *et al*, 2019; Ruparanganda, 2009).

Some adolescent street girls often patronise nightclubs to solicit clients for sex (Chikoko, 2014, 2017; Mhizha, 2010). Some of the nightclubs include AKIZ, Big Apple, Lizzie, Super label, among others (Chikoko, 2014, 2017). The adolescent street girls raise money for survival through *kuaina* (erotic dancing), short time or *zvigwishu* or *pungwe* among others (Chikoko, 2014, 2017). There are businessmen around the Harare Central Business District who hire adolescent street girls for sex. The adolescent street girls supplement their income with sex for food and, in certain instances, cash from male clients (Rurevo and Bourdillon, 2003). There is a close relationship between commercial sex work and substance abuse among adolescent street girls.

Some of the adolescent street girls exchange sex for drugs (Chikoko *et al*, 2020). They exchanged sex for drugs with drug lords selling the substances around the streets (Chikoko et al, 2020). Some of the adolescent street girls were addicted to drugs to the extent that they would not function as normal beings without taking on substances such as cannabis (Chikoko *et al*, 2020). In circumstances where they did not have money to buy the intoxicating substances, they would offer sex to the drug lords in exchange for substances (Chikoko et al, 2020).

Early Sexual Debut and Oral sex

Early sexual debut is one of the forms of sexual abuse or violence common among the street children of the Harare Central Business District (Ruparanganda, 2008). Street children as young as eight (8) years old engage in sexual intercourse. There is also an intricate relationship between substance abuse and early sexual debut among the street children. Some adolescent street girls are initiated into sex when they are highly intoxicated with substances such as cannabis, among others. In his study, Chikoko (2019) cited a certain girl who lost her virginity after she had taken some highly intoxicating substances with her friends and boys' friends. On the other hand, there are cases where some of the street children who had early sexual initiation had to rely on or cope through abusing some intoxicating substances.

Oral sex is another form of sexual abuse or violence among street children. Oral sex is known as a blow job among street children and sex workers. Oral sex is common among the street children who practice commercial sex work (Chikoko, 2014; 2017). Some of the clients of the street children who engage in commercial sex work prefer oral sex, particularly white people or foreigners. Thus, there is a close relationship between oral sex and substance abuse among the street children. To facilitate oral sex, some of the adolescent street children take on substances such as *amarula* (Chikoko, 2017).

Forced Sex/Rape

Forced sex or rape is a reality among the street children of the Harare Central Business District (Wakatama, 2007; Ruparanganda, 2008, Chikoko 2017). There are number of reasons that account for forced sex or rape among the street children. Street sub culture is one of the reasons why forced sex or rape is common or rampant among the street children (Chikoko, 2017; Chikoko et al, 2018). The street subculture is characterised by violence, limited access to services such as food, health, education, among others. There is a link between substance abuse and forced sex among the street children. Some street girls of the are raped as a result of substance misuse. Also, some of the street boys are raped innocent street girls after taking on aphrodisiac substances (Chikoko et al, 2019). Some of the aphrodisiac substances include seven hours and *congo dust*. However, as a result of traumatic experiences and to cope with forced sex or rape some of the street children have resorted to abuse of substances. Some of the misused substances include *chamba* (cannabis), alcohol, and sniffing of glue, among others (Chikoko, 2017).

Pornography and Homosexuality

Pornography is another form of sexual abuse or violence among the street children of the Harare Central Business District (Mhizha, 2010). Street children watch pornographic films at night. In some cases, street children pay a total of two (2) US Dollars to watch pornographic films on the downtown streets, near the Kopje area (Mhizha, 2010). However, such pornographic films are made in areas that are risky for people to move at night. The Harare Kopje area is known to be infested with sex workers and other criminals. Apart from watching pornographic films, street children also have access to social media platforms that expose them to sexual violence (Chikoko, 2017). Some of the social media platforms include *WhatsApp, Instagram, TikTok Tok* among others.

Street children are vulnerable to sexual abuse, violence and exploitation (Mhizha, 2010). There is a close relationship between substance abuse and homosexuality among the street children. As a result of traumatic experiences associated with sodomy, some of the street children resort to the misuse of psycho active substances. Some of the psycho active substances include *kachasu* (a highly intoxicating psycho active substance), *makabe* or *maragada*, chamba and alcohol among others (Mhizha, 2010; Chikoko, 2017). In contrast, some of the street children became vulnerable to homosexuality as a result of excessive use of intoxicating substances, such as sniffing glue, among others (Chikoko, 2017). Such street children become addicted to intoxicating substances.

The State of Child Sexual Abuse in Zimbabwe: A Situational Summary

As highlighted above, street children of the Harare Central Business District are vulnerable to sexual abuse, violence and exploitation. The sexual abuse, violence and exploitation is demonstrated in various forms such as oral sex, pornography, forced sex or rape, multiple sexual relationships, intergenerational sex, sodomy, unprotected sex, masturbation among others. Utilising the empowerment theory, sexual abuse, violence, and exploitation render them vulnerable and powerless. The adolescent girls are powerless as men exercise control over them through economic resources. The social environment in the name of institutions and structures does not provide empowerment to these vulnerable girls. The behaviours of the girls are at variance with some of the key tenets of the empowerment theory, such as social justice, equality, and human rights, among others.

As highlighted above, the street children engage in survival sex. The survival sex comes in many different ways. Transactional sex work occurs between street girls and their male counterparts. The transactional sex could exchange of sexual favours and food. Apart from engaging in transactional sex among the street children themselves, some of them engage in such kind of sex with people from mainstream society. The adolescent street girls engage in commercial sex work to raise money for survival (Chikoko, 2014). Similarly, Sewpaul and colleagues (2012) have observed that some adolescent street girls of Durban, South Africa, engaged in survival sex. The street girls of Durban, South Africa, have also been involved in commercial sex work to raise money for food and other basic needs (Sewpaul, 2012). In addition, some of the adolescent street boys of Durban, South Africa, have also been raising money for survival through selling sex on the streets. The street boys of Durban, South Africa are paid South African Rands 50.00 for eating the bums or sucking of their male clients (Sewpaul et al, 2012).

The street children engage in multiple sexual relationships. Through multiple sexual relationships, they can raise or sustain their lives. In other words, they raised money for meeting basic needs through multiple sexual relationships. Similarly, the street children and youths of Durban, South Africa, are victims or survivors of sexual abuse or violence as they engage in multiple sexual relationships, unprotected sex, and sex work, among others (Osthus et al, 2014). Sex work is common among the girls of Durban, South Africa (Osthus et al, 2014). The street girls of Durban are vulnerable to sexually transmitted diseases as they have little power to negotiate for condom use in those transactional relations (Othus et al, 2014).

The adolescent street children are vulnerable to sexual abuse, violence and exploitation in the form of early sexual debut, unprotected sex and exposure to sexually transmitted diseases, among others. Similarly, street children of Bangladesh are vulnerable to sexual abuse or violence, or exploitation, as evidenced by increases in contracting sexually transmitted diseases, early sexual initiation, unprotected sex among others (Reza and Henly, 2018). Reza and Henly (2018) observed that early sexual initiation is common or rampant among the street children of Bangladesh. Some of the street children of Bangladesh have been historically initiated into sex at the age of seven (7) years or less (Reza and Henly, 2018). In another study of street children of Bangladesh, sexual violence is very common among these innocent children (Kaiser and Sinanan, 2020). Kaiser and Sinanan (2020) observed that majority of street girls of Bangladesh were often raped or had to sleep with their fellow boys on the streets. The street girls are vulnerable to different forms of sexual abuse, violence and exploitation to the extent that there is no one can come to their rescue even when they scream for help at night in dark places (Kaiser and Sinanan, 2020).

Conclusion

As discussed above, the street children of the Harare Central Business District are vulnerable to sexual abuse, violence and exploitation. The sexual abuse, violence and exploitation come in different forms. Some of them include; unprotected sex, multiple sexual relationships, sodomy, bestiality, ritual sex, early sexual debut, masturbation, commercial sex work, forced sex or rape, pornography, intergenerational sex among others. Utilising the empowerment theory, the vulnerabilities of street children to sexual abuse, violence and exploitation demonstrate that they are not adequately protected and empowered by the Zimbabwean society. It illustrates that the Government of Zimbabwe and other key stakeholders are not doing enough to provide protection services to the innocent street children.

Several recommendations to reduce and prevent incidences of sexual abuse, violence and exploitation among the street children can be emphasised. Firstly, there is a need to raise awareness on the sexual rights of street children in the Harare Central Business District. The awareness raising will significantly change people's negative attitudes towards the sexual rights of children in street situations. This could be done through print, electronic, social media and any other platforms. Secondly, there is a need to establish functional Child Protection systems and or structures on the streets. These systems should respond to cases of child sexual abuse, violence and exploitation among the street children. Thirdly, the perpetrators of child sexual abuse, violence and exploitation involving street children should be brought to book as soon as possible. Moreover, there is a need for the Government of Zimbabwe and other duty bearers to fully implement child rights laws, policies and programmes targeting the street children. The Government of Zimbabwe and other duty bearers should fully implement the national legal instruments. Finally, the Government of Zimbabwe and other duty bearers should implement social protection programmes targeting children in street situations to reduce their vulnerabilities to sexual abuse, violence and exploitation.

References

African Union 1999, *African Charter on the Rights and Welfare of Children*, unpublished, Addis Ababa.

Atkinson-Shepherd, S. 2016, 'The gangs of Bangladesh: Exploring organised crime, street gangs and "illicit child labourers" in Dhaka', *Criminology and Criminal Justice*, 16(2), pp. 233–249.

Bhattacharya, A. & Nair, R. 2014, 'Girls on the street: Their life experiences and vulnerability to sexual abuse', *The Indian Journal of Social Work*, 75(1).

Bourdillon, M.F.C. 1991, *Poor, harassed but very much alive*, Gweru: Mambo Press.

Bourdillon, M.F.C. 1994, 'Street children in Harare', *Africa Insight*, 64(4).

Bourdillon, M.F.C. 1995, 'The children on our streets', *Child Care Worker*, 13(3).

Chikoko, W. 2014, 'Commercial "sex work" and substance abuse among adolescent street children of Harare Central Business District', *Journal of Social Development in Africa*, 29(2).

Chikoko, W. 2017, *Substance abuse among street children of Harare: A case of Harare Central Business District*, DPhil thesis, University of Zimbabwe, Harare.

Chikoko, W., Muzvidziwa, V.N., Ruparanganda, W. & Chimhowa, Chikoko, E. 2018a, 'Forced sex or rape and substance abuse among street children of the Harare Central Business District', *International Open and Distance Learning Journal*, 3(2).

Chikoko, W., Muzvidziwa, V.N., Ruparanganda, W. & Chimhowa/Chikoko, E. 2018b, 'The masturbation and substance abuse among the street children of the Harare Central Business District', *Journal of Interdisciplinary Academic Research*, 1(1).

Chikoko, W., Muzvidziwa, V.N., Ruparanganda, W. & Chimhowa/Chikoko, E. 2018c, 'The use of traditional medicine in commercial sex work among adolescent street girls of the Harare Central Business District', *DANDE Journal of Social Sciences and Communications*, 2(2), pp. 75–87.

Chikoko, W., Muzvidziwa, V.N., Ruparanganda, W. & Chikoko, E. 2018d, 'Unprotected sex and substance abuse among the street children of the Harare Central Business District', *Journal of Gleanings from Academic Outliers*, 7(1).

Chikoko, W., Ruparanganda, W. & Chimhowa/Chikoko, E. 2019, 'Multiple sexual relationships and substance abuse among the street children of the Harare Central Business District, Zimbabwe', *Journal of Social Development in Africa*, 34(1).

Chikoko, W., Muzvidziwa, V.N., Ruparanganda, W. & Chikoko, E. 2019, 'Reasons for street girls' entry into commercial sex work of the Harare Central Business District', *Journal of Sociology and Social Anthropology*, 10(1–3), pp. 74–83.

Chikoko, W., Muzvidziwa, V.N., Ruparanganda, W. & Chikoko, E. 2019, 'Oral sex and substance abuse among the street children of the Harare Central Business District, Zimbabwe', *Review of Human Factor Studies*, 25(1), pp. 30–48.

Chikoko, W., Muzvidziwa, V.N., Ruparanganda, W. & Chikoko, E. 2019, 'The techniques of advertising sex and signalling availability among adolescent street girls of the Harare Central Business District', *African Journal of Women and Gender in Development*, 1(1).

Chikoko, W. & Ruparanganda, W. 2020, 'Ubuntu or Hunhu perspective in understanding substance abuse and sexual behaviours of street children of Harare Central Business District, Zimbabwe', *African Journal of Social Work*, 10(1) (Special issue on Ubuntu Social Work).

Chikoko, W., Mhizha, S. & Ruparanganda, W. 2020, 'Sex for drugs: A case of street children of Harare Central Business District', *Journal of Sociology and Social Anthropology*, 11(3–4), pp. 234–241.

Chitereka, C. 2010, 'Child sexual abuse in Zimbabwe: The agenda for social workers', *Asia Pacific Journal of Social Work*, 20(1).

Jera, N.T. 2019, *A study of the Prevention of Child Sexual Exploitation and the Exploration of Social Workers' Perception of Child Sexual Exploitation: A case study of Harare (Zimbabwe) and London (United Kingdom)*, unpublished DPhil thesis, University of Bedfordshire, United Kingdom.

Kaiser, E. & Sinanan, A.W. 2020, 'Survival and resilience of female street children experiencing sexual violence in Bangladesh: A qualitative study', *Journal of Child Sexual Abuse*, 29(5), pp. 550–569.

Manjengwa, J., Matema, C., Tirivanhu, D. & Tizora, R. 2016, 'Deprivation among children living and working on the streets of Harare', *Development Southern Africa*, 33(1), pp. 53–66.

Mella, M. 2012, *An investigation into the nature and extent of economic exploitation of street children in Zimbabwe: A case study of Harare Central Business District*, unpublished MSW dissertation, School of Social Work, University of Zimbabwe.

Mhizha, S. 2010, *The self-image of adolescent street children in Harare*, unpublished MPhil thesis, Department of Psychology, University of Zimbabwe, Harare.

Mhizha, S. & Muromo, T. 2013, 'An exploratory study on the school-related challenges faced by street children in Harare', *Zimbabwe Journal of Educational Research*, 25(3), pp. 350–369.

Muridzo, N.G. 2014, 'Child sexual abuse in Zimbabwe: An agenda for social work', *The Indian Journal of Social Work*, 75(1).

Muridzo, N.G. 2017, *An exploration of the phenomenon of child sexual abuse in Zimbabwe*, unpublished DPhil (Social Work) thesis, University of the Witwatersrand, South Africa.

Reza, M.H. & Henly, J.R. 2018, 'Health crisis, social support and caregiving practices among street children in Bangladesh', *Children and Youth Services Review*, 88, pp. 229–240.

Rumble, L., Mungate, T., Chigiji, H., Salama, P., Nolan, A., Sammon, E. & Muwoni, L. 2015, 'Childhood sexual violence in Zimbabwe: Evidence for the epidemic against girls', *Child Abuse and Neglect*, 46, pp. 60–66.

Ruparanganda, W. 2008, *The sexual behaviour patterns of street youth of Harare, Zimbabwe, in the era of the HIV and AIDS pandemic*, unpublished DPhil thesis, Department of Sociology, University of Zimbabwe.

Rurevo, R. & Bourdillon, M.F.C. 2003, 'Girls: The less visible street children of Zimbabwe', *Children, Youth and Environment*, 13(1), pp. 1–20.

Sewpaul, V., Osthus, I., Mhone, C., Sibilo, E. & Mbhele, S. 2012, 'Life on the streets of Durban: No millionaire ending', *Social Work/Maatskaplike Werk*, 48(3).

Osthus, I.S. & Sewpaul, V. 2014, 'Gender, power and sexuality among youth on the streets of Durban: Socio-economic realities', *International Social Work*, 57(4), pp. 326–337.

United Nations 1989, *The United Nations Convention on the Rights of the Child*, unpublished, Geneva.

United Nations 2006, *World Report on Violence Against Children*, unpublished, Geneva.

Wakatama, M. 2007, *The situation of street children in Zimbabwe: A violation of the United Nations Convention on the Rights of the Child (1989)*, unpublished DPhil thesis, School of Social Work, University of Leicester, United Kingdom.

Chapter Thirteen
Unintended Pregnancies and Substance Abuse among Street Girls of the Harare Central Business District, Zimbabwe

Witness Chikoko

Introduction

Substance abuse and unintended pregnancies are among the global challenges affecting children in street situations. Unwanted pregnancies are a common phenomenon among adolescent street girls the world over, including Zimbabwe. Several reasons account for why street girls end up with unwanted pregnancies, including risky sexual behaviours such as unprotected sex, multiple sexual relationships, and intergenerational sex. Substance abuse can be defined as taking too much of a drug, taking a drug too often or taking drugs or substances for the wrong reasons (Makaruse, 2010). Seemingly, literature is scarce on the relationship between substance abuse and unwanted pregnancies among the adolescent street girls of the Harare Central Business District, Zimbabwe. This chapter analyses the multi-dimensional relationship between unwanted pregnancies and substance abuse among adolescent street girls.

Children in street situations have a greater vulnerability to unwanted pregnancies. The major reasons that account for such high rates of pregnancies among street children include inaccessibility and unaffordability of reproductive health services (Ruparanganda, 2008). In some cases, high rates of pregnancies among street children are associated with risky sexual behaviours such as multiple sexual relationships, unprotected sex, transactional sex and early sexual debut. The pregnant street girls, as social actors, use herbal medicine such as *masuwo* (vaginal opening) to manage their pregnancies. Ruparanganda (2008) has noted that the pregnant street girls chew the herbs to ensure the good health of the foetus. The use of traditional medicine among pregnant girls demonstrates the agency of these children as they can survive in a context where they faced stigma and discrimination in hospitals.

Drawing, from a child rights perspective, the use of traditional medicine by pregnant street girls illustrates acute child rights violations, as these girls could be further exposed to several risks. Ruparanganda (2008) observes that some of the risks include overdosing and others. The use of traditional medicine also contravenes the provisions of the UNCRC, the ACRWC and the national child rights laws, policies and programmes. It also shows that the Government of Zimbabwe, as the primary duty bearer, is not providing adequate protection services to vulnerable street girls on the streets.

Child Agency Theory

Scholars such as Giddens (1984), Crain (1992), Turner (1991), and Cohen (1987) define structure-agency theory as a model in which social practices are determined by the relationship between structure and agency. Agency and structure cannot be separated from one another since they are interlined. Behaviours and activities are not produced by social construction or social structure, but as social actors, people influence both structure and consciousness (Ritzer, 1992). Drawing from the child agency theory, the adolescent street girls of the Harare Central Business District engage in unwanted pregnancies and substance abuse. Substance abuse and unwanted pregnancies could be the only viable options for these children. The behaviours could also be seen as ambiguous agency. Bordonaro and Payne (2012) define ambiguous agency as actions that threaten the existing social order. The unwanted pregnancies and abuse of substances become an ambiguity of agency as they threaten the well-being of the children. Through unwanted pregnancies and abuse of substances, some of the adolescent street girls were exposed to several risks. The ambiguity of agency is also explained in the context that unwanted pregnancies and abuse of substances among adolescent girls are inconsistent with socio-cultural expectations among Shona people. Children, including those in street situations, are not expected to engage in abuse of substances and unwanted pregnancies.

Child Rights Perspective

According to the United Nations Convention on the Rights of a Child (UNCRC) (1989), child rights can be defined through the four broader categories namely, best interest of the child (article 3,) non-discrimination (article 2), the rights of a child to survival and development (article 6) and the right of a child to participation (article 12). Apart from the provisions of the UNCRC, the Government of Zimbabwe is also a signatory to the African Charter on the Rights and Welfare of Children (ACRWC) (1999).

To domesticate the UNCRC and the ACRWC, the Government of Zimbabwe has come up with several child rights legislations and programmes such as the Children's Act (5.06), the Criminal Codification and Reform Act, Zimbabwe National Orphan Care Policy of 1999. The Zimbabwe National Action Plan for Orphans and Other Vulnerable Children (NAP for OVCs) 2004-2008, and the second phase of NAP for OVCs 2010-2015, the third phase of NAP for OVCs 2016-2020 and the Protocol on the Multi-Sectoral Management of Sexual Abuse and Violence in Zimbabwe are some of the policies and programmes that have been promulgated or initiated to promote child rights in Zimbabwe.

Despite the presence of child rights laws, policies and programmes enunciated by the Government of Zimbabwe, children, including street children, do not enjoy their rights, as some are exposed to abuse and violence. The child rights laws, policies and programmes have not been able to be translated into meaningful interventions for children, as the majority of them continue to face abuse in the name of misuse of substances and commercial sex work (Chikoko et al, 2018; Chikoko, 2014). Some scholars have criticised the rights perspective for its Western World orientation. Bourdillon (2009) argues that some of the Western World's conceptualisation of childhood can be regarded as a 'romantic view of childhood'. Children as social actors can construct and sustain their lives even on the streets. Drawing from the child rights perspective, substance abuse and unwanted pregnancies among adolescent street girls of the Harare Central Business District illustrate increased levels of child rights violations. The behaviours are inconsistent with the provisions of the UNCRC (1989), particularly article three, the best interests of the child principle. For example, the Children's Act (5:06) views such children as 'in need of care'.

Unintended Pregnancies and Substance Abuse among Street Girls

Unwanted pregnancies among street girls are linked to the misuse of substances. The relationship between substance abuse and unwanted pregnancies on the streets has many dimensions. For example, increased cases of unwanted pregnancies on the streets are linked with the abuse of psycho active substances. On the other hand, some street girls became addicted to psycho active substance abuse as a result of unwanted pregnancies. In addition, some street girls succumb to unwanted pregnancies as a result of using expired or 'fake' family planning tablets acquired from a street pharmacy.

Unwanted Pregnancies Linked to Excessive Use of Psychoactive Substances

Some street girls acquire unwanted pregnancies as a result of excessive psycho active substances. One of the street girls in Harare Central Business District noted that substance abuse is strongly linked to unwanted pregnancies on the streets. She added that some of the street girls practise unsafe sex, which culminates in unwanted pregnancies:

> *Life on the streets is based on competition. I got pregnant with my child, elder [referring to the author], when I was ill-prepared. That was caused by drunkenness. The days I got pregnant with Talent that was the festive season of 2013, towards Christmas. During those days, unlike these days, male clients had lots of money. I had many boyfriends, and one of them was a soldier. You always know, elder, that when soldiers have money, they buy lots of beer. As a result, we used to stay heavily intoxicated. When the soldier was not around, I was with one of the street boys. We used to abuse burongo [referring to a cough syrup], marijuana or anything intoxicating. As a result of heavy drunkenness, I did not know how I got pregnant with Talent. Sometimes we had unprotected sex. I only realised that I missed my menstrual period. I looked around for medicine to abort, but ironically, this pregnancy was strong. Anyway, it does not matter; I now have my child.*

One of the boys also revealed that the street girls of the Harare Central Business District had unwanted pregnancies. He added that the unwanted pregnancies are linked to substance abuse. The majority of street girls who practice substance abuse contribute to the rising cases of unwanted pregnancies. A street boy also revealed that as a result of unwanted pregnancies, some of the street girls practise unsafe abortion and including baby dumping.

> The majority of girls who are addicted to sex and substances are the ones who get unwanted pregnancies. There are many cases of these girls who abort and sometimes do baby dumping. There is a baby who was dumped along Mukuvisi [referring to a stream in Harare] by these rascals. The baby was taken to the Magaba [referring to a well-known place in Mbare high-density suburb located on the southern side of the Harare Central Business District] police station.

One of the gatekeepers also emphasised that substance abuse has been instrumental in the rising cases of unwanted pregnancies among street girls of the Harare Central Business District. She indicated that at some point, with her organisation, they attempted to assist all pregnant girls through their empowerment programme called Young Mothers. She revealed that some of the street children have been born to girls on the streets.

Psychoactive Substance Use Triggered by Trauma from Unwanted Pregnancies.

Some of the adolescent street girls became addicted to the use of psycho active substances as a result of traumatic experiences associated with unwanted pregnancies. One of the girls living on the street, aged fifteen, indicated that she is an orphan who started living on the streets when she was three years old. She abuses substances as a result of the traumatic experiences she had during the unwanted pregnancy. She added that before she had an unwanted pregnancy, she was not abusing substances, but after the incident, she resorted to abusing substances to cope with the situation. She said, "I used to be sober. I only started abusing substances after I had an unwanted pregnancy on the street. I faced multiple challenges, such that I am always drunk, to cope with the situation." Moreover, a former staff member of Streets Ahead argued that some of the street girls who abuse psychoactive substances have experienced traumatic experiences in their childhood lives. She added that some of the traumatic experiences include forced sex, unwanted pregnancies, and unsafe abortion:

> Some of these girls abuse a lot of substances such that they can cope with their stressful lives on the streets. Life on the streets is very difficult; some of the girls are sexually abused, others experience unwanted pregnancies. Therefore, some of these issues traumatise the girls and end up abusing psycho active substances.

Additionally, some of the street girls take substances such as *chamba* (cannabis) and *bhurongo* (cough syrup), and *chitongo* (a highly intoxicating psycho active substance). One of the street-based vendors selling these substances also revealed that some of the street girls who had been exposed to traumatic life experiences take some of these substances to cope with their situations.

Street-Acquired Family Planning Methods

Some adolescent street girls acquire unwanted pregnancies as a result of using family planning tablets acquired on the streets as part of their reproductive health services. One of the street girls, aged 17 years, noted that she succumbed to unwanted pregnancies on the streets of the Harare Central Business District as a result of using family planning tablets she bought on the streets. The street girl also added that the majority of the street girls rely on buying family planning tablets on the streets as they do not have any other source of the medicine. Street girls are often discriminated against and stigmatised by some of the hospitals as they are considered immoral. In some cases, the stigma and discrimination are also due to the hospitals' demand for payment of money to access their services. One street girl noted that:

> I got pregnant after using some of these family planning tablets. I bought them from the streets. They sell anything on the streets. For a long time, I have been buying and using these tablets from the street pharmacies. As street children, we are stigmatised and discriminated against in hospitals and clinics. I once visited a Poly clinic at Mbare, and they demanded payment up front. So, we have a lot of problems in our lives as street children.

One of the adolescent street boys also indicated that some of the street girls buy reproductive health tablets on the streets. He added that the tablets often cost around one dollar per packet:

> *These street girls do not seek services at the clinic. They buy tablets on the streets. One dollar per packet is the price of the family planning tablets. As street people, we do what is there; that is our life on the streets.*

An informant working for CESVI also revealed that some of the street girls use family planning tablets from the streets, as they find it more convenient and affordable. Some street girls are often found with reproductive health medicines, including family planning tablets, which they access from the street vendors. One of the street vendors said:

> *I sell these items on the streets. There are no jobs, so I survive through the vending of these family planning tablets. Even our government, including law enforcement agents, they are aware that there are no jobs. So that is the way it is.*

Overview of Pregnancy and Drug Use among Street Girls

There is a close relationship between substance abuse and unwanted pregnancies among the adolescent street girls of the Harare Central Business District. The girls demonstrate their agency through unwanted pregnancies and abuse of substances. As sexual beings, some of them end up engaging in unprotected sex and subsequently have unwanted pregnancies. The agency is also highlighted when some of the girls use substances such as family planning tablets acquired on the streets. The abuse of psycho active substances in the name of *chamba* and *chitongo* demonstrates the agency of these girls. The unwanted pregnancy among street girls demonstrates their sexual agency. The abuse of substance also illustrates their agency in the face of multiple challenges, thus reflecting thin agency as noted by Tisdall and Punch (2012). The behaviours could also be explained in the notion of ambiguous agency as it clashes with societal values (Bordonaro and Payne, 2012). Drawing from the Zimbabwe societal value system, girls are not expected to have unwanted pregnancies and also to abuse substances. The unwanted pregnancies demonstrate that the street girls are indulging in premarital sex. Scholars such as Gigengack (2008) view the behaviours as part of the concept of self-destructive agency, considering the deadly risks associated with the practices. For example, as a result of using family planning tablets acquired on the streets, some of the adolescent street girls end up getting unwanted pregnancies.

Drawing from the Ubuntu or Hunhu philosophy (Samkange and Samkange, 1981), substance abuse and unintended pregnancies among street children demonstrate the back of Ubuntu. Ubuntu is defined as the humanness of humanity (Van Breda, 2019). The behaviours show that there is moral decadence on the streets. The behaviours are considered an abomination as children, including those in street situations, are not supposed to have unwanted pregnancies and abuse substances. In line with the child rights perspective, the unwanted pregnancies and abuse or misuse of substances demonstrate serious child rights violations prevalent on the streets. This illustrates how the adolescent street girls of the Harare Central Business District have become vulnerable to sexual abuse, violence and exploitation. The behaviours associated with unintended pregnancies and misuse of substances contravene the provisions of the UNCRC, particularly the principle of the best interest of the child. It also contravenes the provisions of the ACRWC, the Criminal Law (Codification and Reform) Act (9:23), the Domestic Violence (5:16), the Children's Act (5:06) and other child rights laws, policies and programmes. Rather, such children are regarded as 'in need of care' as defined by the Children's Act. The duty bearers should address structural issues that make street girls vulnerable to unwanted pregnancies.

In addition, from a child rights perspective, the use of family planning by street girls bought on the streets demonstrates huge child rights violations. Buying tablets on the streets exposes these girls to a lot of risks associated such as unwanted pregnancies. The behaviour contravenes the provisions of the UNCRC (1989), particularly the best interest of the child principle and article 44 of the ACRWC (1999). The Children's Act *(5:06)* defines such children as 'in need of care'. In addition, some of the child rights programmes, such as the National Action Plan for Orphans and Other Vulnerable Children, also consider street girls who buy family planning from the streets as vulnerable children. They are vulnerable because of the risks associated with the use of tablets that are acquired on the streets. The efficacy of some of the tablets is questionable, as some of them might have been exposed to harsh weather conditions such as extreme heat or cold. The efficacy is questionable given the fact that some of the tablets might also be 'fake'. Therefore, this poses a lot of risks to the users. For example, one of the adolescent street girls ended up getting an unwanted pregnancy as a result of using fake family planning tablets acquired on the streets.

The foregoing discussion suggests that there is a close relationship between substance abuse and unwanted pregnancies. Some of the street girls, who are involved in unsafe sex, culminate in succumbing to unwanted pregnancies. The use of unprotected sex is also associated with unwanted pregnancies. This corroborates with McClelland and Newell (2008) who observed that women who practised street-based prostitution and with problematic substance abuse had the risk of unplanned pregnancies. The unplanned pregnancies resulted from prostitution and drug dependency. De Genna, Goldschmidt and Cornelius (2015) note an increase in unwanted pregnancies among teenage mothers who frequently abused substances such as tobacco, marijuana and alcohol as compared to older mothers.

Conversely, Tucker, Sussell, Golinelli, David, Kennedy and Wenzel (2012) observe that street children have a greater chance of vulnerability to unwanted pregnancies. Some of the reasons that account for such high rates of pregnancies among street children could be inaccessibility and the unaffordability of reproductive health services. Moreover, the high rates of pregnancies among street children are associated with risky sexual behaviours such as multiple sexual relationships, unprotected sex, transactional sex and early sexual debut, among other factors. Zapata and colleagues (2011) have observed that the escalation of unwanted pregnancies among street children of Ukraine is not significantly related to substance abuse but to other factors such as transactional sex work, sexual debut and traumatic experiences such as child abuse and neglect during childhood.

The abuse of psycho active substances can also be regarded as a result of traumatic experiences associated with unwanted pregnancies. As a result of traumatic experiences associated with unwanted pregnancies, some of the street girls resort to abuse of psycho active substances. Therefore, the use of psycho active substances is used as a coping mechanism by adolescent street girls who have had unwanted pregnancies. Some adolescent street girls use family planning methods that they acquired on the streets. The girls resort to the use of these tablets as they face stigma and discrimination in some of the reproductive health clinics and hospitals. In a context where reproductive health services are inaccessible, some of the sexually active adolescent girls resort to using family planning methods acquired on the streets. However, through using the family planning methods acquired on the streets, they end up succumbing to unwanted pregnancies, as some of the tablets would have already expired. There are several risks associated with using family planning tablets acquired from 'street pharmacies'. Ruparanganda (2008) observes that some of the street girls of Harare avoid seeking reproductive health services in hospitals as they fear being known as poor people. He cites a case where a pregnant street girl visited a hospital, and the hospital demanded a lot of requirements, including residential addresses. This is challenging, as some street girls do not meet the requirements of the hospitals or clinics.

Recommendations

Several recommendations to reduce risks associated with unwanted pregnancies and substance abuse among the street girls of the Harare Central Business District can be noted. Firstly, there is a need for full implementation of child rights laws, policies and programmes. The full implementation of the child rights laws, policies and programmes will significantly reduce the incidence of unwanted pregnancies and misuse of substances. Secondly, the Government of Zimbabwe, line ministries, and partners should establish substance rehabilitation centres in the streets. The establishment of such institutions will provide rehabilitation services to children who would have been addicted to the misuse of substances. The Government of Zimbabwe and key stakeholders should conduct more awareness-raising seminars on substance abuse and reproductive health issues should be done targeting the street children of the Harare Central Business District. Through awareness seminars, the adolescent street girls will be empowered, and this will subsequently reduce incidences of unwanted pregnancies and misuse of substances. Moreover, there is a need for increased access to reproductive health services for street children. The provision of reproductive health services can be decentralised at the Drop-in centres to ensure easy access to the street children. Finally, there is a need for the arrest and confiscation of all reproductive health tablets on the streets of the Harare Central Business District. For example, the middlemen or agents who are involved in buying and selling illicit family planning tablets should be arrested because some of their merchandise has expired, and they have the potential to pose health risks to the users.

Conclusion

Unwanted pregnancies and substance abuse among the adolescent street girls of the Harare Central Business District are multi-dimensional. Some of the street girls succumb to unwanted pregnancies as a result of substance abuse. Conversely, some of the adolescent girls also resort to substance abuse as a result of unwanted pregnancies. Substance abuse and unwanted pregnancies among these girls demonstrate agency. The behaviours could be the only viable among these girls, thus thin agency. In addition, the behaviours could also be seen as ambiguous agency. The ambiguity of the agency is at two levels. The first level is when the behaviours are threatening the well-being of the street girls. Secondly, when the actions or behaviours are inconsistent with the socio-cultural value system of the Zimbabwean society. In addition, the unwanted pregnancies and abuse of substances among adolescent street girls are regarded as self-destructive behaviour. Self-destructive agency is based on risks and vulnerabilities associated with substance abuse and unintended pregnancies. As discussed, some of the risks include death, among others. Drawing from a child rights perspective, the unwanted pregnancies and substance abuse among street girls illustrate increased vulnerability of these children. It demonstrates vulnerabilities of street girls as misuse of substances and unwanted pregnancies are in contrast with the international, regional and local child rights laws, policies and programmes.

References

African Union 1999, *African Charter on the Rights and Welfare of Children*, unpublished, Addis Ababa.

Armstrong, L. 2014, 'Screening clients in a decriminalised street-based sex industry: Insights into the experiences of New Zealand sex workers', *Australian and New Zealand Journal of Criminology*, 47(2), 207–222.

Babbie, E. & Mouton, J. 2012, *The practice of social research*, Oxford University Press, Southern Africa, Cape Town.

Bourdillon, M.F.C. 1991, *Poor, harassed but very much alive: An account of street people and their organisation*, Mambo Press, Gweru, Zimbabwe.

Bourdillon, M.F.C. 1994a, 'Street Children in Harare', *Africa: Journal of the International African Institute*, 64(4), 516–533.

Bourdillon, M.F.C. 1994b, 'Street Children in Harare', *Africa: Journal of the International African Institute*, 64(4), 516–533.

Bourdillon, M.F.C. 2009, 'Children's work in Southern Africa', *Werkwinkel*, 4(1), pp. 1–22.

Chikoko, W. 2014, 'Commercial "sex work" and substance abuse among adolescent street children of Harare Central Business District', *Journal of Social Development in Africa*, 29(2).

Chikoko, W. 2017, *Substance abuse among street children of Harare: The case of Harare Central Business District*, unpublished Doctor of Philosophy Thesis, Department of Social Work, University of Zimbabwe, Harare.

Chikoko, W., Chikoko, E., Muzvidziwa, V.N. & Ruparanganda, W. 2016, 'Nongovernmental organisations' response to substance abuse and sexual behaviours of adolescent street children of the Harare Central Business District', *African Journal of Social Work*, 6(2).

Chikoko, W., Muzvidziwa, V.N., Ruparanganda, W. & Chimhowa/Chikoko, E. 2018a, 'Forced sex and substance abuse among the street children of Harare Central Business District, Zimbabwe', *International Open and Distance Learning Journal*, 3(2), Available at: https://www.iodljournal.org [Accessed 22 March 2023].

Chikoko, W., Muzvidziwa, V.N., Ruparanganda, W. & Chimhowa/Chikoko, E. 2018b, 'The masturbation and substance abuse among the street children of the Harare Central Business District', *Journal of Interdisciplinary Academic Research*, Available at: https://www.jiar.org.zw [Accessed 22 March 2023].

Chikoko, W., Muzvidziwa, V.N., Ruparanganda, W. & Chimhowa/Chikoko, E. 2018c, 'The use of traditional medicine in commercial sex work among adolescent street girls of the Harare Central Business District', *DANDE Journal of Social Sciences and Communications*, 2(2).

Chikoko, W., Muzvidziwa, V.N., Ruparanganda, W. & Chikoko, E. 2019, 'Early sexual debut and substance abuse among street children of Harare Central Business District, Zimbabwe', *African Journal of Social Work*, 9(1), pp. 79–87.

Chirwa, Y. & Wakatama, M. 2000, 'Working street children in Harare', in Bourdillon, M.F.C. (ed.), *Earning a life: Working Children in Zimbabwe*, Weaver Press, Harare, pp. 45–58.

Chirwa, Y. 2007, 'Children, Youth and Economic Reforms: An Expedition of the State of Street Children in Zimbabwe', in Maphosa, F., Kujinga, K. & Chingarande, S.D. (eds), *Zimbabwe's Development Experiences since 1980: Challenges and Prospects for the Future*, OSSREA, Ethiopia, pp. 76–93.

Dube, L. 1997, 'AIDS-risk patterns and knowledge of the disease among street children in Harare, Zimbabwe', *Journal of Social Development in Africa*, 12(2), pp. 61–73.

Dube, L. 1999, *Street children: A part of organised society*, unpublished Doctor of Philosophy Thesis, Department of Sociology, University of Zimbabwe, Harare.

Farmer, M., McAlinden, A. & Maruna, S. 2016, 'Sex offending and situational motivation: Findings from a qualitative analysis of desistance from sexual offending', *International Journal of Offender Therapy and Comparative Criminology*, 60(15), pp. 1756–1775.

Government of Zimbabwe 2001, *The Children's Act (Chapter 5:06)*, Government Printers, Harare.

Government of Zimbabwe 2004, *The National Action Plan for Orphans and Other Vulnerable Children 2004–2009*, Government Printers, Harare.

Government of Zimbabwe 2006, *The Criminal Law (Codification and Reform) Act (Chapter 9:23)*, Government Printers, Harare.

Government of Zimbabwe 2010, *The National Action Plan for Orphans and Other Vulnerable Children 2011–2015*, Government Printers, Harare.

Mhizha, S. 2010, *The self-image of adolescent street children in Harare*, unpublished M.Phil Thesis, Department of Psychology, University of Zimbabwe, Harare.

Mhizha, S. 2014, 'Religious self-beliefs and coping vending adolescents in Harare', *Journal of Religion and Health*, 53, pp. 1487–1487.

Mhizha, S. 2015, 'The religious-spiritual self-image and behaviours among adolescent street children in Harare, Zimbabwe', *Journal of Religion and Health*, 54, pp. 187–201.

Mhizha, S. & Muromo, S. 2013, 'An exploratory study on the school-related challenges faced by street children in Harare, Zimbabwe', *Journal of Educational Research*, 25(3).

Mugumbate, J. & Chereni, A. 2019, 'Using African Ubuntu theory in social work with children in Zimbabwe', *African Journal of Social Work*, 9(1), pp. 27–34.

Neuman, W.L. 2011, *Social research methods: Qualitative and quantitative approaches*, 7th ed., Pearson Education Inc., Boston.

Nhenga, T.C. 2008, *Application of the international prohibition on child labour in an African context: Lesotho, Zimbabwe and South Africa*, unpublished Doctor of Philosophy Thesis, Department of Public Law, University of Cape Town, South Africa.

Rurevo, R. & Bourdillon, M.F.C. 2003a, 'Girls: The less visible street children of Zimbabwe', *Children, Youth and Environments*, 13(1), pp. 1–20.

Rurevo, R. & Bourdillon, M.F.C. 2003b, *Girls on the street*, Weaver Press, Harare.

Ruparanganda, W. 2008, *The sexual behaviour patterns of street youth of Harare, Zimbabwe in the era of the HIV and AIDS pandemic*, unpublished D.Phil Thesis, Department of Sociology, University of Zimbabwe, Harare.

Samkange, S. & Samkange, T.M. 1980, *Hunhuism or Ubuntusim: A Zimbabwe indigenous political philosophy*, Graham Publishing, Salisbury/Harare.

Tadele, G. 2009, '"Unrecognised victims": Sexual abuse against male street children in Metkato area of Addis Ababa', *Ethiopian Journal of Health Development*, 23(3).

Tisdall, K. & Punch, S. 2012, '"Not so new"? Looking critically at childhood studies, *Children's Geographies*, 10(3), pp. 249–264.

United Nations 1989, *The United Nations Convention on the Rights of the Child*, unpublished report, Geneva.

Zapata, L.B., Kissin, D.M., Robbins, C.L., Finnerty, E., Skipalska, H., Yorick, R.V., Jamieson, D.J., Marchbanks, P.A. & Hillis, S.D. 2011, 'Multi-city assessment of lifetime pregnancy involvement among street youth, Ukraine', *Journal of Urban Health: Bulletin of the New York Academy of Medicine*, 88(4), pp. 788–801.

Chapter Fourteen
Religion and Scourge of Domestic Servant Syndrome in Some Christian Homes in Southwestern, Nigeria

George Olayeye Olatayo and Abimbola Christiana Ayegboyin

Introduction

Child domestic workers are perceived as one of the antisocial behaviours that are prevalent in modern-day Yoruba societies in the southern part of Nigeria. It is a form of child labour that involves engaging underage children and sometimes young adults in a manner that socially and emotionally deprives those vulnerable children of their growing-up experience in life, owing to their early separation from their immediate families and relations (Rodgers and Standing, 1981:281). Domestic servanthood is adjudged as one of the socially harmful and dehumanising phenomena that is capable of affecting the mental development, and physiological and psychological dispositions of the affected children who are involved in this domestic service. The domestic servant syndrome happens in various forms, scopes and in diverse contexts, depending on the situation in which such children are engaged. In most cases, domestic servants are assigned to look after small children in the home, taking care of aged people, child labour, street hawking, using children for farming or mining activities, taking care of the handicapped in the home, gardening, prostitution, child-trafficking and performing a series of house chores. This is because the process of developing human capital in life begins as early as infancy and continues throughout the life of the individual. The process is incremental, with early choices, inputs and events that have the potential to either debilitate or facilitate development at more advanced stages (Hester, 2010). Concerning the aforementioned areas of the scourge of domestic servant syndromes highlighted, child labour in Christian homes is the focus of this chapter.

However, child labour in this context refers to those young persons who are engaged formally to perform different tasks in the homes outside their immediate family settings. The International Labour Organisation Convention (ILO) classifies domestic work as any form of labour which is performed for a particular household or family in a manner by which the person performing such work is are servant (Hester, 2010). In addition, domestic servants in this context have no freedom of their own and do not have the right to reject the duties assigned to them. On that basis, child domestic servants are commonly referred to as 'house-help'. It refers to children living with families who are neither related by blood nor relatively distant consanguinity but employed to do some wide range of domestic work such as performing house chores, taking care of the children of their master, house cleaning, laundry, going to market, cooking and caregivers to the aged.

The International Labour Organisation Convention (ILO) confines domestic servants as private and personal workers who are providers of caregiving to the homes and families. In this regard, domestic works are performed by underage children below the statutory recommended minimum age to work in any public sector or organisation. It should be noted that this does not necessarily include children who are performing such domestic work and chores under the watch and supervision of their immediate parents. In this context, it is simply the home training to do specific functions under the guidance of the parents or a mature family member who assigns and supervises such duties in the family without being forced or coerced to do it (Bekembo, 1993). This may not necessarily entail any form of abuse or molestation in the course of doing the house chores. Thus, child domestic servant syndrome has been a social mantra in Nigerian homes, especially among the social elites and rich people in the society during the pre-colonial eras and the advent of Christianity.

Domestic Servant Syndrome and Religious Beliefs

As an elusive concept to comprehend, religion can be regarded as a belief and worship of the Supreme Being and superhuman agency (Chinecherem and Ozoh, 2017). Dawkins opines that religious beliefs and teachings are one of the ways by which child abuses are commonly perpetuated in the world today under the guise of helping less privileged children from socially vulnerable homes (Dwarkins, 2012). In Christian contexts, for instance, one of the supportive doctrines for the engagement in domestic servanthood is religious teaching that compels religious adherents to train up their children in the ways of the Lord. For example, Proverbs (13:24, KJV) says, "Spare the rod and spoil the child". But whose duty it is to perform these sacred family duties in the homes is not clearly stated. Is it the biological parents, adopted parents or strangers? Nevertheless, these theological assertions are distortions of the Biblical teachings as regards the training of children. In the Yoruba culture of Nigeria, particularly the sub-Yoruba dialects in the Southwestern part, adults and those who are categorised as older people are assumed to be persons who have customary rights to control, correct and reprove the wrongdoings of the children and young adults (Fadipe, 1970:3).

However, this position does not generally recognise the view that even some of the adults could be badly raised and uncultured with moral deficiencies. Therefore, lack of such moral effronteries and grounds to perform such social tasks in society. Nevertheless, the traditions in Yoruba society affirm that, so far, such adults are older, the Yoruba culture naturally arrogates such social rights to their mature adults to correct their young ones in the society. That is why an adage in the Yoruba language says, *Bi eyi kekere ko gbon, ewo ni ti eyi to dagba*, meaning that 'if this small child is a novice, what of these fully grown adults'. This assumption seems incorrect and sociologically faulty, error-based and insensitive to the fact that the environment where children are raised, who influenced their growing up and all types of training they received in their formative ages usually define who they would become in the future and perhaps form their social inclinations. Therefore, in some cases, religious dogmas and cultural superstitions encourage the practice of domestic servant syndrome in many Christian homes in Yorubaland. By implication, it is not strange to see some children living with their extended family members, such as uncles, aunties, religious priests, and distant relatives in the family.

In most cases, some domestic servants were brought from far places, and other ethnic tribal groups came to come and perform domestic service in the homes of the rich because their parents could not afford to give them basic education and training due to the poverty level in the country. Nevertheless, it is not unjustifiable for a child to live with other families, because children need to be taught some aspects of social values, moral beliefs and social practices. However, the problem is that when disciplining and guiding children become abusive, where punishment is meted out accompanied by furious anger and transferred aggression, it, therefore, becomes child abuse. In some cases, domestic servants are mistreated, exploited, assaulted, molested, raped tortured killed for ritual purposes or denied their basic fundamental human rights either directly or indirectly because of religious beliefs, practices and cultural traditions.

The Booming of Domestic Servant Syndrome in Christian Homes

The history of domestic servant syndrome in Nigeria is as old as the country and humanity. To have a grasp of a comprehensive understanding of the domestic servant phenomenon, this chapter traced the historical antecedents of domestic servant syndrome to the precolonial period, colonial eras and contemporary times. During the precolonial time, children would be sent out willingly by their biological parents to go and live with their wealthy family members or distant relations, either to learn a particular trading skill or to be an apprentice under a master artisan (Kaushik, 1998). In some instances, children were forced and used as financial collateral for the family. They were to go and live with the wealthy people in the society whose parents owned large sums of money or valuable property (Akiwowo, 1972:32). Children were used as surety against the indebtedness of the family. This practice in Yoruba traditional social practice is known as *'won fi omo ya owo'*, meaning that the child is used as collateral for the family's indebtedness.

The who is indemnified by his or her parents may not gain freedom; perhaps, the debt collected by their parents is neither paid nor written off by creditors. This development implies that their freedom may not be given, and such children would be perpetually in unending slavery. Around that time, domestic servants were usually used to perform domestic works and house chores such as fetching firewood, fetching water, providing fodder for their master's horse or camel, washing clothes, cooking, following their masters to the village market to sell goods and keeping home fronts when their master is not at home. Those families who could afford domestic servants by that time were only rich people, powerful warriors or warlords, as well as community leaders such as local chiefs and kings (Adegunwa,1987:41). Therefore, there was no clear way to check the social menace of domestic servant syndrome in the community at that time.

During colonial times, the coming of white Europeans to Africa made the domestic servant syndrome take a different turn. By that time, there was little exposure to education, especially how to read and write, as well as to foreign civilisation. This freely gave some of the colonial masters access to as many domestic servants as they wanted. Then, by that time, it was a positive thing for the native parents to see their children living with the white settlers in their official residence. White Europeans also needed servants who would look after them and perform domestic work and other necessary work in the home. In addition, some educated elites in the society who were public servants also hired domestic servants in their homes. The general practice at that time was that it was better to have a child who stayed with educated people so that he or she would be educated as well. There were limited schools at that time where black African children could acquire formal education.

The only available opportunity is to place their children in the homes of the Whiteman and educated elites to help them in the house and learn the arts of education as well. Therefore, the main reason for giving out the children to the Whiteman and other educated families is to gain new knowledge from them and better living conditions (Akinjogbin, 1988). It should be noted that some of the generous masters of domestic servants could give the parents of their house cleaner some gift items like foreign alcoholic wine, a mirror, gunpowder, a face-cap, an umbrella, a walking stick, clothes and money, depending on how rich the person was. More so, it is reliably informed that many of the domestic servants at that time who lived with Europeans and public civil servants were the early recipients of modern education at least up to the primary school level. This consequently provides available hands for the local administrators to have someone who could help them as clerks, interpreters, messengers and cook (Fafunwas, 1981:35). Thus, it was an aid to relieve the parents of the domestic servants of the burden of caring for their children. More so, in the postcolonial time, the practices of domestic servant syndrome were a bit similar to the colonial times, but the only difference is the way modernity and contemporary civilisation dictate the pace of living of people's lives and their homes.

By this time, there were social mechanisms and formal legal procedures to follow as regards child adoption in society. This is because, in the post-independent eras, the structure of society changed as the social class of the people and families equally changed due to the level of social exposure, education and postmodern civilisation, which made people agitate for better living conditions. In addition, world bodies and regional organisations such as the United Nations International Children's Emergency Fund (UNICEF), World Health Organisation (WHO), International Labour Organisation (ILO) and African Union (AU) are keenly interested in preserving the fundamental human rights of the people (DaSilva, 1994:53). These world organisations and bodies should make necessary recommendations for formal agreements among the countries to enter a treaty on how to regulate and formalise the process of child adoption in the family, with specific conditions to meet (Kaushik, 1998:63). However, due to the level of poverty in the country and the social gap in the class structure in the society, which were created because of the acquisition of the Western education value system, some homes still lag and cannot necessarily provide for their children's needs. Therefore, it is observed that domestic servant syndrome is still booming in some Christian-educated families and homes in some parts of Southwestern Nigeria.

Indeed, reflections on the experience of domestic servants in educated Christian families in contemporary times are very different from what was obtainable in the precolonial and colonial eras. Most of the family who engages in domestic servant syndrome are doing so to have a 'house-help' who would look after their children because of the nature of their job demands, which could not permit them to oversee their family affairs regularly. Hence, because of the trust that people have in ministers of God in society and some Christian believers, many people think that their children are in safe hands to be trained in the ways of the Lord, morally and need the proper education. Nevertheless, the dreams of such parents do not usually come to pass when they later see what their children are going through in the homes of the so-called ministers and believers of God.

Many times, the reports of both print and electronic media are aghast at news of the engagement of the domestic servants. The domestic servants are killed for ritual purposes, sexually molested or seriously tortured for being accused of witchcraft (Aboderin, 1991).

In most cases, the domestic servants would be denied access and the right to learning and formal education. Many domestic servants may not learn any trade or be allowed to be apprentices. The main duties of domestic servants in such homes are to look after the children of their master and do the house chores and cleaning. This, however, by implication, encourages a high rate of out-of-school children and school dropouts in the country. This makes the domestic servants inferior to their peers and sometimes even look like outcasts because they domestic servants are socially stigmatised. This invariably lowers their self-esteem and personal self-worth as a human person. Besides, the majority of domestic servants are abused and their natural fundamental rights are denied in various forms, such as prohibiting them from socialising with other children in the neighbourhood, putting them in confinement, depriving them of food and sexual assaults, among other things (Abdullah, 1995). In addition to this, it is observed that some domestic servants are found to be engaged for very long hours of working with either little or no rest, regardless of sleeping. Thus, these occurrences may have a long time effects on the domestic servant's social and spiritual growth and development. The normal and constant ways of correcting domestic servants in such homes are through verbal and physical assaults when such children make mistakes (Okunade, 2004:67).

Causes of Domestic Servant Abuse

The predisposing factors that propel the increasing rates of domestic servant syndrome in the country are multifaceted, and are different in form and context, but range from demographic conditions through poor income, insecurity, to the poverty level due to the unfavourable economic conditions and hardship, as well as poor living conditions in the country. Demographically, the population growth rate and human densities are undeniable human capital, which makes socio-economic conditions relatively difficult and scarce. The magnitudes of poor economic conditions explain the reasons why available social amenities could not be distributed sufficiently go around or are too expensive for the average homes and families. When a family cannot afford the bare basic needs of life at home, then the children need to fend for themselves, and the best way to go sometimes is to begin to engage in child domestic labour (Bekembo, 1993).

Furthermore, income level and assurance of social security are also parts of the social needs that aggravate the level of unemployment and underutilisation of substantive economic hours daily. This forms serious domestic servant problems and child labour issues in society. This situation comes because of either unemployment or underemployment of parents who need to cater for their dependents in the family. The family income may not be enough and often not even secured, as retrenchment may scare them in the face. To make up for this economic shortage, sending out children for domestic service and child labour is inevitable.

Another very important factor is the level of ignorance on the part of the parents. Some parents push their children to work because they are not aware of the danger or great consequences of the act to the child, the family and society in the future. This condition is often reinforced by the availability of needed resources to cater for the expensive education that seems unaffordable to the parents of those vulnerable domestic servants.

Furthermore, poverty is another factor that causes child domestic servant syndrome. The article of ILO 1992 clarifies and maintains that poverty is one of the greatest single forces, which creates the flow of children into the place while they are supposed to be under the care and love of their parents. The serious economic needs make it nearly impossible for households to invest in their children's social and educational needs. Besides, the money needed to send the children to school for a good education is not available in the family, regardless of the price of education, which is not within the reach of the average home and family. Indeed, it is obvious in the country's socio-economic scenario that the price of good education can be very expensive and unaffordable for poor families. Meanwhile, some of the relatively poor families and households tend to have more children and larger family sizes than they can be catered for. This already provided ample ground for the available children to engage in child labour and domestic service in other homes. This irrevocably lowers the school attendance and completion rates. This directly shows the implication of poverty on many issues that, in turn, create a condition in which the children are engaging in domestic servant work.

Moreover, there is the issue of socio-cultural norms that are associated with domestic servant syndrome (Bashir, 1998:76). This succinctly posits that the decision to send children to work is partly a matter of socio-cultural traditions and tribal indigenous beliefs of some people that are cherished as their social norms and value system. This is stated that if a parent lives in a society where everyone desires to send their children to work as a domestic servant, it is worthwhile for each parent to send their children to work, and if not everybody sends them to work, each parent may find it not worthwhile. Some societies, especially in Nigeria, tend to hold this view.

The Consequences of Domestic Servant Syndrome on National Development

There are serious effects of child labour and domestic servant syndrome, which transcend personal, family and societal needs. The extent of the consequences of domestic servanthood seems to vary from one level to another other depending on the level of involvement from the individual level to the state level. At the individual level, child domestic services impair the physical and mental development of children. This situation brings about an increase in the number of children who are mentally demented and stunted in society. This condition spells doom for society. According to Bashir, he posits that there is a "child labour trap' that the family is likely to fall into. He contends that an increase in child domestic labourers frequently causes a decline in the acquisition of human capital in society. He further explains that if a child is engaged all through the day, it is likely that the child will remain uneducated and have low productivity later in life as a grown-up adult. This implies that those domestic servants who work more as teenagers usually have very low social productivity when they become adults. That is, child domestic service is likely to diminish their adulthood productivity due to protracted hours of service as children (DaSilva, 1994). In addition to this, it is observed that many forms of unskilled labour at present practically open children not only merely fail to train, but also to be positively untrained for future needs and productivity.

Solutions and Workouts for Child Domestic Servant Syndrome

Several approaches could be adopted to reduce the menace of the phenomenon of child domestic servant syndrome to the barest minimum in society, and some of the ways include the following. Firstly, there should be concerted efforts to tackle the rate of poverty, hunger and economic backwardness in African societies. Most of the victims of Child labour are lured into the practice because of the poverty and economic hardship that confront their families. Most families are not economically empowered, and so those families find it difficult to be able to cater for their household's basic needs. The widespread poverty is one of the major causes of the social pandemic of human exploitation in contemporary African societies. If the poverty level of every household were reduced, then child domestic servant syndrome would be reduced drastically.

Moreover, assurance of good quality and affordable education that must be compulsory for all the children who are within the school age in the country, especially in rural areas, will go a long way to solve the problem of child domestic servant syndrome in the country. All children ought to be allowed to go to school and encouraged to have an education as a viable way of preparing them for mental, emotional and physiological needs and development for their future lives (Fafunwa, 1971:34). Perhaps, if all children were in school, learning in the classroom, they would be formally informed about the dangers that are inherently associated with different forms of human exploitation and different kinds of abuses which children are going through in society.

Another solution to the problem of domestic servant syndrome is the provision of support services for children who are currently working as domestic servants in different homes in society. Those children should be allowed and encouraged to go to school and combine schooling with their schedule of work. This is because the immediate and actual causes of some children who are working as domestic servants for other families are unknown. Some are orphans who are still depending extensively on other families for the provision of basic needs for their support and survival, for their livelihood. The domestic servants in this category need to be given some palliative measures like scholarships, good feeding schemes, provision for clothing and other things that can enhance their level of literacy. In addition, another important factor is raising public awareness and enlightenment campaigns against the child domestic servant syndrome in society. This includes improving children's knowledge of work hazards and raising parental awareness of human capital for effective productivity in the future. In addition to this, the public should be sensitised about the dangers that are associated with domestic service done by relatively underage children. For instance, the risk factor that domestic servants are likely to be sexually assaulted, molested, used for rituals, contracting deadly diseases, trafficking illicit drugs and even become drug addicts, armed robbers, prostitutes and so on are higher than those children who are living with their parents with adequate home training and formal education in school.

Lastly, the government must make efforts to support international organisations and world bodies to make good policies and effective legal instruments, which will enhance children's lives and protect the young ones in society. In addition, the government must make laws that would prohibit child domestic labour and ensure that the laws that would criminalise such practices are domesticated in the country's constitution and applicable to the general use by the populace, and whoever violates such laws should be punished accordingly. This legal framework would regulate child labour and at the same time enforce to stoppage of families from sending their children out to work as domestic servants.

Conclusion

From the foregoing, it is evident that the phenomenon of child labour and domestic workers' syndromes is an inevitable social menace in different societies today because of the rate of poverty and socio-economic conditions of the families which push children out of their comfort zones to go and get an alternative for survival in the strange homes. However, when there are significant improvements in the living conditions of the people, then this menace would stop or be reduced to the barest minimum. The parents must understand that they own their children's duty of taking good care of their basic needs, home training and getting good and proper education so that they would have all-around development and become acceptable in society. Hence, if parents fail to perform their expected duties of nurturing and providing for their children's needs, then it is a form of breaching social agreement and is bound to the larger society. This is because poor-raised children are likely to be deviant and social miscreants who would eventually become hardened criminals to the larger society (Obinaju, 1996). Besides, several untrained children who do not have proper education and adequate care usually pose a natural threat to the peace of society by becoming ready-made and prepared foot soldiers for insurgency and chaotic civil disorder in society (Ukaga, 2005:16).

Conclusively, this paper has attempted to justify that domestic workers are on the increase, and it is a bane to children's development in some African societies. It presents the history of child domestic workers, its booming in Christian homes, causes, rights of the children and ways out. Among other things, it was discovered that poverty is a major cause of child labour and domestic servant syndrome in the country. However, other causes are peripheral and still linked to poverty rates in society. Thus, the government has a major role to play in making life meaningful for people to live. This is one of the processes by which this social problem could either be reduced or eliminated.

References

Abdullah, M. 1995, 'A Study of Child Labour and Mining Work in Northern Nigeria: Islamic Perspectives', *Journal of Arabic & Islamic Studies*, vol. 3, no. 5, pp. 75–90, 'Uthman Danfodio University, Sokoto, Nigeria.

Aboderin, Y. 1991, 'Literacy for all: How to kindle and Sustain Literacy Interest in Nigerians', *Journal of Literacy and Reading in Nigeria*, vol. 6, pp. 140–165.

Adegunwa, I. 1987, *The Practice of Indemnifying Children as Loan Collateral in Yorubaland*, Hope Publishers, Ibadan.

Akinjogbin, A. 1981, 'Alajogbe or Alajobi: A Yoruba Sociological Study', *Odù: University of Ife Journal of African Studies*, vol. 9, no. 2, pp. 70–89.

Akinjogbin, A. 1982, *The History and Sociology of Yoruba People*, University of London Press, London.

Akiwowo, A. 1972, *The Sociology of Traditional Societies in Africa*, Oxford University Press, London.

Bashir, A. 1998, *Effects of Child Abuse on Family, Society and Nation Building*, Global-Smart Publishers, Abuja, Nigeria.

Bekembo, M. 1993, 'The Child in Africa and Socialisation of Education', in P. Dasgupta (ed.), *An Enquiry into Well-being of African Children and Destitutions*, Oxford University Press, London, pp. 81–96.

Chinecherem, U.M. & Ozoh, J.N. 2017, 'Child Labour and its Determinants in the Informal Sector of Onitsha, Nigeria', *Journal of Research on Humanities and Social Sciences*, vol. 7, no. 20, Nnamdi Azikiwe University, Awka, Nigeria. Available at: https://www.iiste.org [Accessed 3 April 2023].

DaSilva, H. 1994, *Children at Work: Poverty and Malnutrition Issues*, UNICEF Bulletins, East Asia and Pacific Regional Office, Bangkok.

Dwarkins, Z.H. 2012, 'The Impact of the Out-of-School Children on Socio-Economic and Educational Development of African Children', in O. Emejulu & I. Isiugo-Abanihe (eds), *Cross-Disciplinary Perspectives in Literacy and Language Studies: Essays in Honour of Chukwuemeka Eze Onukaogu*, IDAC & Afrika-links Book, Kampala, Uganda, pp. 234–245.

Fadipe, N. 1970, *The Sociology of the Yoruba*, Onibon-Oje Press & Books Industry, Ibadan, Nigeria.

Fafunwa, B. 1981, *History of Education in Southwestern Nigeria*, Macmillan, London.

Federal Government of Nigeria & UNICEF Office. 1996, *Early Child Care Project in Nigeria: A Training Guide for Lead Trainers*, UNICEF Publication, Lagos.

Federal Government of Nigeria. 2004, *Policy on Education Reforms*, NERDC Publication, Lagos.

Hester, V.H. 2010, *The Link between Poverty and Malnutrition: A South African Perspective on Health SA Gesundheit*, Available at: https://hsag.co.za [Accessed 20 April 2023].

Kaushik, B. 1998, *Child Labour: Causes, Consequences and Cure: With Remarks on International Labour Standards*, Available at: https://ssrn.com/abstract604927 [Accessed 15 April 2023].

Mahammad, M. 2005, *National Programme on the Elimination of Child Labour in Nigeria*, Agenda for International Labour Organisation National Millennium Goal & Nigeria Vision 2020, NMGA Annual Reports, Abuja.

Obinaju, Q.I. 1996, *Early Childhood Education: Theory and Practices*, BON Universal Ltd., Calabar, Nigeria.

Okunade, O. 2004, 'Synergy Not Proper: The Roles of Parents and Well-Meaning Adults in Child Upbringing in Some Selected Communities in Ijesaland, Nigeria', Unpublished Master's thesis, Department of Sociology and Anthropology, Obafemi Awolowo University, Ile-Ife, Nigeria.

Rodgers, G. & Standing, G. 1981, *Child Work, Poverty and Underdevelopment*, International Labour Office & UNFPA Publications, Geneva.

Tyndale House Publishers. n.d., *The Life Application Study Bible, King James Version: Proverbs Chapter 13 Verse 24*, Tyndale House, Wheaton, Illinois.

Ukaga, R.C. 2005, *Teaching Children to Write and Read*, Career Book House, Owerri, Nigeria.

UNICEF 1994, 'Children at Work: Poverty and Malnutrition Issues', *UNICEF Bulletins*, East Asia and Pacific Regional Office. Available at: http://unicef.org/childev/povertyinfo/malnutritioninasian/vol12/15no/chil4.html [Accessed 1 April 2023]

www.ingramcontent.com/pod-product-compliance
Lightning Source LLC
Jackson TN
JSHW021529281025
93244JS00006B/49